# The Currency of Connection

How trust transforms life,
relationships and work

BY TERESA MITROVIC

Published by New Generation Publishing in 2020

Copyright © Teresa Mitrovic 2020

First Edition

ISBN 978-1-78955-736-7

**www.newgeneration-publishing.com**

New Generation Publishing

# Contents

How This Book Began........................................................................ i

'BEFORE WE BEGIN' ..................................................................... 1

    Why Trust?................................................................................ 3

    Is This Book for You?............................................................... 6

    How the Book is Laid Out........................................................ 8

SECTION ONE: HOW TRUST WORKS............................................. 9

    The Basics............................................................................... 10

    Why Trust Doesn't Always Seem So Easy .............................. 15

    Our Relationship to Trust is Personal.................................... 17

    Transforming Self-Serving Behaviours ................................. 18

    The Neurochemistry of Trust................................................ 19

    How is Trust Built? 4xC's to Remember ............................... 22

    Trust and Trustworthiness ..................................................... 25

    Vulnerability vs. Predictability .............................................. 26

    Vulnerability: Building Trust Fast.......................................... 27

    How We Make It Hard ........................................................... 29

SECTION TWO: WHY NOW? ......................................................... 31

    Trust by Default or Design..................................................... 32

    A Crisis of Trust .................................................................... 35

    Trust Feeds Culture................................................................ 37

    Trust Enables Growth ............................................................ 39

    First, Self-Trust, Then Connection ........................................ 40

    Easily Said (or How We Mess it Up) ...................................... 42

    From Inertia to Influence ....................................................... 45

SECTION THREE: SELF-TRUST....................................................... 47

    Why Self-Trust Matters.......................................................... 49

Why Anxiety Feels Inescapable ...............................................52

Derailing Distractions ..............................................................55

Reflection, Humility and Learning from Mistakes ..................56

Balancing Tension and Trust.....................................................58

Trust, Tension and Our Overworked Nervous System...........62

Trust, Patterns and Emotional Sabotage .................................65

Reframing Fear to Tap into Self-Trust.....................................69

Trust and Trauma ....................................................................71

The Biology and Physiology of Trust........................................74

The Neuroscience of Trust .......................................................78

Amygdala Hijack.......................................................................82

Emotions: Energy in Motion.....................................................84

Shaping Mindsets .....................................................................87

To Trust Is to Let Go................................................................90

Changing Beliefs ......................................................................91

When We Get It Right...............................................................92

Ideas to Begin With..................................................................96

SECTION FOUR: SOCIAL ..............................................................103

How Trust Acts as a Social Eco System..................................105

Co-creating Cultures: Why Your Influence Is Greater Than You
Think.......................................................................................108

The Power of Connection........................................................110

What Does Love Have to Do with It?......................................113

How Differences in Our Personalities and World Views
Influence Trust.....................................................................116

Trust and Our Relationships ...................................................120

How Our Behaviour Impacts Other Peoples DNA...............123

How the Way We Engage with the World Shapes Our
Approach to Trust.................................................................125

Wired for Safety: Our Wiring for Threat is Acute and Constantly Alert........................................................ 128

Energy is Contagious............................................... 131

The Role of Emotions ............................................. 132

Social Pain: Does Losing Your Cool with Others Really Matter? .................................................................. 135

How 'Mindreading Misassumptions' Impact Trust ............. 136

Ideas to Begin With ............................................... 138

SECTION FIVE: ORGANISATIONAL ............................................. 143

Organisational Health ............................................. 144

What Does a Fear Free Workplace Look Like? .................... 145

Is the Absence of Trust a Liability? ...................... 150

Why Your Engagement is Often Highest on Day One......... 154

Trust, But Verify ................................................... 158

Enabling Agility in a Fast-Changing World.......................... 160

Why Work is Personal ............................................. 162

Relationships and The Link to Motivation ........................... 168

Nested Systems: The Systems That Bind .............................. 171

Culture:................................................................. 174

What Your Culture Reflects About Trust.............................. 174

Cultural Differences at Work: What Distinguishes Us? ........ 178

Leadership: ........................................................... 184

The Evolving Role of Leadership........................................... 184

Trust as a Leadership Advantage ........................................ 188

Leadership Blind Spots........................................... 192

Letting Go of Expertise to Embrace Emergence.................... 194

The Evolution of Leadership and the Trend Towards Teams ........................................................................... 196

Management: The Managers Mindset: Championing Trust. 198

Teams: Why High Performers Aren't Always a High

Performing Team ................................................................203

Accountability and Trust ....................................................208

Change as a Catalyst ..........................................................216

Constant Change vs. VUCA Environments ..........................227

What is VUCA? ..................................................................228

Ideas to Begin With ...........................................................230

What to Look Out For ........................................................236

SECTION SIX: CONVERSATIONS ............................................240

Caroline - Head of People & Talent, Tourism .....................242

Chris - Managing Director, Consumer Goods ......................244

Chris - CEO Consumer Goods Retail ..................................248

Dee - Senior Director HR, Not for Profit ............................257

Dominic - CEO SaaS Start Up.............................................267

Eleni - Managing Partner, Advertising .................................276

Fiona - Head of Marketing Communications, Tertiary
Education ...........................................................................282

Helen - COO Government...................................................287

Jason - Director, Technology...............................................299

Jim - Managing Director, Entertainment .............................306

Katie - Head of HR Centre of Expertise,
Telecommunications ...........................................................309

Ralph - Leadership & Coaching Consultant / Programme
Director Tertiary Education .................................................324

Silao - CEO Healthcare .......................................................329

Anon - (Disruptive) Recruitment Start Up Co-Founder........334

Wendy - Snr Managing Consultant, Consulting ...................336

Sam - CEO, Consumer Goods Retail....................................340

Martin - Executive Director, Government ............................349

David - ex CEO, Government...............................................354

ACKNOWLEDGEMENTS .......................................................365

To my parents, Elizabeth and Tomo who taught me about the power of love, forgiveness and perseverance.

To my son Milan, who has taught me compassion, grace and resilience; and who I will forever be grateful to for changing the course of my life.

And to my husband Mark, who has taught me about the strength and beauty of vulnerability, of second chances and of unconditional love.

I am eternally grateful to each of you for your love and support, through all of life's adventures. There's no one I would rather be on this journey with.

*"You must trust and believe in people,*
*or life becomes impossible."*

*Anton Chekhov*

# How This Book Began...

For a long time, I have been fascinated by relationships. From the complexities of how and why we engage a little differently with different friends, colleagues and family members to the – sometimes starkly different - sets of rules we have for how we treat ourselves and each other.

When I began my professional career, I was already the parent of a school aged child; I wanted to excel in my career, but I also wanted to understand how I could create a life that felt balanced and rewarding. I wanted to understand how to craft and align healthy beliefs and behaviours to make life feel more energizing and less like a series of difficult decisions to be made about competing, urgent – and seemingly equally crucial – priorities.

I wanted a fulfilling corporate career that would be rewarding and stimulating but I wanted to be a wonderful parent; present, engaged and available for my son too. I didn't want to feel like an imposter waiting to be found out, or a failure as a professional *or* a parent. What I wanted, was to carve out a sense of identity and strength that would feel real to me, while I managed the tension between navigating the working world and raising my young son.

While I was a young single mother, my career progressed into management and the need to create a work environment that felt engaging, meaningful and rewarding for both myself and the team stepped up a notch. I felt driven by a genuine desire to be a good 'boss' and by the equally ever-present worry that I'd make a complete mess of it.

What I learned over the more than 20 years that lies between first feeling that until now, is the knowledge that the times I felt most confident, most courageous, most capable and most 'on purpose' – in any realm of life - were those times when I trusted myself deeply.

More interesting, to me was the realisation that at work, the one key difference between those relationships which unlocked deep collaboration and remarkable competitive advantage, and those that were only ever operational, was the degree of trust that existed between us.

Not the predictive kind of trust we're all most familiar with which allows us to gauge how someone will respond based on our previous experiences with them, but the vulnerability-based kind where communication is transparent, honest and non-judgmental. Where both parties can see and sense the genuine interest and care each person expresses in the others' professional and personal success and wellbeing.

I knew that trust was the game changer.

What I loved was that it didn't just make our team more effective and efficient, it made everyone feel something much bigger than they were used to feeling at work. It changed the way we felt about ourselves and each other, about what we were working on, and about what became possible through working together. It mined energy and enthusiasm in ways nothing else did. When we trusted each other enough to give – and receive - open and honest feedback from each other, we tapped into our collective intelligence and energy, and the possibilities for us, both individually and as a team, expanded exponentially.

I knew trust was crucial, I just couldn't figure out how to make it happen if it wasn't happening organically, or if the seed didn't already exist for me to build on. Through willpower and desire, I learned how to plant small seeds that slowly became trust, but I still lacked the understanding around why it worked so well in some situations and took so painfully long in others. It kickstarted a lifelong curiosity in trust, and a desire to make that elusive skill of creating it and nurturing it, a part of my everyday life.

At a deeper more personal level, since childhood, my life has been underpinned by experiences that left me feeling isolated, unsafe and alone. Hurt and shame, a need to never feel unsafe again, or to be dependent on others, shaped my world view and I think was the key driver throughout my commercial career. That relentless drive created a tension between who I was at work, and the person I wanted to be for my son at home. The tension was at times creative and generative, yet at other times slipped into an emotional tension which I wasn't always aware of, or able to navigate as well as I would like.

I only began to appreciate the distinction as my commercial career switched into consulting. My appreciation of the need for safety - as a basic instinct we seek out and protect against - deepened. The more I worked with people from all industries, from front line managers to CEO's and founders, the needs remained the same - safety, control, acceptance. I have watched trust enable all three in a way in a way no other practice does.

A caveat here. Abraham Maslow once said that if the only tool you have is a hammer, it's tempting to treat everything as though it were a nail. When you realize the extent to which trust underpins our lives, it would be easy to see trust as that hammer - the one tool with the power to fix everything. It's powerful, but it's not the only tool we need to forge great relationships and cultures. There are other soft skills (like empathy and listening) which sit alongside trust and boost our interpersonal skills and our emotional and social intelligence far beyond anything we imagine possible from what - on the surface - are seemingly simple practices.

Trust though, is where it all begins. It provides a rich,

deep, robust and flexible foundation from which everything else sources the strength and security to lay down roots before redirecting energy into outward growth.

It's the one principle which is enduring, relevant and flexible enough to help you create healthier relationships. Not just with yourself, but throughout your work and social lives. Better yet, it's a practice that is self-fulfilling, sustainable and surprisingly rewarding.

## A Disclaimer

This is (deliberately) not a textbook. You won't find it peppered with statistics or research references. What you will find is collected wisdom, insights and ideas from a review of the literature, more than 20 years of personal experience and client work, and some of the world's most inspiring and dedicated advocates of trust and social connection.

My intent is not to create the final word on trust, but instead to offer a starting point which challenges your thinking, encourages you to reflect, triggers the curiosity to behave a little differently and in doing so, forever changes your corner of the world for the better.

Here's to that journey,

_Teresa_

BEFORE
WE
BEGIN

*Trust transforms the
quality of our relationships,
and by association, our lives.
It changes our relationships
with our self, each other
and our places of work.*

# Why Trust?

*"When people honor each other, there is a trust established that leads to synergy, interdependence, and deep respect. Both parties make decisions and choices based on what is right, what is best, what is valued most highly."*

*Blaine Lee*

Several books already exist about trust. So why this book and why now? In short, whether instinctive or experienced, we know trust matters. We know we work better, and easier when it's present, but we've forgotten – or maybe never really considered – how to make it work, what prevents it and how to regain it when it's lost. This book covers that from a very human perspective. Why we need trust now, where to begin and how to extend it into each area of your life.

More specifically, there are four core principles behind this book:

- Relationships are the foundations of our lives. We create, achieve and grow through our interactions with others. The quality, strength and flexibility of those relationships relies on the degree and depth of trust between us.

- Change is frequent, fast and can be destabilizing. It's not a matter of whether we'll experience change – but rather when. Trust can help us to embrace change with curiosity, resilience and realistic optimism.

- Trust and fear can't coexist. Even the perception of risk or fear is enough to jeopardize trust. Building trust means creating safety at a psychological, emotional

3

and physical level whether in relationships at work or at home, or within ourselves.

- We tend to adopt a paradoxical, ad hoc approach to trust. We are usually more inclined to expect and seek trust from others, than to actively gift, or cultivate it, ourselves. We tend to focus on our role in building trust only when its absence is being keenly felt. Even then, we tend to approach it based on what we need, rather than partnering to enable trust to build.

If you're reading this book, it's a fair assumption that you've experienced relationships or working environments so bad - or so good - that you know what you're missing out on when trust is absent. You may not appreciate yet all the ways in which trust is built and broken, but you'd like to know more so you can make trust a conscious choice in each of your relationships.

Or, you may simply sense that trust is important and something you want to know more about and be more conscious of day to day.

Whether we are active in building trust or not, one fact remains. All humans share the core psychological needs of feeling safe, having a sense of control and feeling valued by the people around them. With our survival instinct inescapably linked to our 'tribe' (whether at home, socially, or at work), our need to be a valued member of a group is so wired into our neurology that 'social' pain (such as being excluded, reprimanded in public or shamed) is felt as distinctly, and viscerally, as physical pain.

Though we rely less on our 'tribe' for our survival these days, our connection to them - and the way that connection underpins or undermines our well-being - remains hardwired and instinctive. Healthy, generative relationships are a major determinant in how quickly and how greatly we thrive and succeed in work and in life. And trust is the core element that either enables the safety to connect to others, or, by virtue of its absence, triggers self-protection instead. Trust is the foundation of healthy relationships at every level; with our 'selves', each other and within our places of work.

This book is an invitation to get beyond the static and noise of everyday working life, to understand and remedy the root cause of misunderstanding, disconnection and misdirected efforts in relationships.

We explore why it matters that we have this conversation now, what fear breeds and what trust unlocks. And we highlight some simple steps to rebuilding and fostering greater trust in the relationship arenas that matter most; your 'self', the people you live with, and the organisations you work within.

# Is This Book for You?

This book has been written for people who are working with others, in close quarters, or tense situations, and who want to create relationships that feel energised, respectful and resilient.

It is for the managers of teams who are doing all in their power to create a healthy and high performing work environment but who are experiencing some recurring problems that seem difficult to shift.

It's also for people who have been recipients of management or leadership development but who may not have experienced the full benefit of adult development from the inside out.

From a keener self-awareness about your own personality and how your preferences shape your way of working and engaging; to knitting together more effectively as a team for sustainable engagement; to aligning personal aspirations to team and organisational performance. Trust enables each step; from the seemingly small yet unbelievably hard discipline of 'letting go', and the discomfort of vulnerability, to finding peace with becoming more 'emergent' in a rapidly changing working world.

Most of all, this book is for people who don't have time to waste on things that don't work, whose businesses are lean, whose hearts recognize a piece is missing, and whose minds are open to learning and experimenting with new ways of thinking and doing.

In essence, this book is for you if:

- You are in a toxic or challenging work environment and you're looking for a fresh approach to equipping a

6

team to become more resourceful - both individually and collectively.

- You have experienced the joy, engagement and seamless success that is made possible by virtue of high trust relationships, but you've found the moments fleeting and difficult to replicate.
- You have felt the frustration, futility or sense of loss that comes when trust is low or broken, or seemingly irreparably lost, and you'd like to know how to recover it.
- You are a manager or leader who instinctively feels, or knows, that more is possible within your working relationships, but you aren't sure how to help your peers, clients and team members open up to seamless collaboration.
- You believe (as I do) that relationships sit at the centre of our ability to experience greater ease, enjoyment, and enrichment in our work and social lives and you want to make trust a bigger part of your everyday life.

# How the Book is Laid Out

This book is divided into four core sections: an **overview** that explores the topic of trust; '**self-trust**' which looks at our own individual relationship with trust and trusting in ourselves; '**social**' which delves into our personal relationships; and finally, '**organisational**' which examines the multiple ways trust is built, risked or broken in our work lives from the processes and culture inherent in our workplaces to the behaviours of our peers, managers and leaders.

Each section is broken down into smaller subsections designed to make it easier to find the pieces you're most interested in hearing more about. The self-trust, social and organisational sections each close with ideas for action you can take. Dive in there if you want to deepen your experience of trust, whether that be with yourself, the people you share your life with or the people you work alongside.

My hope is that this book opens your eyes to the value that trust can have personally, socially and commercially, and that you feel inspired to begin building more trust wherever you are.

I recommend reading Why Now? and What Is Trust? before you skip elsewhere. Partly to ground you in the thinking behind the book, partly because it's where I explain concepts that I build on in each of the following sections.

# SECTION ONE:

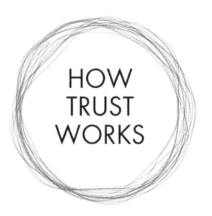

HOW
TRUST
WORKS

# The Basics

If trust is so vital to our relationships, why isn't it prioritized more? And why haven't we mastered it already?

**Fear sells:**

Multi-billion-dollar industries rely on fear to sell products and services. Countless organisations employ fear as a leadership strategy or performance tactic. Fear is the fastest way to motivate people. It may be a short-term tactic but it's a powerfully primal one.

**Trust is dynamic:**

Human behaviours and emotions are complex and constantly shifting, so trust isn't static. Instead, it is a daily dynamic of belief and behaviour, of expectation and evaluation. Our beliefs about what trust and trustworthiness looks and feels like shapes our behaviour. Our expectations of how others 'should' behave to earn and keep our trust, is subject to constant re-evaluation. We are always alert and gauging who, and how much we can trust.

**Trust is a personal choice:**

It is given and withdrawn – sometimes without our knowledge - at least until its presence or absence becomes unmistakable. We can't assume others will trust us, nor can we make others trust us, we simply have to earn it, value it, and continually nurture it.

## Trust is an individual experience:

We are all a unique (and evolving) mix of personality preferences, life experience, upbringing, and culture. So what is acceptable to one person, may be confronting to another. Sometimes surprisingly so. While some of us are more open and ready to trust than others, others need more time to warm to one another. One is not better than the other, both are natural and worthy of respect. Expecting people to trust us faster - or to act the way we would - can slow trust down or undermine it altogether.

## Trust requires vulnerability:

Trust, in its purest (and its most rewarding) form, requires us to make ourselves vulnerable in the face of perceived risk. Yet vulnerability-based trust is elusive and deeply challenging; giving others the opportunity to judge, reject or abuse our vulnerability makes us hesitate, or stop altogether. Achieving this deep level of trust requires a leap of confidence.

## Trust needs space:

Trust isn't built at speed, or when we're talking tactics or engaging on a surface level. It is built in the course of having bigger, deeper conversations about crucial and often challenging topics. Conversations that are often avoided in favour of artificial harmony, or derailed by a lack of time or a reluctance to contribute – and to challenge - without hesitation.

**Trust touchpoints are everywhere:**

Touchpoints where trust is tested, built or broken permeate our work and private lives. We all navigate conversations and events daily that test us - even in relationships which have previously felt high trust. Our success in maintaining or strengthening trust along the way (whether we are aware of it or not) hinges not just on the context surrounding those events and conversations, but on our emotional, social and conversational intelligence.

**Trust is contextual:**

We may trust people in some situations but not all. We may extend trust more willingly or feel more open to trusting in environments where we feel safer (our own homes, close relationships or secure workplaces) and less so in environments that make us feel insecure (new relationships, new workplaces, moments of high stakes or close scrutiny).

**Trust is both fragile and flexible:**

Because we're each unique and trust is so personal to each of us, we can behave in ways that are innocent to us but challenging for others which means trust can be easily - and unexpectedly - tested. A foundation of mutual understanding and appreciation in a relationship gives trust the flexibility to bend under strain. When we're with people we believe understand and appreciate us, we drop our assumptions and defenses and engage from a place of positive intent and curiosity rather than assumption and judgement.

**Negative behaviours are often more common than high trust behaviours:**

Whether you're aware of it or not, the effects of trust, or proof of its absence is always being felt and as social creatures, we can sometimes fall into bad habits purely through trying to fit in. Rather than encouraging openness and collaboration in groups, we join the quiet sidelined conversations in the background. We avoid the difficult conversations rather than engaging in spirited debate that results in better understanding and wholehearted support.

**Trust is a whole-body experience:**

Our brains are on alert 24/7/365 for signs of safety so we can adjust our behaviour in order to sustain our survival. Our bodies are always fully engaged in the process of listening, sense-making and response so we're ready to react appropriately when the need arises. And that need is assessed and responded to swiftly - whether the stimulus is real, or perceived. Trust is dynamic and all encompassing; it's instinctive, intellectual, emotional and behavioural.

Trust is as vital to the health and success of relationships as it is complex. Trust can transform our relationship with our self, with the people we live and work with and even with the organisations and systems we work within. It has the power to connect people, to increase capacity and to foster collective wisdom and competitive edge. At best, its absence can cause artificial harmony and at worst, dysfunction or outright destruction.

At the macro view, changing the culture of a society or an organisation can feel like a big place to start. While it's certainly easier to facilitate change from the top down in any system, you can play a role no matter where your place in that system is.

# Why Trust Doesn't Always Seem So Easy

Take a moment to think about someone at work who you trust deeply. You know you could be open and honest with them if you're unsure or unclear on something, or if you have concerns about a course of action. You know your relationship equity is strong enough with them that any requests you make, or any feedback you give, will be met with a degree of openness and understanding. You are confident that trust, respect and good intent sets the context for your working relationship.

Would you also trust that person with concerns or challenges from your personal life? Would you share with them the more personal insecurities and fears you have? Or would that seem inappropriate?

Trust is contextual. And context, as we've seen, can be a game changer. Though the principle of trust is fairly universal, what it feels and looks like varies depending on the specific scenario.

While we may deeply trust someone in one arena of our life, we may dial back that trust if we imagine them in a different context entirely. There are boundaries around what feels natural and right for each relationship depending on the people involved, the environment we are in, and the nature of what we are exchanging, or expecting of one another. It's natural, and it's how we build up relationships - a little at a time.

It's natural to misjudge sometimes too, to overshare in a relationship we feel safe in. Overshares are characterized by those moments where you've shared something and suddenly felt very exposed. Or when you've heard something that's left you feeling like a deer trapped in headlights, frozen, shocked and unsure how to respond.

A relationship can only carry the degree of vulnerability it has grown to hold. Too much vulnerability in a relationship can be too much pressure for the recipient if that vulnerability itself is out of context or bigger than anything the recipient has fielded in the past, or bigger than what they were expecting. Those moments can stunt or deepen relationships depending on how we respond to them; whether we close off and retreat to protect ourselves, or allow each other space to understand each other more.

Trust, like relationships is dynamic. In some relationships, usually those which have been tested through either time or trials, it can feel big and encompassing, flexible and resilient. In others, usually those that are new and still developing, it can feel fragile, shallow and tentative.

Like walking onto a rope bridge, the surer we are of our safety, the further we are likely to venture.

# Our Relationship to Trust is Personal

We all have an understanding of what trust means in a social context, without that common view relationships would be remarkably hard work. But our relationship with trust is slightly different depending on our life experience, world view and our personality. We take those assumptions and expectations into every relationship we enter, yet they often remain hidden until something stirs the need to begin explicitly expressing what trust looks and feels like to us. Even then, having the conversations that bridge the gap between what we - and the other person - needs to feel safe and confident enough to trust again can be a difficult process.

That's because trust is a complex system of largely subconscious expectations and evaluations which slowly develop to alter our confidence, our sense of safety, our experience of relationships, our aspirations and our expectations of the world. It's such a powerful combination that it even has the potential to alter us at a genetic level.

Understanding how our unique view alters our experience of trust, and gaining insights into how others might approach trust themselves, is one of the fastest and most powerful ways to improve our relationships.

When we can better identify which challenges to our ability to trust stem from our view of reality vs. which stem from someone's behaviour towards us, it becomes a lot easier to articulate what we need next. The heat drops out of difficult conversations and we can begin to find a way forward together.

# Transforming Self-Serving Behaviours

The opposite of trust, is of course, distrust or fear. It is something we tolerate when we have to, but which is damaging at best and toxic and dangerous at worst.

When we're with people we don't trust, our defenses automatically fire up. We instinctively start behaving in ways that distance us (avoiding spending time with them, limiting how much work we have to do together, opting for email and messaging rather than talking in person). Or which allow for pre-emptive defense or self-protection (limiting our emotional, reputational or financial investment).

Our involvement with those we distrust becomes characterized by the desire to protect ourselves from whatever perceived risk we feel we face rather than a desire to connect with, understand and work – or live – alongside them.

Our natural instincts tell us that if we distrust someone, we have something to lose, or something to fear. Whatever the case, it makes doing anything other than protecting ourselves difficult. So, while we will do what we have to survive, we're often reluctant to go any further. It means the energy we could be using to create, resolve, initiate or collaborate is being redirected to self-preservation.

In short, when we distrust, we focus on our own survival, success and wellbeing over that of the people we live and work with.

# The Neurochemistry of Trust

We, like everything else in the universe (including the organisations we work in) run on energy. Our brains, though tiny in terms of mass (taking up approximately 2% of our body's mass), draw 25% of our body's energy. That energy moves around our brains, redirecting from 'protect' (our primitive response to self-preservation and survival) to 'connect' (our social bonding and creative, constructive mode) based on cues it's getting from our environment.

Trust is the lever that directs that energy towards connection and collaboration or protection and withholding.

As trust gains popularity as a topic that underpins leadership and organisation health, new research is finding its way into how our neurochemistry alters our thinking and our behaviour, exploring the hidden impacts on both ourselves and others.

Emotion, and its role in thought and behaviour has been the subject of neuroscience studies since the 1970's. Now though, scientists are exploring how our emotions influence how effectively we function day to day.

The way our brains have evolved means that, in a nutshell, our emotions precede our thought processes. Our emotions begin in an ancient part of our brain - our amygdala - which (amongst other features) plays a fundamental role in survival, which gives it the power to override our thinking and logic. And even if the emotions we are experiencing aren't strong enough to override our thinking, they will shape how we interpret what's happening, and in the decisions we subsequently make.

Our brains never stop learning and adapting to our environments, the events we go through and the people we share our lives with. In a process called neuroplasticity, our emotions, our experiences and what we learn from them continue to alter our brains throughout life. Healthy connection unleashes healthy chemicals like serotonin (high levels of which are linked to happiness, while low levels link to depression), oxytocin (also known as the hug hormone due to its crucial role in social bonding) and dopamine (which causes feelings of pleasure and reward and which can keep us 'hooked').

Fear creates more of what is commonly referred to as the 'stress' chemical cortisone which our body needs in small doses to support digestion and rest. It becomes damaging when it's released too frequently or for long periods. Fear also triggers the release of adrenalin which is sometimes referred to as the 'fear' hormone. In situations of extreme fear, it can cause permanent changes in our brains over time, with some sources stating it can change the size and shape of the amygdala.

Both sides of that hormonal spectrum are necessary for vital functions in our bodies, but our bodies were designed to shift state between safety and protection. To drive, and then brake our system. To give us energy to move at speed, and then to downshift into a rest state. The rhythm of our modern life can tip us into existing for too long in that heightened, energised, alert state, without the requisite respite to adequately rest, digest and metabolize those hormones. Fear originates not just from what is happening, but also what we expect, or worry might happen.

While neurochemistry may sound like more than you need to know, a better understanding of what happens mentally and emotionally during trust or mistrust makes reframing people's behaviour easier. It helps us appreciate and understand how and why we – and others – act as we do and enables us to become more emotionally, conversationally and socially intelligent.

# How is Trust Built? 4xC's to Remember

Trust is often felt as an attitude yet expressed as a behaviour. How we feel about trust, our attitude toward it in any moment, is a result of:

- Our beliefs: we may extend trust freely, or wait for it to be earned;
- Our evaluations: weighing the degree to which we might trust someone in a given circumstances, and;
- Our expectations: of whether we 'should' be able to trust certain people or institutions.

We express trust as a behaviour through the choices we make and the actions we take as a result of those choices. When you reflect on the relationships in your working and private life, you'll see expressions of trust - or distrust - in people's behaviour. Those expressions are based on whether the situation - or people within it - is deemed to be safe, or risky. When we trust, we open up (sharing information and insights, being candid and vulnerable) and move towards greater interdependence; we begin relying on and supporting others and letting them rely on and support us. When we mistrust others, we hold back, we become defensive, protective or argumentative.

At its simplest level, when we evaluate trust, whether at a personal or institutional level, we're looking for two key factors; character and capability. To get a little more granular, character and capability is refined to; Competence and Consistency, Credibility and Connection. A combination of qualities which are variously attributed to Mayer, Blanchard and Covey. Here's how I remember them:

**The 4 C's of Trust**

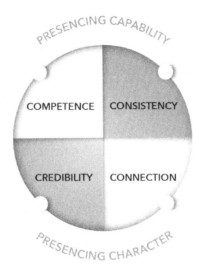

Our character is about who we are as humans. Whether we are credible and able to connect with people. In other words, are we inherently honest and reliable? And do we genuinely care about others and take time to understand and relate to people? Sometimes, between our desire to please, and our being overcommitted, we can 'counterfeit'. Pretend that we are addressing or changing things but never adjusting our behaviour long enough to lead to lasting change. Whether we're being genuine, or counterfeit can be seen in the results of our actions.

Character acts as a psychological, often unspoken promise of what you can expect from someone. We start reading those cues from our first experience of someone and keep updating our evaluation of them as we engage with and begin placing our faith in them.

Our capability stems from our degree of competence *and* how consistent our output and our behaviour is. In other words, can we do what we say we can, and are we able to continue to meet the standards we have set for our performance or our behaviour? Capability is the follow through on the promise of our character, the evidence that faith in a person was well placed.

Trust needs both sides of the equation – character (credibility and connection) and capability (competence and consistency) - to provide the familiarity, security and resilience to remain strong and flexible over time.

# Trust and Trustworthiness

*"He who does not trust enough, will not be trusted."*

*Lao Tzu*

Trust – like all things in relationships – goes both ways. It isn't just about our trust of others, it's also about how trustworthy we are in their eyes.

Building our trustworthiness is about being attentive to those four C's; who we are and how we behave. We can get a sense of how trustworthy others find us by noticing the extent to which people feel they can be themselves and open up in our presence; and the degree to which they rely on us to act with integrity and honesty.

It can be a human tendency to think first about the trust we're placing in others, but trust is both our assessment of, and our response to, others and their assessment and response to us.

Creating relationships and organisational cultures which generate trust rather than uncertainty, insecurity or anxiety means paying attention to both sides of the equation – to our ability and willingness to extend trust to others, and to working on earning trust ourselves.

# Vulnerability vs. Predictability

*"Trust is built when someone is vulnerable
and not taken advantage of."*

*Bob Vanourek*

Ask people what they think of when they think about trust and you will usually hear definitions based around how we expect others to behave. A concept referred to by Patrick Lencioni (sought after consultant and multiple best-selling author) as 'predictive trust'.

Predictive trust is surface level trust. Transactional. It's often our first evaluation of trust and it's how we instinctively learn of our exposure to possible risk. For work that sits at a transactional or operational level, where the risks are smaller, or engagements are brief, it's absolutely sufficient.

The key to great, open and generative relationships and cultures is a different kind of trust altogether. A trust Patrick Lencioni terms 'vulnerability-based trust'.

Vulnerability based trust breaks through barriers and creates a frictionless way of working and relating to each other that enables experimentation, learning, growth and exceptional performance and achievement. It's the kind of trust that's present in relationships which grow together through adversity and has been attributed to financial results in high trust companies which are 2.5 times higher than the norm.

# Vulnerability: Building Trust Fast

Sitting in tandem with the concept of 'vulnerability-based trust' is the reality that we usually only realize the importance of trust when we're feeling vulnerable and it's made conspicuous by its absence. Up until that point, a number of things may have been happening without us even noticing.

We may have been coasting on the previous goodwill of our relationship, or on implied or transferred trust (through our belief and trust in a mutual third party) which we've placed in others without seeing clear proof we can trust them ourselves. Or it may be that our relationship was such up until that point that we never felt enough risk or doubt to warrant mistrust.

Trust is linked to safety, so it's only when we're evaluating risk and fear that we start to value its importance and assess its depth or resilience.

Fear, and perceived fear responses, are triggered when we are about to do something that has caused - or reminds us of - pain or humiliation that we've experienced before, or watched people we love experience. It doesn't need to be exact to trigger the memory.

The good news is that we can build trust quickly when we need to. The bad news is that we can't do that without allowing ourselves to become vulnerable in the process.

Paving the way for vulnerability means creating enough safety in a conversation, or in a relationship, as is required for people to feel their contribution will be heard and respected, rather than judged or betrayed. And because safety and fear are so closely linked (and so viscerally experienced), the concept of what creates safety can be as personal a construct as trust. It's not enough to create safety based on our own need – we have to understand what constitutes safety for the people we want to trust us.

Brene Brown (shame researcher and best-selling author) explains the need to gauge how much vulnerability a relationship or a conversation can sustain before sharing our views or our feelings. Going too far can feel like an overshare, leaving the 'sharer' feeling exposed and the listener feeling awkward or out of their depth. Testing the waters slowly and building up gradually is a strategy that protects both parties.

Navigating vulnerability with care is instinctive, careful and considered work. It involves creating the space and time for conversations where judgements can be set aside, and people can listen and ask questions to deepen their understanding. It's where conversations switch from being transactional to transformative. And though the process seems slow, it accelerates everything that follows.

# How We Make It Hard

While we're building trust, stumbling on any one of those four areas (competence and consistency, credibility and connection), can set us back. If we say one thing and do another, we weaken our credibility. If we act dismissively, cruelly or disrespectfully, we weaken our connection. If we can't do what we agreed to, we weaken our perceived competence. And if we behave erratically – reliable some days and not others – we're viewed as inconsistent. On the other hand, when we have built a history of being connected, credible, competent and consistent, the occasional slip is seen as human, inevitable and ultimately forgivable.

While there are always people who can paint a convincing picture of their character; leading us to believe that they care (connection) and that they will deliver on their promise (credibility), cracks always, eventually, show through. Though we might want to believe them, we can look back and see whether or not they delivered, how they treated us when they things got tough (connection) and in hindsight, there is always a pattern to their behaviour (consistency).

And sometimes, it's possible to be so overloaded or distracted, that even with the best of intentions you'll briefly lack credibility, your ability to connect with others will falter and you may be lack lustre in your efforts. In those times, what matters is consistency. When the pattern of your behaviour over time has been predominantly strong across competence, connection and credibility, it provides a safety net around the relationship. People understand lapses.

It's consistency over time that anchors trust, which

explains why trust can take time to build and why it can sometimes feel fragile, or be easily - and unexpectedly - lost. It explains why once established, trust becomes incredibly strong, enduring, flexible and resilient.

# SECTION TWO:

WHY
NOW?

# Trust by Default or Design

In simple and small ways every day; in families, friendships and workplaces across the world, conditional and contextual trust is being expressed. We just don't usually dwell on it.

The interesting thing about trust is that we instinctively know when it exists and when it doesn't. We can feel it, even if we're not labelling it as trust. If we feel safe being vulnerable in someone's presence, we have trust. If we find ourselves openly and willingly supporting someone, even when it exacts a cost, takes valuable time or adds to our workload that relationship has trust. When we give or receive feedback that is honest and frank, but which lands with care and consideration, there is trust.

We know when we've lost it too.

We may not realize the point at which things changed, but it's clear when trust is no longer present. They, or we, retreat. Whether it's obvious, like avoidance, withholding information, short responses, sharper than usual feedback or exclusion; or subtle, like the sense that things have 'cooled' between us. If you're used to having trust then you lose it, you will feel its absence keenly.

Trust makes everything both feel better and work smoother. Yet we frequently leave it to chance rather than making a conscious choice to engage in actively fostering it.

In a reflection of our own personal experience and our own intuitive knowing, a growing body of research shows that where there is high trust, there is more openness and honesty which, in our lives, leads to stronger, richer more loving and more forgiving relationships. In our work, it leads to improved engagement, greater collaboration, reduced costs and higher returns on investment.

In his book The Moral Molecule, Paul Zak, neuroscientist and author shares that "Compared with people at low-trust companies, people at high-trust companies report: 74% less stress, 106% more energy at work, 50% higher productivity, 13% fewer sick days, 76% more engagement, 29% more satisfaction with their lives, 40% less burnout."

High trust builds stronger relationships, families, teams and organisations. It counteracts stress and promotes meaningful and joyful experiences. So why, if it can make our lives more meaningful, joyful, productive and abundant is there not more of it around? Great question.

Until it becomes a focus, we tend to build trust out of habit. And acting from habit is essentially consigning our behaviour to autopilot.

Autopilot is incredibly helpful. It enables us to take care of the basics of survival whilst conserving energy. But where trust is concerned, it means we tend to extend, build and reciprocate trust, without ever actively engaging our minds beyond the most basic conscious thoughts and responses.

When we're acting foremost from habit, building or breaking trust is like an exercise in minimum viable effort. We do it well enough to survive. But that's where the path diverges - separating those who do it well and thrive, from those who simply do it well just enough to survive and get by.

When we act on autopilot, the trust we build is often predictive rather than rooted in vulnerability. It's not the type of trust that can withstand tension or ambiguity. Unless of course, our habits have been built consciously or created with care. The difference lies in the quality of our habits.

Building the kind of game changing trust that you not only feel, but which you can see the effects of, requires self-awareness, conscious thought, practice and discipline. Like all things related to great relationships, though it sometimes comes naturally, keeping it alive and healthy requires some focus. It requires us to be attentive to connecting with the person we're with, rather than taking a 'one size fits all approach' based on our own defaults or preferences.

# A Crisis of Trust

*"Learning to trust is one of life's most difficult tasks."*

*Isaac Watts*

Trust is woven through the fabric of our lives. It is what holds our relationships, workplaces and ultimately our society together. Yet our trust in our workplaces, governments, financial institutions and our media outlets has fallen dramatically worldwide and can often feel fragile at best.

In the years since the global financial crisis and the ensuring recession, we have witnessed a feast of organisational and political scandals. We regularly hear about corporate tax avoidance on a global scale, politicians on the take and seemingly endless revelations of widespread and lengthy historic child sex abuse from people in positions of authority and civic trust.

But trust is still such a fundamental part of the human experience, that despite the evidence to the contrary, we still have an expectation that we should be able to trust our leaders, our peers and our significant others. Except, it's a need no one has taught us how to meet - in ourselves, or in each other.

No one teaches us how to initiate the kind of deep and abiding trust that sustains flexibility and faith within relationships, leaders and institutions. We're never taught how to rebuild it when it's broken, or how to nurture it into that powerful and rare slice of magic that is so deeply engaging and empowering to everyone it reaches.

Despite the importance of trust in relationships, our lives

have become so busy, and our attention so thinly spread that even when we know how to create the environments and initiate the conversations, we can struggle to find the time or energy to follow through with anything close to the consistency trust relies on to establish itself.

We work flexibly and remotely and under increasing time and resource pressure, giving us fewer opportunities to connect, build familiarity and mutual understanding and discover shared likes and dislikes.

We socialize in snapshots – snatched phone conversations, texts, and messaging or simply 'connecting' with friends across Facebook, Pinterest, Snapchat and Instagram. It seems, once you have a career or business, a family or social life and a home to maintain, the one to one quality connections and conversations that lead to deep trust don't happen without some serious organisation skills. Yet trust is the one thing we could all benefit from practicing more of.

# Trust Feeds Culture

Our relationships all sit within a wider context of culture, be it family, team, organisational, religious or ethnic; and culture presents a catch 22 of sorts.

The health of any culture is determined by which behaviours are valued, encouraged and reinforced. Whether there is openness or self-preservation, trust or suspicion, the way in which its members treat themselves and each other creates the cultural climate. That climate in turn creates a reinforcing loop which influences the behaviour of new members who join the group or organisation. Whether new members slowly integrate, or inevitably begin to feel like square pegs in round holes - who unsuccessfully agitate for change or eventually move on - the influence of culture is universal. The environments we work and live in, impact us whether we're consciously aware of it or not. Wherever our workplace, or family, sits on the spectrum between trust and suspicion, we feel and respond to it instinctively. It's human nature.

We know from personal experience the difference in working, or living, with people we know we can be open and honest with, and those with whom we feel we need to watch our back. Where there is vulnerability-based trust, we can relax in the knowledge that people know us, believe our intentions are good and are likely to listen to us without judging. There is a certain flexibility and freedom in these relationships. We know they may not always be smooth; we know there may be times where we may not always 'like' each other. Still, we are confident that we can speak up and be listened to. We know that within these relationships, people are interested. They are invested. They care. We interpret their behaviour through an assumption of good intent and we can reasonably expect to receive the benefit of the doubt in moments of bad judgment, when we've made mistakes, or when our comments land a little clumsily.

Within cultures, relationships remain dynamic even when we feel or believe our relationships are strong. There is always change, whether we want – or initiate - it or not. Whether there is growth, decline or apathy though, is determined by the people within those relationships. Everyone has a part to play whether we're ready to admit, or fully own, our role or not.

# Trust Enables Growth

Growth feels expansive and rich with opportunity. But growth requires innovation, change and the ability to venture into new arenas. Together. All of which requires a commitment to interdependence of members within the group, trial and error, the active and regular evaluation of risk vs. reward and open and frequent communication. All of which becomes significantly easier when trust exists between the members.

Strong, vulnerability-based trust shifts cultures and enables growth by changing the way we work, and live, together. With trust present, we feel more able – and encouraged - to share our` ideas, and our concerns, no matter how crazy they may seem. We foster a culture of collective contribution, responsibility and encouragement, where different perspectives are sought, explored, valued and built on.

Though trust – like culture - sits below the surface of our everyday awareness, it has the power to subtly influence all that we do. Whether we are opening up to collaboration and the sharing of ideas, energy and resources, or tempted to hold tight, play our cards close to our chest and stay quiet, trust is the driving force.

# First, Self-Trust, Then Connection

*"The best way to find out if you can trust somebody,*
*is to trust them."*

*Ernest Hemingway*

The paradox is that trust creates the ultimate double standard in relationships. We want openness and honesty from others, we want them to embrace a little vulnerability so we can gauge how much we can relate to and connect with them, so we can allow ourselves to trust them, but we don't want to risk being vulnerable ourselves.

Self-trust, and the capacity to build deep trust requires vulnerability. To be vulnerable, you need to know what you want, what you can give (without fear of losing a little of yourself) and you need to be vividly – even viscerally - aware of what constitutes a step too far.

Like all emotional energy exchanges, you can only comfortably give what you are able to lose. If you don't trust yourself, extending trust to others will always feel slightly uncomfortable. You may find yourself making decisions you later question the wisdom of.

Self-trust is characterized by a handful of traits that make for a powerful core of confidence;

- knowing that the beliefs you hold are consistently expressed through your behaviour;
- knowing your behaviour will be consistent, no matter who you are with or what pressure you are under;
- having the courage to try, and to make mistakes;
- being honest about your mistakes and choosing

candour, humility and learning in the face of shame or
embarrassment;

- comfort in extending compassion and care to the
people you work and live with even when you know it
may not be reciprocated;
- appreciating that you are making the best decisions
you can at the time you're making them, even if things
look different with hindsight.

When you trust yourself, the need for reciprocation lessens.
The desire may not completely disappear, but it stops being an
essential trade off which determines whether – or to what degree
- you collaborate with someone.

Though it can sound counterintuitive, the less we expect
others to 'give back' the more forthcoming people tend to
become. Generosity creates generosity. Released from the
expectations of others, we often find ourselves wanting to give
more. And when we do, the giving feels different – to both
giver and receiver. Acts of trustworthiness and generosity
both spawn more of the same. You simply have to create the
confidence that enables you to go first.

# Easily Said (or How We Mess it Up)

We tend to focus on solving the symptoms of a problem rather than the source. We try to fix people's thinking (to make it more like ours) rather than repair relationships.

Knowing there is a problem in a relationship isn't the difficult part. What's difficult is tracking the symptoms that show up back to the source of the problem.

We often attempt to solve an absence of trust by working on solving what we can see - the topic, or event - rather than seeing it as an opportunity to invest in understanding the relationship better. We cajole, discipline, argue, defend, sell, exclude and judge people when we could be listening, exploring, sharing and ultimately, resolving.

**We judge our behaviour, and the behaviour or others, by different standards.**

When we behave in ways that undermine trust, we attribute it to how stressed, tired, or concerned we are. We often assign our behaviour to our environment, rather than who we are as a person. When it comes to judging others - we can default to making it about who they are, rather than what they may be in the middle of. It's the fundamental attribution error at work. It can create double standards that blind us to the conversations we need to be having to create more human workplaces and more supportive homes.

**We assume that trust is either fixed, a given, or impossible to build.**

Trust is a choice. It isn't granted with status (although

expectations of trustworthiness are) and it can't be demanded through greater scrutiny and tighter control. It's an intrinsic quality which is earned and gifted. We can't make people trust us, but we can work on earning it.

## We assume that trust, once broken can't be rebuilt.

It can be hard to come back from a breach of trust, but it isn't impossible. In fact, in some cases, trust can return even stronger. When you know what you've lost and you're eager and committed to regaining it, your newfound respect and humility for the value and fragility of trust can make a relationship stronger and more durable. It depends on intent, credibility and consistency.

## We don't create space for it.

We take for granted that once people know us and have some experience of how we behave, that trust has been built and will continue to be a feature of our relationship. That's not always the case. We are all human, busy, juggling and all perennially caught up in our own work and lives. There are multiple opportunities for us to misstep in relationships without ever intending it, and sometimes, without even realising.

The underlying point I'm trying to make? Be genuine in your intent to create high trust relationships. Not all relationships require high trust to work well, just the ones that are close, or critical to your success in work and life. Sincerity is felt. So is insincerity. Aim to be quicker at recognizing your assumptions and your habits and moving instead towards being curious, respectful and genuine.

# From Inertia to Influence

In a world where almost everyone finds themselves questioning the trustworthiness of media, corporations, religious leaders and politician it's easy to feel distinct or separated from what is happening. And it's that feeling that disconnects us from the influence we can have, leading us to rely on others to take the first steps. As the saying goes – when you're complaining about the traffic, it pays to remember that you <u>are</u> the traffic. Or, in the case of societies, organisations, or families that feel like they've gone rogue, <u>you</u> are a part of that culture or dynamic.

Whether you acknowledge - or believe - it or not, you have influence on the people and the world around you simply by virtue of your presence. And though you may question how much one person can achieve, it's worth remembering that many incredible shifts and movements began with a single, committed person. Think about Rosa Parks who quietly and resolutely started a revolution in response to racial segregation; Steve Jobs who forever changed the way we communicate, connect, relax and manage our lives; and Nelson Mandela who campaigned for freedom of rights. Each had different backgrounds, different aspirations and vastly different lives, but what they had in common was a single-minded maverick approach to standing by their beliefs.

And though our aspirations in terms of how we expect to live and work with others may seem so much smaller by comparison, they are no less grand or necessary. We all have the inherent capability to move the dial and create more trust and trustworthiness within ourselves, our private lives and our professional lives. We can – if we choose to – become great role models for trust and enjoy our lives more in the process.

In a world where trust in institutions, media and senior leaders is declining, and where our human need to connect and to feel safe remains inherently strong, we have the potential to create a shift that makes a real and noticeable difference. All any of us needs, is the desire to begin and the skills and motivation to continue. Change – at any level – begins with us.

# SECTION THREE:

SELF-TRUST

*Trusting ourselves emboldens us
to live with greater courage and conviction.
It keeps us focused, in flow, and allows us to
develop strength and flexibility.*

# Why Self-Trust Matters

*"Just trust yourself, then you will know how to live."*

*Johann Wolfgang von Goethe*

If there were no crisis of confidence, no imposter syndrome, no self-doubt and no midlife crisis, there'd be no need to explore self-trust.

But enduring self-trust is what sense checks our decisions, buttresses a leap of faith, emboldens us to make decisions others may hesitate over, and enables us to swiftly navigate the self-confidence hiccups that affect most of us at one time or another in our lives.

Decision fatigue, tiredness, overwhelm, uncertainty and significant life changes can rapidly deplete our self-trust. Humans were never designed to live in constant stress, or insecurity, yet in the architecture of our modern lives, that is precisely what many of us do.

Whether it manifests as persistent worry or anxiety, or full-blown burnout, the combination of career security, the safety and health of family and friends, financial freedom, our own health, and our home environment combine to keep us fully alert to risk every waking moment.

If we're lucky, our lives don't begin that way. If we're lucky the responsibility, and our exposure to adversity, is light through our childhoods and into adulthood. Typically, a great deal of the early part of our adulthood is spent shaping who we are and carving out our place in the world. We slowly graduate from a life of study and familiar social and family circles into a career we hope will be pivotal in creating a fully lived life - however we define it.

With our career trajectory or aspirations in sight - and in motion - we tend to turn our attention to building out the life around us. Turning houses into homes, creating our own family units, broadening our social circles and branching out into new hobbies and passions, side careers, and more.

And along the way, we're taking cues. From our friends, our family members, lecturers and teachers, bosses, colleagues, teammates and a host of role models we aspire to emulate. Whether subtle or maverick, jarring or congruent, their influences shape the decisions we make. We compare ourselves to them and test out aspects of their life to see what fits. We test new ways of thinking and behaving to see what feels like us - or at least the 'us' that we aspire to become.

Then things begin to gradually change. Sometimes not always for the best.

We say yes to promotions that challenge our competence and confidence and which sometimes lead us into the grip of imposter syndrome.

We say yes to relationships that - on the surface - make sense but never quite feel right and steadily result in self-doubt, low self-esteem, or harm.

We wake up and realize the life we've created might look good on the outside, but it no longer feels like the right fit. Sometimes, we wake up realising that we've followed a blueprint that feels out of touch with what really matters to us. Sometimes we're so disconnected, we're not even sure what matters to us anymore.

And sometimes, we find ourselves trusting others more than we trust ourselves. It's not uncommon to treat someone else's judgement as more trustworthy than our own. It's a natural step in learning and a natural part of relationships to sometimes let others take the lead on a direction of travel.

When it comes to our instinct and intuition however, these are such perfectly designed and precisely tuned instruments that it's also not uncommon to regret deferring to others despite its warning signals.

When your instinct is telling you to sit up and take notice, it's better to learn from your own judgement (whether it's right or wrong) and to build your self-trust than to solely put your trust in others.

The environments that we live in are critical. Humans are adaptive creatures, we adjust our behaviour to be able to survive in work and life. Our brain is always sensing, making sense of, and triggering reactions in response to our environment. That process of continual subtle adaptation shapes our thinking, our behaviour and even the way our genes express themselves. Adaptation redirects and changes the energy flow in our brains and results in a process of neural plasticity, creating new pathways for anything which repeatedly holds our attention with disciplined focus and energy.

Simply put, we can literally change the shape and strengthen the function of areas of our brains through stress and fear; and equally, through safety and optimism. Just as living in prolonged fear heightens our senses, living in safety calms them.

Rediscovering self-trust enables us to reframe the situations that otherwise hamper our self-belief and limit our ability to access our resourcefulness. It enables us to transform those difficult situations into learning curves that build our strength, confidence and resilience.

# Why Anxiety Feels Inescapable

We start learning in life by modelling others, so it makes sense that even as adults moving through our 20's and beyond, we're modelling the lives of others. It's natural to draw comparisons between the lives we are leading and the lives we imagine others have. It gets messy when we confuse the aspirational value of positive role modelling with direct comparisons which can be misinformed and corrosive.

Comparisons, whether they make us feel better or worse, aren't healthy unless they're inspiring us with enthusiasm and a positive desire to stretch ourselves a little further. To test our own limits in the pursuit of meaning, enjoyment and fulfilment.

Even in the pursuit of our own ambitions we can lose sight of what really matters to us as we find ourselves being socially and professionally conditioned by the people we spend our lives with. It's too easy to find yourself on a path where you wake up wondering whether the life you're in is the one you really wanted after all.

Self-trust helps us regulate the ways in which we benchmark ourselves against others to keep it in perspective. The aspects of self-care and credibility that make up self-trust, enables us to step back from keeping up with 'The Jones's' and dial back any creeping feelings of imposter syndrome. Self-trust acts like a compass, helping us recalibrate after significant change and rebalance our equilibrium after difficult experiences.

A life of pushing, pursuing, and competing can test our mental, emotional and physical strength. Yet when we free our mental, physical and emotional energy from toxic habits, we regain the bandwidth to take the steps we need to look after ourselves properly. And to avoid, or self-correct our thoughts and behaviour when we notice them taking us in directions we know don't work for us.

However, to live life fully we do need a degree of tension. It keeps us striving, focused, energised and on our toes. It's when the pressure seems never ending (when you can't see the light at the end of the tunnel) or when it feels so big that it overwhelms our ability to effectively deal with it, that it becomes maladaptive. That pervading sense of risk pulls our focus from thinking and behaving in ways that are constructive and connected towards destructive, disconnected and protective. It replaces open trust with wary evaluation.

The more time we spend in survival mode, rushing to get things done, reacting automatically, rather than taking a moment to choose what feels right, the more we feed the cycle of tiredness, insecurity, fear, suspicion and social comparison that can feel difficult to escape. It's in that place that self-belief, self-trust and self-efficacy begin to slowly and steadily erode, undermining our mental, emotional and physical health.

What is more harmful, is when we gradually acclimatize to all of those influences over time to the extent that it becomes our new normal. We put our tiredness and constant distraction down to the pace of life, rather than our inability to generate enough energy through our work and life to balance what we're burning through, and to create the necessary focus and certainty to live how we really want to.

However, even when faced with pressure, being able to trust ourselves and others, is the difference between getting the space or support we need to navigate the situation in healthy ways, or faltering under the weight of it. Even in times of trauma, there is the possibility of positive, generative outcomes (referred to as Post Traumatic Growth) which is every bit as real and as powerful as Post Traumatic Stress.

Life is not a static proposition. It's unpredictable and sometimes chaotic. At the most basic and fundamental of levels, the only 'elements' you can control is you; how you think and act. The only person you can ever rely on to be there for you - forever and always - is you. And in that sense, the practice of trust begins with you. Trust in yourself enables the resilience to roll with what life brings.

Building self-trust creates greater belief in your own strength and self-efficacy in the face of pressure. Of your belief in being, or of becoming equal to the task, being able to find the support or resources you need to make it through, or to simply view the pressure or stress as an opportunity for growth or expression.

When we can begin trusting our own instincts again, and to trust that the world - and our relationships - won't fall apart if we make some changes, we can begin to tune out the things we know aren't healthy for us and tune back into the signs our mind, emotions and body are sending.

If we want to tap into trust as a way of reframing the challenges we're facing, we need effective ways of recognizing when we're in the grip of negative tension and strategies for stepping back from it to allow our bodies time to return to a rest state.

Building self-trust gives you the perspective to identify, establish and enforce the boundaries that are required for carving out that rest and restoration time.

# Derailing Distractions

The demands on our attention and time mean that mastering self-trust becomes a daily discipline that slowly gets easier over time. Like any new habit worth nurturing it takes desire (to want to make it work, but also to be open to failing sometimes) and persistence.

The road to self-trust is littered with diversions and distractions, so it pays to be aware of what they look like and how to meet them head on, so they don't slow you down.

In a hyper connected world where many people hold multiple roles or pull double shifts (moving from work, to carer or volunteer) there's little time to reflect on what is and isn't working for us in life. Without that regular, reflective practice, it's easy to slowly lose the relationship with ourselves. It becomes easy to simply spend so much time facing outwards that we never sense check that the decisions we make, and the action we take, is consistent with who we want to be and how we want to live. Being true to who you are and how you want to live – being credible with consistency - builds strength and confidence. It's a powerful and liberating mix.

# Reflection, Humility and Learning from Mistakes

Building self-trust can seem unimportant and inconvenient. Self-reflection can feel awkward, meandering and inconsequential. It's much easier to focus on other people, or other things. Yet the best way to fully understand any concept that involves human relationships is to begin with your relationship with yourself. Knowing what brings you joy, what grates your nerves, your triggers, your strengths, your foibles, your aspirations, who you are at your best and your worst, when to be disciplined and when to be gentle with yourself, even *how* to be gentle with yourself. By knowing ourselves well, we can more closely align what we are doing, with who we want to be, and we become more graceful and present with everyone else.

Genuine self-trust requires reflecting on whether we're extending ourselves the same degree of relationship care and consideration we would to a close friend. It means taking the time to take stock of whether we're doing what we say we will, both well and with consistency. Reviewing whether the way we *want* to behave as people – and the way we actually *do* behave – are aligned and grounding our credibility.

It means knowing what each of those things looks like to us in the context of our lives so we can recognize the contrast between what happens when we're on track and what happens when we're not.

It means knowing that we won't always get it right, especially when we're new to practicing it, and holding the faith that we will get it right. That with practice comes not perfection, but progress; and a consistency that helps us find an authentic way of behaving that better fits the best version of ourselves.

## Balancing Tension and Trust

*"Between stimulus and response there is space. In that space is our power to choose our response. In our response lies our growth and our freedom."*

*Viktor E. Frankl*

We know that being at our best, whether it's how we perform at work or how well we live life, means being free from persistent worry or stress (not to be confused with regular pressure which in bursts can be great for us), energised, physically fit and geared for resilience.

So what stops us from turning what we know into real, practical, sustainable change?

The paradox is, our daily lives which demand we connect more effectively, more often, and to be more open and embracing of trust, slowly nudge us out of thriving mode and into 'surviving' mode where we default to self-preservation. The more time we spend in survival mode, the more tired and discouraged we tend to become. It's where self-belief, self-trust and self-efficacy are slowly and steadily eroded.

In contrast, self-trust and a more trusting outlook on the world we inhabit, engenders a sense of self-worth and security which allows us to feel connected to the people and events around us, without being unduly swayed by them.

We begin trusting our own instincts again, we tune out a little more to the things we know aren't healthy for us and we begin tuning back into the signals our mind, emotions and body are sending.

With our mental, physical and emotional energy freed from toxic habits, we have the bandwidth to take appropriate steps to look after ourselves properly and to avoid, or self-correct our thoughts and behaviour when we notice them taking us in directions we know don't work for us.

Yet it's not actually the pressure inherent in our lives that is the enemy, at least not in finite bursts. Studies have shown that pressure is healthy for us and that even the effects of stress can be largely determined by whether we view stress as positive or negative.

In fact, to live fully we need a degree of tension – it keeps us striving, focused, energised and on our toes. It's when the pressure seems never ending (when you can't see the light at the end of the tunnel) or when it feels so big that it overwhelms our ability to effectively deal with, it that it suddenly becomes corrosive.

Even when faced with pressure, self-trust and the ability to feel safe trusting others, can be the difference between getting the space or support you need to navigate the situation in healthy ways and faltering under the weight of it.

When we feel tired and overwhelmed, it's tempting to think the answer is to find some down time. And while that helps, it's a short-term solution to a potentially longer-term problem. Too much unrelenting pressure is as damaging for us as too little (the result is rust out – which is every bit as real as it's opposite – burn out).

As well as finding time out to catch your breath, working on building your self-trust will give you a stronger sense of your own strength and self-efficacy in the face of pressure. Of being equal to the task, or being able to find the support or resources you need to make it through, or to simply view the pressure or stress as an opportunity for growth or expression.

The reality for many of us is that we now exist in a

permanent state of high alert, yet we haven't honed the skills to trust ourselves to respond in ways that bolster our confidence and competence. Or the skills to foster trust in the nearest and most important relationships which we rely on to help us get the time, space and support we need to work and live at our best.

Instead, we check our devices with feelings ranging from anxiety to expectation, we race to meet deadlines, say yes when we'd really love to say no, try to be all things to all people (the consummate professional and the loving parent / friend / sibling / offspring, supportive and engaging partner). Most of us are doing double time simply to make our professional and our personal lives work. Time for ourselves, for reflection for recharging our energy is often at best, hard won, and at worst, de-prioritized in the face of those competing demands.

If those scenarios feel familiar, then you'll already know that persistent stress or worry can be emotionally, mentally and physically exhausting. When our bodies are under that degree of sustained demand, without respite, we are effectively living in a perpetual state of fear. Our brain is in a heightened state of awareness, our emotions are primed, and our body is reading us for battle or a fast escape.

Suddenly every little thing is scanned for its potential to harm us. Small things seem big, perspective becomes elusive and we become more concerned with protecting ourselves than connecting with others.

We all need to be able to step back from that tension, from time to time. Not just to allow our bodies time to recover and return to a rest state (which is vital for resetting our system), but to avoid longer term changes to our bodies.

Building self-trust gives you the perspective to identify,

establish and enforce the boundaries that are required for carving out that rest and restoration time.

# Trust, Tension and Our Overworked Nervous System

*"Fear is the easiest emotional response to trigger and the fastest route to burnout."*

*Brown, Kingsley, Paterson (Fear Free Organisation, 2015)*

Viktor E. Frankl's quote is a powerful reminder of the grace we are capable of when we pause before responding. He wrote this from the perspective of us having more power over our mind and our subsequent behaviour than we realize. In life, finding that space, when we're busy, tense or faced with confrontation, can be hard because of how instinctively we respond to threats, stress and pressure.

While the world around us changes dramatically from generation to generation, increasing the demands on our time and attention, our internal wiring is still prompting us to respond to the world - and its steady pace of change and challenge - as though we were cavemen.

Our bodies - well designed though they are - were never meant to cope with unrelenting pressure. They are designed to keep us safe and alive. By being tapped into stress, uncertainty or pressure, we are playing havoc with its natural rhythm.

We have within us, a remarkable set of nervous systems. A vast and complex internal communication and control network which sends messages throughout our body to keep us alive, alert and responsive to our environment.

Within that nervous system network is the Autonomic Nervous System - a system that controls the involuntary and subconscious actions and reactions that enable us to live without having to consciously think about every breath or heartbeat. The Autonomic Nervous System contains the two regulating systems that are designed to work together to keep us safe and healthy, flipping us from safety and trust to fear and mistrust.

The Sympathetic Nervous System drives our fight, freeze or flight response to fear or perceived threats while the Parasympathetic Nervous System drives our 'rest, repair and digest'. The two work in tandem to stimulate (when we need to act quickly to defend or protect ourselves) and deregulate our system (to allow us the time to recharge, repair and heal when we can do so safely).

The difficulty comes when persistent pressure tips that healthy balance into a Sympathetic Nervous System dominance instead. Where fight, flight or freeze begins to feel like our default setting. That imbalance leaves the Parasympathetic Nervous System less time to correct our bodies systems and restore order after that stress response.

In Dr Libby Weaver's book 'Rushing Women's Syndrome' she talks about the effects of Sympathetic Nervous System dominance. She cites some simple patterns which cause exhaustion and which, left unchecked, can lead to Sympathetic Nervous System dominance:
- Inability to say no
- Seeking approval, acceptance and love
- Not putting yourself first
- Lack of sleep
- Over exercising

- Lack of solitude
- Excess liver loaders (such as sugars, alcohol, caffeine, trans fats, synthetic substances and infections).

According to Dr Weaver, even trying to release stress by running can reinforce the message that you're in flight mode.

When things get out of whack with our stress levels, we can end up being dominated by our Sympathetic Nervous System. Our heart rate stays high, our breathing remains shallow and rapid, our digestive function is impaired, and we find ourselves more prone to food cravings, hunger, overeating and deep tiredness.

Strong boundaries that allow us to retain a healthy control over our own time, energy and commitments, plus the standard staples of good diet and nutrition, regular exercise, rest time and good sleep are all critical in activating the Parasympathetic Nervous System and our 'rest, repair, digest' functions.

While Sympathetic Nervous System dominance may not directly impact your inclination to trust, it can give you a much shorter tolerance, making you more defensive, more reactive and less open to others. And while people who know you will wait it out, if it doesn't change, it can cause lasting damage to you and your relationships.

# Trust, Patterns and Emotional Sabotage

Being aware of where our emotions are taking us - and how the chemicals they release can hook us into autopilot - can help us initiate the first step in regaining our composure. The step of pulling ourselves back from triggered behaviour which is as disruptive to ourselves as it is to others, and to behaving in more resourceful, productive and positive ways.

Once an emotion becomes a feeling, the chemical reaction that floods our body can leave us a little emotionally drunk. Our first five emotions - fear, anger, disgust, shame and sadness - result in survival responses which release adrenalin (to trigger an instant response) and cortisol (to redirect blood flow and alter biological processes, slowing down some functions, while speeding up others more necessary for fight or flight). The collective result is to effectively kickstart our body's fight or flight processes.

Most of the time we're in the grip of these feelings, we're not really going to run or physically fight, but the shifts in our behaviour screams (to anyone near us) that we're in survival mode. We become defensive, argumentative. We withdraw, withhold, or sabotage ourselves and others in small and subtle ways.

The two emotion combinations; excitement/joy and trust/love result in attachment behaviour which motivates us to support, engage and connect with others. The attachment emotions release dopamine (which brings us a sense of reward and pleasure), adrenalin (which prompts us to take immediate action), serotonin (which relaxes us and makes us feel more confident) and oxytocin (which prompts us to socialize and bond with others).

Surprise – as we've mentioned earlier - can push us either way depending on the nature of the surprise. It can move us towards the survival end of the spectrum where we focus on putting our own needs first and self-protection. Or towards attachment, motivating us to be with and connect to others.

Though it might be unreasonable to expect that we could spend the majority of our life feeling pleasantly surprised and basking in joy, trust and love, it helps to know a little about this natural spectrum we all move back and forth along. It's also helpful to realize that just as we swing towards one end, like pendulums we can swing back too.

Attachment emotions are a great incubator for trust. Ideally, we need to create more moments where those feelings can prevail. All emotions though are a source of feedback and learning. And sometimes, depending on your personal history or circumstance, you may find that you spend more time in avoidance mode. Both avoidance and attachment emotions can create more of the same. Both create changes in your brain (remember neuroplasticity?). But when you can recognize and understand the patterns that take you there, and release yourself from them using strategies based on your strengths, you begin to free yourself from them.

Self-reflection is one of the ways to create shifts. The trick here is not to overthink it, but to view the pattern that grips you with curiosity. Our survival patterns are there for very good reason – once they were what your body believed was necessary to stay safe. It's disingenuous to suggest that positive thinking alone, or an iron clad discipline, will override them. Though they may in time, it can be a path that leads to more struggle, disappointment and pain. Instead, recognize that these patterns were - once - here to help. Take an objective look at them through the lens that is your life today and weigh what information is important for you to know right now. In this moment. Then hold and acknowledge that, be grateful for the nudge (as strange as that sounds there is science to back choosing to acknowledge your innate wisdom rather than dismissing it). Then let the rest fall away.

Another way to transcend patterns that no longer work for you - or which you now recognize never have - is knowing your triggers and your strengths. Most of us can point to one particular 'button' which when pushed unleashes the beast within us. Being triggered is human and it would be impossible to expect to ever live life without the interruption of triggering events or people (tempting though it sounds!). So, work with what you have. There is a wonderful psychometric tool I use with clients, which - as part of the practice - has an exercise called 'The Journey to Composure'. The exercise encourages you to choose one 'overextension' which you know you find yourself in the grip of. You're encouraged to think about what you notice when that happens. The thoughts that run through your mind, any physical sensations you experience and any ways in which your behaviour changes. That step is important because pausing while you're mid rant, or reaction, is hard, so having multiple ways to recognize you're in the grip is helpful. Then you look at two core strengths you possess which you could lean on to help you regain your composure, and what you would tell yourself to help access that quality.

Fighting to overcome something can feel energy and effort intensive and can feed the negativity. Conversely, simply seeing it (rather than being in it), listening to any instinctive nudges or reminders it's giving you, deciding what is relevant and then letting go can be a surprisingly gentle and powerful experience. As with many things in life, observing, embracing and then releasing, or letting go is one of the most profound interactions we can have.

# Reframing Fear to Tap into Self-Trust

Fear, stress and anxiety are all a necessary part of our body's survival regulation. We can't switch them off, but to restore self-trust, we do need to be able to differentiate between them; to understand when we're in their grip and to know how to release ourselves. Because although they're distinct, they each draw our energy away from our executive brain and back to a place of self-preservation.

Our brains primary function is sustaining our survival, yet the energy in our brains cannot be at full strength, in two places, at once. So, if we're scared, stressed, or worrying about the uncontrollable, we diminish our ability to fix the very problems we're facing.

We know we're stressed when the removal of the 'stressor' (the event or circumstances) removes the feeling of the stress. Brief periods of stress can be a good thing for our productivity, and positive stress (eustress) is a core component of growth and resilience. Stress, little and often can build our competence, our confidence and our resilience. It becomes distress when we pass the point of positive impact and can feel only the downsides.

Anxiety is the perception or anticipation of risk or danger. It's future based, outside of our immediate control, sometimes shapeless and can feel immobilizing.

Fear is what we feel when we know or sense something is wrong. It's what we feel when we are or may be in danger.

In her book Playing Big, Author and Coach Tara Mohr shares how Rabbi Alan Lew wrote about the way in which in biblical Hebrew, fear is known by different words; Pachad and

Yirah. Pachad is similar to anxiety; it's worry, whether real or imagined, about things that have yet to happen. Yirah is that feeling you get when you're in the presence of something bigger than yourself. Yirah is the kind of fear when you feel scared and excited at the same time. It's what you feel when you're on the brink of something big.

Simply naming and reframing what you're feeling can be enough to bring a fresh perspective and new levels of resourcefulness.

# Trust and Trauma

Most of us have an awareness of Post-Traumatic Stress Disorder and an understanding or appreciation of how it can turn someone's world upside down and forever alter their world view. We accept that there is no way someone can experience traumatic events without being altered in some way by them.

But seemingly 'small' things can leave a surprisingly big impact too. A concept known as 'little T' is slowly gaining awareness. It refers to those traumas which, though they may not have proved life threatening, called our safety into question in such a strong and indelible way that it shapes our future perceptions of the world.

Those 'little T' traumas, which include experiences such as withholding love or affection, neglect, abuse and isolation, divorce, redundancy and extreme stress can leave you battle scarred and wary. We all experience those events differently, but when they leave you feeling insecure and guarded, being thrust into – or reminded of - those experiences makes it harder to resist the temptation to protect yourself which automatically threatens interpersonal trust.

How safe we feel in the world unavoidably impacts our capacity to trust - whether the object of our trust is people or institutions. Trauma – even of the 'little T' variety - can leave you with a sensitized antenna when it comes to interpersonal relationships, changes or simply daily life.

When we experience something as traumatic, the sensations are so painful and our brains so eager to protect us from ever encountering it again, that we quickly file the information away. Unfortunately, in our brains' haste to store the memory away and promptly move on, we miss the essential step of processing those memories - and the feelings they triggered - properly. Instead, they get filed in a chaotic emotional jumble and when something we're experiencing in our life triggers the recall of even a small slice of that memory, our brain dives in to retrieve it fully. That full retrieval comes from a place of service - our brains are expecting to find a helpful reference there for us, and as it brings that (intentionally helpful) memory out of storage, it brings with it all of its original emotional heat.

Trauma is a deeply personal experience that can surface years after the fact, finding expression in small and uncomfortably surprising ways. Getting to the heart of the hurt or fear, unpacking the experience with a trusted professional who can help you emotionally, mentally and physically process – and move through – the memory can help you get to a place where it's hold on you is released. It may not be possible to lose the memory, or the pain of it, but sometimes it's possible to ease the intensity and get to a place where you can have the memory and the emotions without 'being had' by them.

We may not always see the scars of little T trauma or know whether someone's capacity for trust is related to something deeply frightening in their life. What we can do is practice the compassion, inclusion and openness that fosters the psychological safety which leads to trust.

Early childhood trauma can make trust harder to build as an adult.

Studies have shown that children who miss out on safety and security in their formative years can struggle to fully trust others as adults. Those early experiences shape their world views, making trust a much harder gift to bestow.

It's been reported that when children's needs aren't being met by the people charged with their care, the situation is experienced by children as a direct threat to their survival by virtue of the fact that their survival relies on the support of their caregiver.

Does that mean you will never fully trust others? No. It will likely mean you may need work a little harder to opening yourself up to the vulnerability of trust. Developing strong self-trust and then building a small '1%' circle of people you can bring in close and begin gently establishing reciprocal vulnerability with are good places to start.

# The Biology and Physiology of Trust

As we move through our lives, we are constantly evaluating whether to trust or not, whether we're consciously aware of those moment to moment evaluations or not. That experience is reaching us on a mental, emotional and physical level, shaping or reinforcing our beliefs, our behaviour and ultimately, creating lasting changes in our brains and our bodies.

When you live in a heightened state of stress and worry, several things can happen;

- You can become addicted to adrenalin (think 'workaholic');
- Your brain changes shape; your amygdala (the part of your brain which regulates the release of stress chemicals into your body) can enlarge;
- You alter your genes (transcription genes pick up 'memories' of your environment to help you evolve);
- You create pathways in your brain that results in those 'negative' connections becoming a faster, more natural and more automatic subconscious response, meaning you may end up becoming more risk averse and/or pessimistic whether you intend to or not.

You may have already experienced the addictive nature of adrenalin without even realising it. If you have ever panicked if your day isn't spent running from meeting to meeting; realized your short-term memory is shot; found it hard to relinquish control; or been on holiday and found it incredibly hard to unwind you'll know what adrenalin feels like. A senior (and quite brilliant) woman I once worked for admitted to me

74

she had jumped back onto her blackberry within half an hour after giving birth. We don't do these things when we feel safe, or when we genuinely trust ourselves, others and our place in an organisation.

Work addiction may be a little easier to grasp – it's no longer the preserve of the egomaniacs or control freaks. Instead, it's something most of us have experienced, or teetered on the edge of at some point throughout our career. Combine a period of consistently high-volume workloads and a strong desire to do all you can to sustain quality of both work and relationships and you have a recipe for resetting the way you work. Without the social and systemic support that allows you to pull back, to catch your breath and return to a more 'normal' pace, you can become stuck in a cycle of feeling as though you are constantly in fifth gear. There's a place for trust in these tense environments, but rarely the space to foster it.

Part of the reason patterns can become so hard to break is thanks to our body's incredible capacity for creating habits. If you have habits that are so ingrained, it takes significant energy and focus to behave differently, you'll have experienced the full force of your brains incredible ability to autopilot those behaviours you repeat most frequently. It's a way of conserving energy, of releasing you from the need to consider everything you do. It consigns the frequently worn, deeply trodden paths to the far reaches of your subconscious, to free up energy for your conscious brain to concentrate on the variables in our life which require our full awareness and attention. It works incredibly well, unless those paths (our patterns) are damaging, in which case, changing your patterns essentially means upgrading your biology. Not impossible, just purposeful, committed work.

So, what happens under your skin when you're in a state of trust vs. distrust?

By now, you're probably realising that by the time we're acting out either trust or safety vs. distrust, stress or fear - a series of changes has already taken place without you even being consciously aware. Your brain is sending signals and pumping chemicals through your body, designed to either put you on alert, prepare you to fight or flee, or to regulate those initial shocks and reassure your entire system that you are safe from harm.

When we're feeling fearful, or stressed, the chemicals released by our brain means our sympathetic nervous system springs into action. It's this system which subconsciously drives the fight or flight responses throughout our body; burning sugar for fuel, saving fat for survival further down the track and speeding up our heart rate. It relies on the Parasympathetic Nervous System to counterbalance it once it gets messages of safety from your Central Nervous System. Once your brain sends the signal you're out of danger, the role of the Parasympathetic Nervous System is to provide your body with the rest and repair activity it needs to restore balance. To slow your heart rate and respiration and to allow your digestive processes to return to normal function.

Cortisol is one of the chemicals most frequently mentioned for its role in responding to stress. It isn't damaging though when it's doled out in the small doses our body was intended to release. It's designed to help us by regulating our sleep and waking cycles, and by following the release of adrenalin (also in small doses) to restore our body to a normal state after a stressful experience.

But cortisol can stay active in our body long after a

stressful event has occurred. While the effects of cortisol can reduce by half in as little as an hour or 90 minutes, we can find ourselves still reeling from breaches of trust hours, days and even weeks later. Reliving the memories, whether we're replaying them in our mind or talking about what happened with others, keeps us experiencing the event long after it's actually taken place.

The role of cortisol in a sympathetic nervous system response - when our amygdala has been triggered - is to help shut down unnecessary functions so our full resources can be turned towards dealing with the imminent threat. It enables glucose to be released and mobilized in our blood stream giving us the fuel to run or fight. This stress-based response is supposed to be short-lived. But when cortisol is high, it does a number of things which are unhelpful when they don't switch off. It:

- partially shuts down our immune system;
- stops muscle and bone growth (by inhibiting the uptake of amino acids into muscles and inhibiting calcium absorption in the intestine);
- drives up blood pressure by making the body more sensitive to noradrenalin (norepinephrine) and adrenalin (epinephrine);
- disrupts our reproductive systems;
- causes intense hunger and food cravings;

Most crucially, when cortisol remains high for prolonged periods, it can stop the feedback mechanism that allows our Parasympathetic Nervous System to step in, address the chemical overload and restore balance.

# The Neuroscience of Trust

We know how trust and distrust feels and we're aware of how it changes our behaviour. What neuroscience has uncovered is that our mental energy shifts depending on whether we feel we can trust or not, literally opening up, or closing off areas of function in our brain.

We know from experience that when we trust others, we are more likely to:

- Assume good intent;
- Remain open minded and be more likely to request - and hear -the viewpoints of others;
- Find creative solutions to problems which take into consideration – and, ultimately aim to meet - the needs of others;
- Evaluate information in a clear and logical way which factors in emotions without being trumped by them;
- Employ abstract thinking skills;
- Seek and volunteer support;
- Visualize and weigh a range of possible solutions or future outcomes, rather than settling for what is known, or safe;
- Engage with curiousity and interest rather than judgement and opinion.

The ability to do all of those things rests in our Pre-Frontal Cortex (PFC), or what is commonly referred to as our Executive Brain. They are (both literally and metaphorically) the higher brain functions.

Our PFC is the most recent evolutionary step in our brain

development. Its where we move beyond our basic survival needs, beyond the pull (not influence) of emotions to reflect objectively on what's before us. It's where we have the capacity to look a little further and a little broader for possible options. It's the part of our brain that allows us to evaluate, rationalize, plan, moderate our behaviour and connect with others.

On the flip side, when we're stressed or fearful, our energy is immediately drawn back to, and centred in, the Limbic Brain (sometimes referred to as our emotional brain), the part of our brain tasked with keeping us safe from threats. This is the place where we assess and respond to risks. The place where adrenalin and cortisol are released and where our triggers originate to switch our emotions and behaviour from 'connect' (when we anticipate trust) to 'protect' (when we anticipate distrust).

Trapped in that instinctive state of auto pilot, where our higher need (whether perceived or real) is to protect ourselves, we naturally put our own needs ahead of others and take evasive and defensive action to keep ourselves safe. Building strong relationships and collaborating with co-workers is the least of our worries – suddenly our focus in on saving our own skin. Our mindset shifts, our ability to think suffers, our behaviour changes, and our health, relationships and work all suffer.

It might not seem like much of a leap to think that if we feel safe, our system relaxes, and our mental attention moves back toward our executive brain where (if we have peace of mind) we can openly and unguardedly connect with others. However, patterns of mistrust can be deep seated, unconscious and difficult to override without some awareness, reflection and disciplined practice.

Our brains are intricate, amazing pieces of anatomy that scientists are still unravelling the mysteries of. When it comes to the brains we most commonly think of (since there's now reference to the gut brain and the heart brain which contain 100 million neurons and 40,000 neurons respectively) there are three areas; the reptilian brain, the limbic brain and the neocortex. Each work together to sense, process and react to both fear and safety.

The reptilian brain (our 'survival' brain) is an ancient part of our hardwiring that drives our survival by regulating and sustaining our bodily functions. If you've heard people refer to 'lizard brain' behaviour, this is where that behaviour is stemming from. Emotions begin here - visual emotional stimuli registers in this part of our brain (the brainstem) before travelling to the frontal cortex which is where we first become aware. That happens in less than 1/10 of a second.

The Limbic brain (our 'emotional brain') houses our senses and our memory and processes the emotions from our lizard/survival brain. It influences trust by assigning meaning to our emotions based on previous experience and expectation, and by triggering the motivation to behave in a certain way.

The neocortex (our 'thinking' brain) is the most recent evolutionary development in our brain. It drives our thinking and is sometimes referred to as the thinking brain. It connects the other parts of brain function and brings thinking and comprehension to the mix of emotions. The Pre-Frontal Cortex (PFC) that sits at the front of this part of our brain acts as our modern-day command and control centre. It plays one of the most important roles in trust in action by evaluating our responses and moderating them for the environment before we physically act.

Ultimately, this is where we tend to act rather than react. When we instinctively feel safe, it's easy for our attention to reside here, being creative, intuitive, proactive, social and relaxed. When we can recognize the signs that we're deep in mistrust territory, we can switch to observer mode. We can begin interrupting our natural responses to change our behaviour, and actively bring ourselves back to a place of safety where we restore the full use of our 'thinking brain'.

# Amygdala Hijack

Amygdala hijack is an experience many of us have had, even if we've never heard the term. If you've ever felt yourself react to something in ways that feel totally disproportionate, you will know what it is like to be in the grip of this increasingly common phenomenon.

It's that uncomfortable '0-100 miles an hour in 2 seconds' experience of responding with more emotion and heat than you expected. It can happen when your patience has worn thin, when you're too tired to be socially sensitive towards a situation, or because the experience you're in is triggering an emotional memory you have yet to fully resolve (possibly a 'little T' experience you haven't fully processed – read 'Trust and Trauma' to find out more about little T).

Our amygdala is where emotions are learned, and emotional memories are held. Our emotions create strong neural pathways in our brains and unfortunately, our brains aren't concerned about whether we're feeling pleasure or pain, nor do they filter what they learn. All of our experiences are recorded. It's the extreme experiences and repeated patterns which become the 'go to' responses when our brains start pattern matching in an attempt to prepare us for what lies ahead - good, bad or ugly.

But our emotional wiring and our amygdala are linked to survival which is why bad experiences seem so much slower to leave, and so much quicker to return, than the good ones. We're programmed to prioritise and remember threat for the sake of our survival. Sights, sounds, words that we associate with fear, tap straight into our amygdala and instantly trigger our defenses

Amygdala hijack matters. Not least because losing our cool is the last thing we need, but because it's emotionally and physically exhausting to redirect your energies into reacting when you could be working on something more proactive instead.

Amygdala hijack can also alert you to unresolved issues that become triggers for us which become more raw and sensitized the more tired and stressed we become.

Realising that we're in the throes of something that's been triggered by, but isn't solely related to the situation in hand, can help us restore a little perspective. The first step to dialing down the amygdala hijack is bringing yourself back to the present moment and what is happening now.

Sometimes those unexpected outbursts highlight our need for rest and distance to regain our equilibrium. Sometimes they highlight a bigger unresolved emotional memory that requires our attention - and the right support - to unpack and resolve them properly.

# Emotions: Energy in Motion

For years, emotion has been viewed as something akin to weakness. We would avoid being emotional in front of others and were advised against being 'too emotional' at work. As the world has slowly evolved from mechanized and industrial ways of working into knowledge-based ways of working, where passion and purpose are key to engagement and performance, a new appreciation for the way emotion connects and drives us has developed. The science is clear; embracing our emotions is key to our ability to function effectively as human beings, to create healthy workplaces and safe, generative communities.

Emotions are vital to our ability to reason and to make sound judgements. When we're trying to read and understand the behaviour of others - and to adapt our own behaviour if necessary - it's our emotions that we lean on. Emotions are how we learn as humans, and how we build and develop relationships.

Our feelings also play an important role in problem solving, decision making and creating strategies for moving forward. Our ability to notice, observe how we're feeling and then think about what that means, is what drives our emotional intelligence and maturity. And it's that interplay between our thoughts and our emotions that propel and brake our responses and behaviour.

Our emotions help us to experience the world, our mind - and our ability to think and process those emotions - helps us to understand it.

We have eight core emotions which drives us either toward attachment, or avoidance. Attachment emotions (excitement/joy, trust/love) drive our energy outward, enabling us to connect with others. They're natural enablers of trust.

Avoidance emotions (fear, anger, disgust, shame, sadness) drive our energy inwards, to focus on protection and self-preservation. They make building, sustaining, or restoring trust, hard work. Surprise, unsurprisingly (no pun intended!) is an emotion that sits on both sides. The context (whether it's a good or bad surprise) determines whether it works to reinforce attachment or turn us towards avoidance.

Each emotion generates a series of chemical reactions which trigger fast shifts in our thinking and our behaviour. Some of those reactions are subtle shifts. We have thousands of emotional reactions every day which never break through to our conscious awareness, but which drive our beliefs and behaviour anyway. It's only when those emotions are strong enough to for us to notice - when they've broken through to become 'feelings' - that we can start to take an active role in becoming more self-aware, and emotionally mature and intelligent.

While emotions themselves are brief (some scientists say an emotion lasts no longer than 90 seconds in our bodies) a feeling can seem overwhelming. Persistent feelings become moods which can last for hours, days or weeks, and which influence not just us, but the people we live and work with too. It's when heavy feelings go unaddressed, as they sometimes do when conversations feel too risky, or too hard to have, that dysfunction sets in and we move away from attachment toward avoidance. We choose self-protection by withholding, becoming defensive, arguing, undermining and sabotaging.

There is a knack to noticing you've been triggered into avoidance, and to taking a breath to enable you to respond, rather than react. It takes practice and is always harder when you're tired, or particularly riled, but it is possible. In fact, it's foundational in creating the emotional stability that underpins self-trust, because it allows you the space to process those feelings, and to address the source of them constructively.

# Shaping Mindsets

Our world view is the lens through which everything else passes. Our perceptions of ourselves and others (and how we anticipate they will treat us) and of the world (and how welcoming or difficult we expect it to be) is the filter through which we make sense of the world around us; our place in it, and our relationship to others.

What many of us know from our own personal experience is that when the world feels a safer and more trustworthy place, we feel more relaxed, take more chances, extend trust more readily, and laugh off embarrassment and mistakes a little easier.

While our world view might share certain characteristics with friends or family, the full frame is something that remains uniquely our own. No one else sees the world in quite the same way as us.

Our unique world views start taking shape as infants, as we test the boundaries and relational ties that bind us to our carers. Those early influences – whether they are of neglect or nurturance – set in motion a way of interacting with the world which can impact the wiring in our brains, our emotional landscape and in turn, our behaviour into adulthood.

It establishes the foundations of trust – whether we feel safe in, or fearful of our world, and our responses to it. If we feel unsafe, we become more vigilant, intuitively warier of everything around us – our natural inclination is biased towards an expectation of risk. If we feel safe, our mind and our behaviour open up to the world. We engage more, we are biased towards optimism and positive outcomes.

Initially shaped by our experiences with our carers, our worldview continues to be reinforced and shaped by the environments and relationships we inhabit, and by our own determination to learn a new way of relating to the world.

By the time we reach adulthood, our world view simply feels like part of the fabric of who we are. We identify with being optimistic and energised, of always expecting the best. Or we become used to waiting for the other shoe to drop, of expecting and planning for the worst, of suspecting that every good experience must be followed by something bad to balance out the scorecard. Our mindsets' feel habitual and relatively fixed. An ingrained facet of our identity, rather than a view of the world which is dynamic and flexible.

As adults, bad relationships, persistent pressure or stress (whether at work, privately, or in balancing work and private life) can cement our perspective even further, creating a mindset referred to as 'learned helplessness'. However, even as adults in the face of learned helplessness (which, given the number of people who 'cope' with life may be more common than we realize) we have an opportunity to change our view.

We have the power to switch our view of the world from automatic to conscious or intentional. To take back control by virtue of a little awareness, choice and discipline. That's where trusting ourselves enters the picture.

The good news is that our mindsets needn't remain fixed. Our minds after all, are our own and neuroplasticity tells us that our minds never stop learning and adapting. All we need to do is create change. In even the smallest of ways, we can begin testing and stretching our mental boundaries and assumptions - challenging ourselves to get curious and experiment with new ways of thinking and behaving.

By reaching beyond our current mindset and opening ourselves up to new experiences we start to reset our beliefs. We start to become more of the person we want to be. We begin to act more intentionally and purposefully in pursuit of our future, rather than giving in to our past. We start to know - and trust - ourselves more.

# To Trust Is to Let Go

Trust requires the ability to let go. It requires flexibility, vulnerability and being open and willing to embrace whatever the future brings.

Modern life encourages us to own, possess, hold on to and control as much as we can possibly manage. The busier and more stretched we become, the more we hold onto what we have, attempt to control as much of the life around us as possible, and preserve our precious attention for the many other places it is required. But the more we control, the less space and agency we give others, and the less they feel trusted.

Ironically, sometimes a simple mindset shift can help change our outlook. 'Trying to be flexible' can sap our energy and leave us feeling exhausted. 'Being flexible' on the other hand, can leave us feeling resilient and energised. Language is both an indication of whether we are feeling capable or stretched, and the key to turning our experience around.

# Changing Beliefs

Real changes in self-belief happen through insight, and insights mean taking the time to reflect on what we are experiencing and why. Understanding the patterns behind how and when we react - what triggers our emotions - is how we learn and grow as people. And it's that learning that changes the pathways in our brains and creates new ways of engaging with the world around us.

Whether we're feeling trust or distrust, we're in its grip and responding instinctively before we begin to intellectually process the situation we're in.

Reflection is essential to allow us to pause, and sense check that our beliefs and behaviour are aligned, and most importantly, that they are congruent with our aspirations.

In the process of reflecting, we update our way of being - how we hold ourselves in the world - we reinforce our intentions, and we begin to learn and understand more about ourselves. We develop a stronger sense of self, and a more grounded trust in our internal wisdom and intellect; what drives us, and our default behaviours. We learn to discern the difference between intellect and wisdom, intention and action, mistakes and lessons. Ultimately, we learn to understand, appreciate, and trust ourselves more.

# When We Get It Right

**We prove to ourselves what we're capable of.**

Self-trust is a remarkable thing. Knowing that you are capable, that you can rely on yourself to make good decisions that create joy and meaning in work and life is an intoxicating feeling. Possibly because it seems so rare or fleeting.

It's liberating to realize that amidst the push and pull demands of connectivity, responsibilities and our own aspirations, we can create a central oasis of calm. An inner place, where we feel in control yet flexible. Responsive rather than reactive. We have a greater appreciation of our own needs, capabilities, possibilities and boundaries.

**We stop comparing ourselves to others.**

Rather than looking outward to anchor our sense of self and level set our aspirations against those of our peers or 'role models', we consult our own internal GPS. The values, dreams and codes of conduct that we know are authentic to us.

Self-trust opens us up to paying greater attention to what those are. It allows us to reflect on what we've been told vs. what we believe and in doing so, it allows us to connect – and restore the relationship between - what we believe (at a cognitive level), what we sense (at a physical level) and what we feel (at an emotional level). It stops us living to a set of rules mapped by others and gives us the permission to set out a new roadmap for a journey that feels right for us.

Armed with self-trust, the benchmark for a good life stops being the highlight reels we see in social media, and instead becomes our own aspirations and authenticity. Our highly tuned self-awareness alerts us when we're off track and gently nudges us towards a course correction. No sense of self-loathing, no shame. Just awareness, reflection and a subtle redirection. It's a self-fulfilling cycle of self-esteem building.

## We develop self-respect; we begin to like ourselves and to feel comfortable in our own company.

You create a relationship with yourself where you appreciate and value your competence. Where you know your behaviour is consistent, irrespective of the people you are with or the situations you find yourself in. Where you genuinely care about your own wellbeing, and where you act with credibility and authenticity. You elevate yourself to that rare position of self-knowledge where you can genuinely appreciate who you are and how you work. A place where authenticity comes more easily and more consistently. Perhaps best of all, when you build self-trust, self-respect isn't far behind.

## We become a great role model to the people we live and work with.

When it comes to relationships, nothing is more inspiring, energizing or enjoyable as being in the presence of someone who is comfortable in their own skin. Someone who embraces their faults and acknowledges their talents. Someone who has mastered the art of being vulnerable without being weak. Someone who is so secure in themselves, that connecting with others appears fluid and deeply genuine. With self-trust, self-respect and the art of vulnerability mastered, we become that person to others.

## We get clearer on the situations and relationships we want

**to invest in and those we're ready to leave.**

In their book Coaching for Resilience, writers Adrienne Green and John Humphrey identify the two greatest stressors in our lives as being the desire to control and the desire for approval. In life, they posit, we often seek to control too much (or rather things we have little hope of influencing let alone controlling), and we seek love and approval from a much wider sphere of people than we really need to. Instead, they encourage us to consider what we really must control, and whose approval or support we really need in order to deliver our commitments with competence and confidence. When you bring it back to the basics, the lists are not as long as you might have thought.

The complexity there is that while we can edit back what we worry about in terms of what we control and whose approval we seek, we still need to be able to manage the expectations of other people.

Self-trust – being able to listen and respond to your own internal dialogue about what matters most in a way that is authentic and considered - makes recognizing which situations and people you want to invest in, and which you need to gracefully exit clearer; and how to handle the difficult moments in between with more grace.

**We regain the energy that has been lost to self-doubt.**

Without self-trust we can begin to second guess ourselves, even if the feedback or circumstances around us indicate we have nothing to fear. Being promoted, or simply becoming more visible at work, can trigger feelings of uncertainty and discomfort and – in the absence of specific and trusted feedback - have us questioning whether we're behaving in the 'right' or 'expected' way

The mental and emotional load of keeping those thoughts and feelings at bay while you focus on your work eats valuable energy. In the longer term, left unchecked it can create a self-fulfilling loop where you begin to believe your own press rather than seeking counsel from trusted advisors.

**We tap into a healthier and more optimistic way to live; we trust our instincts and our judgment more and release ourselves from the angst of second guessing.**

With self-trust in our repertoire, we have enough critical awareness to notice our instinctual reactions. We have the presence of mind to seek and listen to our own judgement and the confidence to ask for clarity or solicit feedback. Crucially, with practice, we can cultivate an attitude of openness and perpetual learning that makes life feel more like a series of adventurous learning curves, rather than a test of right or wrong.

# Ideas to Begin With

**Be choosy.**

Make fewer commitments to yourself and make sure you really mean them. Be clear about why they matter to you, so you'll be very aware of what you'll be giving up by letting them slip.

**Start small.**

Make and keep small commitments. A pattern of small, regularly kept commitments trumps one wonderful, but one-off commitment. Consistency sends a powerful message to yourself.

**Value your self-made commitments.**

Treat them with the same degree of sanctity you reserve for the commitments you make to others. If you can't reschedule self-made commitments, don't. It might mean saying no instead of yes, and it might be socially uncomfortable for a while, but it with be worth it if you're upholding a self-made commitment which really matters.

**Take stock.**

What brings you joy? What grates your nerves? What are your triggers, your strengths, your foibles, your aspirations? Who are you at your best and your worst? How do you practice being gentle with yourself? How do you choose when to be disciplined and when to be gentle? Know your love language. It speaks to your needs.

## Recognize the patterns.

What still serves you? What is past its use by date? What beliefs bob to the surface and steal your strength? Did someone else give them to you? If so, was that person always right? Did they begin as a way for you to stay safe or in control? Do you still need that response because those circumstances still exist around you today? What strategies or skills have you developed since then that can take their place to keep you safe instead? If your subconscious is reluctant to let go - ask yourself, is there anything it is drawing my attention to that I may still need to be aware of?

## Breathe.

Attempting to maintain control while under fire is often accompanied by faster paced, shallow breath. It's the stress response which switches your entire being away from being open and connecting, towards closing down, escaping, avoidance and protecting yourself. Slowing your breathing reverses the fight/flight response and calms your nervous system so you can relax into the moment.

## Scan.

When the ability to stay mentally and emotionally open to trust is hardest, you may find your body harbouring tension in preparation for fighting or fleeing the source of your discomfort. It's a natural response your body engages to help you stay safe, but physical tension reinforces the other messages your brain is getting that whatever situation you are in, it can't be trusted. If you want to open up, scan your body for tension and actively relax all the muscles you find that are tight.

## Get present.

Bring your attention back to the moment you're in. Let yourself be totally absorbed by it for a few moments. Let the smells, sights, senses soak into your consciousness. You can plan for the future, take steps today to get closer to it, but the only influence and control you have is what you can wield in this moment. Plan for the future, but leave space for things to evolve – they do.

## Be grateful.

Rather than focusing on gaps, look at the progress. Sometimes while focusing on what we're aiming for, it can be easy to forget or discount what we've already done, or what is already happening in the same space as the goal or dream we're chasing.

## Use language wisely.

As Yoda says, "Do, or do not, there is no try". The language you use might sound harmless enough, but words carry meaning and whether you're consciously aware of it, your mind is listening and aligning what you say with how you feel. It's keeping you in harmony. 'Try' indicates effort. 'Do or do not' is a choice. One contains power and one does not. Trying to be flexible is energy taxing. Being flexible is energy enriching.

## Choose.

Being overwhelmed is one of the fastest ways to unleash self-doubt and destabilize your sense of self. Pause for a moment and consider the fact that – like it or not - everything that is on your plate is there because you said yes to it. So, what would you remove? Give yourself permission to push some things back and to push others off. Sometimes it is all you need to unlock the energy and drive to recommit to getting it done.

### Rocks, pebbles, sand, water.

Like the famous analogy about rocks in a jar, prioritise. Imagine your life is a large clear glass jar. You can fill it with rocks, and it seems jammed full. But there's still space – for pebbles, sand and water. The truth is, you have more capacity than you realize but you may have put the sand in before the rocks and pebbles. Prioritise your work and life – make space for your rocks and pebbles first and add the sand and water only after they are in place.

### Change what you mean by 'help'.

There is a slim and sometimes faint line between helping and assuming responsibility or absolving others of responsibility. If you're a natural giver, chances are you are overextending yourself in support of others. Instead of leaping in, check what they need to get to where they need to go. The answer may require less of you than you'd expected but mean a great deal more.

### Say 'no' more.

Decide what 'hard no's' you need in your life to stay resilient and resourceful. Then use them firmly and when pressed, change the subject. Get clear on those things you usually default to saying yes to that you later regret, and then create a couple of ways to defer your response: e.g. Let me digest that and come back to you. How soon do you need an answer? What have you already tried?

### Say 'yes' to new things.

Throw caution to the wind. Occasionally. Say yes to things you wouldn't usually. Try new social adventures. Try things that extend your comfort zone (not dangerously so – just enough to test and stretch your limits) so you experience something unusual while proving to yourself that it is absolutely survivable. Let other people take charge and instead of judging the experience, observe it. What do you enjoy, or appreciate that you hadn't expected to?

### Reconnect to nature.

In whatever way works for you. Spend time at a beach, or near or on the ocean, lounge in a park, camp, go for a walk or ride through the forest. Soak up how 'big', enduring and at ease nature is.

### Volunteer.

Spending time being with and helping others, gives you space from - and perspective on - your own life.

### Consider the fact that the only thing you can genuinely hope to control is yourself.

Your own thoughts, feelings and behaviour. Everything else is a waste of your precious energy. Also, marvel at the irony that whilst you've been focusing on trying to control everything outside of yourself, you've probably been allowing your thoughts, emotions and behaviour to run riot on autopilot.

## Introversion and Extroversion - be the best version of yourself

Introversion and extroversion refer to the way we engage with others and to how we draw energy from our social situations.

Briefly, more introverted people are more energized by solitude, prefer to socialize in small groups or one to one, can prefer deep conversations rather than small talk and often appear emotionally measured and reflective. Extroverts are energized by larger groups, are usually very expressive and outgoing, tend to be fast paced and quick to take the initiative, or take the lead in making things happen and getting things done.

There is a school of thought that we are predominantly either extroverts, introverts or ambiverts (a relative balance of both). Carl Jung, the psychologist who first coined these terms suggested that to be either purely introvert or extrovert would make us crazy, suggesting that, as most of us have experienced, we usually reside somewhere along the spectrum and move slightly depending on the contexts we are in.

You may find as you build self-trust, that your leanings towards either extroversion or introversion shape which practices work best for you. Here are a few things to try:

If you're an introvert:

- Practice asking and speaking up, even if it's to say you'll come back with an answer, or to ask for more information. If you know you will be expected to have answers in a meeting, buy yourself some reflection time in advance.

- Understand that extroverts are fast movers and stepping forward comes naturally. Their speed and volume may sometimes be overbearing, but their energy is vital to getting traction and maintaining momentum.

- Appreciate that you will usually know where you stand with an extrovert - take expressiveness as a sign of enthusiasm, involvement and passion. Welcome the influencing skills of gifted extroverts.

If you're an extrovert:
- Practice patience and curiosity. Leave space for introverts to voice their views. Try layering your messages and requests. Build in time for your introverted counterparts to digest news and ideas and to reflect on their views. Check that their silence means they are processing what's happening.
- Understand that introverts are often reflective and want to make wise, considered moves. Don't mistake a slower pace or lack of verbal participation for disengagement, invite them to share their perspectives instead.
- Appreciate that introverts make great observers and may see things you miss. Appreciate that time to reflect means you will get a more considered response.

# SECTION FOUR:

SOCIAL

*Humans are social creatures. Everything we do, we do with – and through – others. Remember how it feels to be excluded from social gatherings, or meetings and you'll realize how core a need human connection is.*

# How Trust Acts as a Social Eco System

*"Trust each other again and again. When the trust level gets high enough, people transcend apparent limits, discovering new and awesome abilities of which they were previously unaware."*

*David Armistead*

While self-trust sits at the core (because of its power to ground you in confidence and enable appropriate degrees of assertiveness) the ability to engender trust in your social relationships is the ecosystem that forges sustainable change.

Trust is constantly toggling in the depth of our mind. We scan, appraise and respond 24/7/365. Becoming more attuned to building trust means becoming more aware of the situations where it is tested and becoming used to pausing to choose your response, rather than just acting out of habit or raw emotion.

Developing trust in our closest living and working relationships helps us to redefine 'normal'. It gives us the potential to change the environment around us – one relationship at a time.

One of the hardest steps in building trust in our relationships is embracing vulnerability. The deepest trust develops between people when there is an active environment of safety which enables the ability to become vulnerable. To make mistakes, admit weakness, express doubt and fear, and to share what makes us anxious or excited. When the relationships around us provide us with the freedom to be human, we stop spending energy on being perfect, being right or looking good in the eyes of others. Instead we redirect our energy into participation, contribution, engagement and collaboration.

When we're no longer covering our butts and doing double time trying to second guess what our significant other, our friends, boss, team or clients need, we free up the emotional and mental space to become increasingly, naturally, enthusiastic and creative.

Ultimately, it's the trust between us and the people we live with that provides the foundation for meaningful and constructive social connection. It is the difference between well adjusted, healthy relationships and relationships which foster isolation, insecurity and self-doubt.

Becoming who we have the potential to be, depends not just on our own self-awareness and self-development but on our ability to connect with others. To find our place in the world, a place we can be ourselves, where our personality, talents and attributes are appreciated and valued, we need to find our tribe. The people we identify with, whose company we enjoy, and who bring out the best in us. The people we feel safe enough with to just be ourselves.

Be it family, friends or our work mates, when we find that fit, we blossom. Why? Because all of our energy is focused on the positive side of the emotional, physical and cognitive spectrums. Our body, conditioned to scan for threats 24/7 still scans, but the sensitivity drops. Our attention, our energy and our thoughts are focused on positive emotions and efforts that (by virtue of the environment we're in and the people who create the culture of that environment) are reciprocated, creating a virtuous circle.

In family relationships, it feels like family members you would just as easily call friends. In social circles it feels like a close community who share in each other's joy and step up to support each other when things get tough. At work, it feels like having the space, agency, air cover and encouragement to do your best work while continually developing.

Trust helps us generate understanding, appreciation, respect, reciprocity and appreciation.

Our lives become easier, simpler, smoother, more supportive, less challenging places to be when we have clarity, honesty and open communication. When we can be clear about what drives and what derails us and when we can communicate that with a degree of eloquence and emotional awareness and social sensitivity. When we can ask for what we need and share our ideas without feeling silly or stupid.

We might wistfully hope for - or frustratingly moan about - how much we want to live in a world where life seems to run smoothly. Where there's less stress, less rush and more enjoyment and time to spend our leisure hours doing the things we really want to do. Yet we are unaware of (or maybe conveniently forget) the role we play in creating the dynamic we crave.

If we want others to behave in more trustworthy ways, we have a responsibility to them (and to ourselves) to help create an environment between us that makes trustworthiness possible. Someone has to go first and if our need or desire is strong enough, then we have everything to gain by being that someone.

# Co-creating Cultures: Why Your Influence Is Greater Than You Think

*"It is mutual trust, even more than mutual interest, that holds human associations together."*

*H.L.Mencken*

Trust plays a critical role in our social life, because - simply put - we don't live in vacuum. Our world revolves around relationships. Healthy and productive social systems, whether they are families, communities or companies, are sustained by a degree of interdependence on each other. The quality of our relationships often dictates the degree of success and fulfilment we experience whether it's at home, in our social lives or at work. Frictionless collaboration – on any front - relies on trust.

If you're living in a city, it's fair to assume that you are living alongside, and interacting with, dozens if not hundreds of people every week. Together, we create and alter the environments we live in and shape the experiences of the people we share it with (whether they're close to us, or strangers) simply through our behaviour. Remember the last time someone aggressively cut you off in traffic or scowled at you on public transport? Or the last time the generosity of a stranger restored your faith in human nature?

It's not just society that demands we get relationships right to create a seamless social experience in life. Evolution deliberately hardwired us for social connection so we can access the support, love, protection and skills of others in order to - at the very least - survive, but ultimately, to thrive.

Unfortunately, that hardwiring has become both a blessing and a curse in our modern hyper-connected lives.

On the upside, it still drives us towards building relationships, sharing our skills, knowledge and resources so that together we can have - and do - more than we could on our own. It encourages us to help others when we think or feel that they need support. It helps us to show compassion and empathy when it's needed, and to find joy and comfort in each other's company.

The downside is that this innate built-in need often misfires in our modern hyper connected, busy world. We seek inclusion and connection, but we look for it in two dimensional endorsements (think, Facebook likes, retweets and hearts on Instagram). We build our relationship networks wide and shallow, and we share what feels safe in that fragile and shallow environment. The shared vulnerability that builds deep, abiding, reciprocal trust never has the time or the opportunity to grow.

Relationships are an essential rite of passage to adulthood. Our experiences in relationships help to shape and build our brain by altering our perception and by adding to our repertoire of responses. Our exposure to relationships provides the psychological growth and development we need to successfully engage in the world.

# The Power of Connection

*"Love and belonging might seem like a convenience we can live without, but our biology is built to thirst for connection because it is linked to our most basic survival needs. Connection is the first of three adaptations that support our sophisticated sociality, but our need for connection is the bedrock upon which the others are built."*

*Matthew D. Lieberman*
*(Social, Why our brains are wired to connect)*

Humans are heat seekers. Evolution has hardwired us to seek warmth and connection. We all want to matter, to be loved and to make a difference. So much so, we'll seek and prioritise connection over sustenance.

At the most basic (and brutal) level, without human interaction we can survive, but we won't develop fully. A study of orphans found that babies who were fed and clothed but never cuddled, or played with, failed to develop even basic language skills and died while still in childhood.

A separate study of infant monkeys who were given the option of a wooden mother figure with bottle attached, or a wire statue clothed in soft fabric with no feeding ability, found the infant primates chose the soft option. When given the choice of physical sustenance or physical connection, they chose connection every time.

But it's not just monkeys and infants that crave connection. Human brains are hardwired for connection. We crave the connection and inclusion inherent in relationships because relationships are an integral part of our personal growth and expression. It's a need so great that we even build relationships with jailors.

110

What's remarkable, is that we know from our own – both painful and pleasurable - personal experiences that one of the most basic human needs is to be accepted, to matter, and to be loved.

In the 1950's John Bowlby created the concept of an attachment system in infant hood, cleverly designed to register and respond to the proximity of our caregivers.

Attachment relationships are the relationships we build early in life. The intense emotional bonds we create in infancy form neurobiological connections that can influence our future intimate relationships. (e.g. When we get blamed by our partners for enacting the same behaviours on them that their parents did). Our parent's treatment of us has a powerful influence on our childhood development. And irrespective of whether we experience neglect and separation, or safety and encouragement, the influences of our early caregivers reaches into adulthood.

Physical closeness meant we felt connected, while physical distance led to variable degrees of separation anxiety. John Bowlby's view was that we never lose that attachment system or the very real social distress it causes when we're separated from those we've become close to.

And that is where it gets messy. Human relationships are intricate, complex and full of surprises.

We have to trust that we're safe in relationships. That when people leave, they'll return. That we can voice opinions, good and bad, without being misunderstood (at least for too long) and that there is enough elasticity in the relationship that we're confident we'll pull back together when life, or circumstance, pulls us apart.

In short, we need to trust. Studies have found that social pain, the kind of pain that comes from being rejected, judged and found wanting, or humiliated, is registered in our brains in the same place as physical pain. Our need to connect – to be part of a 'tribe' - is so fundamental to our survival, that the experience of not having it results in very real physical pain.

Every time we reach out to someone, we're seeking connection, while also risking rejection. There is a vulnerability inherent in human social connection. On the other side of that vulnerability lies the inclusion, support and sustenance we crave. Trust is the safety net that enables us to wade into our vulnerability with increasing confidence and depth, while we build the remarkable relationships that sustain and support us.

Healthy relationships make for stronger mental, physical and emotional health.

# What Does Love Have to Do with It?

We usually share a sense of familiarity with the people we love and live with, whether they are the family we inherit or the friends we choose. There is shared heritage, shared experience, shared aspirations or passions. But even in our closest relationships there are areas of difference – sometimes vast – which can at times either inspire or divide us.

Our ability to sustain trust is linked to the quality of the connection we have in each relationship. And although we might be drawn together by commonalities, it's our ability to communicate, to navigate change and resolve differences that enable us to keep moving forward together which strengthens those connections. It's about knowing how to treat others the way they want to be treated, not how 'we' want to be treated. The concept of The Five Love Languages created by Gary Chapman highlights the different ways we might be communicating around love – the closest relative of trust. It explains the confusion behind someone telling you that you don't love, respect or appreciate them, when – in your own view – you've done nothing *but* demonstrate that.

Chapman posits that we each have a preference for the ways in which we interpret the affection and endorsements of others; Physical Touch (which includes touch, physical presence and accessibility), Quality Time (undivided attention, quality conversation and quality activities), Words of Affirmation (unsolicited compliments, encouraging and kind words), Acts of Service (taking over responsibilities to ease their burden), Receiving Gifts (physical reminders that you're thinking of them).

Think back for a moment to an occasion where you were

trying to show someone you cared, yet it fell on deaf ears. Can you pick which language you were speaking and distinguish what your intended recipients' language might be instead?

People give us clues all the time about what matters to them. They demonstrate what they value most through their language and their behaviour. It shows up in the things we prioritise, and the things we respond to.

What does this have to do with trust?

We're told as youngsters to treat others the way we would like to be treated, but that doesn't always work. Though we might agree on basic foundational principles such as treating others respectfully and fairly, those principles are defined slightly differently by each of us. That's because we use our own personal histories and world views as the context for how we create meaning around them. You and I might have a similar desire to respect each other, but we may value different things. If I value punctuality and you value spontaneity, your approach to time keeping might feel disrespectful to me.

However, love and trust are trump cards which change how we view those perceived transgressions, adding a flexibility to the relationship we wouldn't otherwise allow. If I feel a degree of 'love', warmth, or connection between us, I will assume your behaviour is about you, and your habits and priorities; rather than seeing it as a lack of respect or thought for me.

Building and sustaining strong trust in our close relationships is about continuing to reinforce the connection (whether it's love, warmth, or just positive regard) between us. It's about letting people know that you see and understand them. How better to demonstrate that than to spend a few minutes thinking back to understand what they recognize as love and appreciation, so you can speak to them in their own 'language'?

# How Differences in Our Personalities and World Views Influence Trust

What makes us so unique from each other are the differences in our world view which is shaped by both our personality and by our experiences. Like life, our thoughts and behaviours are never static. We're changing all the time; influenced by, and responding to, the people and events in our lives.

Difficult relationships, challenging home environments, pressure, support, neglect, love - all of these things and more shape our understanding of the world and what we can expect from it, as well as the part we play in it.

We begin shaping our attitude towards life in childhood and build on that frame of reference as we develop. Our personalities, which may be defined as part nature, part nurture, take root too and develop, evolving through adolescence into adulthood. Though traditional thinking was that personality was fairly fixed throughout life, recent research over the past decade is proving that not only is personality change possible, it may even be the route towards a more meaningful and 'self-actualized' life. After all, why focus on 'growth' if change isn't possible?

The differences between us can build connection when we value the skills and attitudes others bring to a relationship that we don't have. It provides balance and helps us see possibilities and challenges from a whole new perspective. As Einstein said, "you can't solve a problem with the same thinking that created it."

When there is disconnect, or when trust breaks down -

whether through misunderstanding, disrespect or insecurity - appreciating the value in the difference becomes harder. It becomes easier, almost instinctive, to just see the difference instead. We debate, rather than acknowledge differing views. We block ideas from others and defend our own. We stop listening because we're hooked on selling our own story. While we argue to be heard - and to be right - our relationships, quality of thinking and the integrity of the solutions we are seeking all suffer.

Bridging the gap means taking a step back - and down - to recalibrate. It also means understanding the differences we each bring to the conversation – and the inherent value in those differences - so we can add value, rather than argue it.

Different personality styles may unintentionally trigger fear - rather than inspire trust - through their interactions with peers and colleagues. It can occur quite incidentally through communication, pace of thinking, spoken or unspoken expectations, and body language.

One of the easiest ways to identify, understand and appreciate those differences in personality is through using the Big5 dimensions of personality. The Big5 is a set of continua that underpins a wide range of personality profiling tools. No matter who you are, or what personality profiling you have participated in in the past, you will recognize some of your behaviour as sitting somewhere on the continua of these five dimensions.

- Openness to experience; creative, conceptual and open to change vs. fact and detail focused, practical and secure in the status quo.
- Conscientiousness; spontaneity, letting things evolve organically, a relaxed approach vs. setting ambitious goals, reliably delivering, organisation and precision.

- Extroversion; sociable, energised through interaction with others, demonstrative and seizing the initiative vs. measured, serious minded and energised by solitude, one to one or small group conversations.
- Agreeableness; collaborative, empathetic and striving for harmony vs. logic, competitiveness and forceful arguing.
- Neuroticism; sensitivity and nervousness vs. assurance and confidence.

These aspects of our personality shape how we respond to pressure, how we seek reward, how we gather and use energy, what we need to fully thrive, and what triggers stress and upset. As complex beings who continually respond to our environment to stay safe, our outward behaviour can (and does) move along the spectrum depending on the context we're in.

When we understand our own orientation and can guess the preferences of the people we live and work with, we begin to understand why we sometimes clash and where we align. We start to understand that seeing things from different perspectives means we each have a valuable role to play in conversations. It brings creativity to problem solving, introduces ideas or alternatives we would never have thought of, and helps us see the opportunities or risks in situations that we might have overlooked.

Ultimately, if it's the similarities which provide warmth and comfort, it's the differences that provide interest and stimulation. The fact that our friends, siblings, offspring, parents, neighbours, significant others see the world differently means we get to explore the world through their eyes a little piece at a time.

When things are going well in relationships, differences balance the dynamic and make us stronger, more resourceful, more adaptable and more resilient than we might be on our own. When one or other of us is feeling challenged or triggered, those differences can feel like barriers to being heard and understood.

Understanding dominant styles - ours and others – and understanding our synergies and points of separation - is invaluable for interrupting and redirecting conflict into constructive conversations. Conversations that continue to reinforce trust.

You can build deeper trust through simply understanding, acknowledging and valuing the differences between you and the people you live closely with. Explore your differences, how they change your world view and how they work together to make your relationship uniquely special.

# Trust and Our Relationships

Our relationships shape the choices we make, the patterns we fall into over time, and our concept of what life looks like to us – the meanings of right, wrong, fair, successful, love, hope, ambition, power, kindness.

Relationships have the power to bring out the very best – and the very worst – in us. Successful relationships give us the encouragement, safety and support to test our boundaries, explore, seek adventure, build confidence and awareness in social situations and to learn and grow from our mistakes. The greatest relationships have the power to help us shape futures we might never visualize on our own.

Yet none of these things happen in the absence of trust. Trust enables us to share, and to hear others, without defensiveness. And to be open to asking for - and accepting - guidance, wisdom, help.

All of our relationships have the potential to shape us if we remain in them. Yet our most important relationships for growth, are the ones we feel we can be both vulnerable and safe in.

Anyone who had a difficult early family life will tell you that your environment shapes the person you become by virtue of the way you adapt your behaviour to survive. Those early family relationships hold significant sway because they happen at such an early - and vital - stage of our development. As we mature and start building friendships through life, our inner circle expands and we find ourselves opening up to others, trusting them with our hopes, dreams and fears. How others respond to us is what shapes our choices - and ultimately - our lives, by nudging us to adapt to whatever we're experiencing.

When we're busy and pushed for time and attention, it's easy for our close relationships to become functional first and relational second. We unconsciously lean towards creating shallow, functional relationships that help us to get things done. Whether it's managing a family, juggling our lives, fitting in exercise or social and leisure time, or doing our day job. Without quality time and attention, the people whose understanding, support and friendship we rely on to feel loved and supported, only get our attention only when we need something, or something is going wrong. We can unintentionally find ourselves taking the kinds of shortcuts in our relationships which effectively edit out the vital steps which build trust.

Busy work lives and social commitments can deepen the desire to protect some solitary leisure time for recharging our batteries. And for some, for whom tiredness seems to creep into every emotional, mental and physical nook and cranny, the time we spend with loved ones becomes the space where we relax, where we hope to draw support from others rather than give something of ourselves. Though our personal relationships are often the ones we value most, we can find ourselves giving them less quality time and attention rather than more.

As our lives have become more digital, more driven by tangible and visible achievement, we have become technically smarter, increasingly effective 'doers', but our social skills have atrophied. We are rapidly losing the ability to genuinely listen to and value each other and to connect in ways that go deeper than the pure function or mechanics of daily life alone.

Yet strong relationships require our presence. Life is full, it moves fast, and connecting is easier done digitally rather than in person. In a world where we're facing unprecedented levels of anxiety and depression, it's time to get back to basics. To reprioritize our time, to be clear about what we want to give and receive in life, to reflect on what we expect and where we're settling. To be intentional about what we are saying yes - and no - to.

# How Our Behaviour Impacts Other Peoples DNA

*"Humans are built to be influenced by those around us, to follow their lead. In the west we call this conforming, something looked down upon. But in the East, the same behaviour is called harmonizing, something essential for group living."*

*Matthew D. Lieberman*
*(Social: Why our brains are wired to connect)*

The argument over nature vs. nurture is a long and exhaustive one. To what degree are we shaped by our nature and to what degree do the environments we're raised in, or live through, shape who we become?

It's a debate too big for us to venture into here, but when it comes to trust, to the way we handle ourselves and the way we behave towards others, there is one thing worth noting. We possess two very different types of genes – template genes and transcription genes. Our template genes are fixed – they are determined right at the start and undeniably shape who we are. Our transcription genes are designed to be influenced and imprinted by our environment. They help us adjust, to learn from the people and places around us, to thrive in our world.

It's our transcription genes that mean not only are we susceptible to other people's behaviour; when we stay immersed in it, we're slowly encoding it into our DNA. In fact, research (albeit using mice) shows that changes in values and behaviour can be passed down through three generations. Our values, and how we live them matters. Our interactions with each other don't just affect our day to day experience - they can alter our biology over time. Changing not just how our genes adapt but altering the level of chemicals our brain releases into our body.

What does this mean for trust? It means we may just be learning fear and distrust from our nearest and dearest. That - in turn - our behaviour is slowly conditioning their behaviours while also altering their biology. It means that the patterns of avoidance or attachment we have, may be reflected by the people we share our lives with.

It means that it's worth considering what trust looks and feels like to us so we're creating the kinds of environments around us that reflect our intent. The kinds of environments where if people were learning from us and modelling our behaviour, it would mirror trust back to us. It means practicing consistency, rather than good intentions paired with poor discipline.

# How the Way We Engage with the World Shapes Our Approach to Trust

Though there is arguably no such thing as a pure extrovert or a pure introvert (according to Freud who created both terms), most of us tend to identify more with one end of the spectrum than the other. We tend to gravitate towards a certain way of engaging with the world which influences how we 'show up' in the world, what generates and depletes our energy levels and what we need to feel really content. When you read the multi choice options below, which feels most natural to you, A or B?

A.   A night out partying with friends
B.   A quiet night in with a book

A.   Standing in front of an audience
B.   Being in the audience

A.   Hosting a party with lots of new people
B.   Hosting a dinner party with close friends

A.   Hot desking
B.   Having your own desk

A.   Spirited debate in the moment
B.   Time to reflect and consider your response

A.   Spontaneity
B.   Structure

If you answered mostly A's you're likely to be extroverted. Outgoing, social, vocal, outwardly confident and energized by variety, newness and change.

If you chose mostly B's you're more likely to be introverted. To prefer socializing with smaller groups of people you know, to have time to think and reflect and to listen rather than hold the floor.

Introverts are prone to sensory overstimulation, meaning they need less activity around them than their extrovert counterparts. While extroverts will find attention, loud spaces and large groups energizing, introverts can find them overwhelming and exhausting.

Extroverts are quick off the mark, love activity, are highly responsive in conversations and are quick to share and express their ideas. Whereas introverts find value and energy in small groups of trusted people, solitude and reflection.

When you see the ends of the spectrum, the differences are obvious and it's clear to see how profoundly those natural tendencies can impact peoples' behaviour in relationships.

In reality though, it's often difficult to tell an introvert from an extrovert. That's because an introvert who is in their element – socializing with a small group of close friends, or leading a meeting on a subject on which they're an expert – can become animated, spirited and (if only briefly) be comfortable being the centre of attention in a room.

Why does that matter? Because for us to genuinely trust each other, whether in life or work, we need to understand how to build rapport with each other. We need to make a greater effort to understand, appreciate and value each other a little more than we usually do.

It's easy for introverts to feel pressured, humiliated and

overruled by extroverted colleagues and friends, whose urgency or excitement can feel heavy handed. It's also easy for extroverts to feel frustrated by introverted counterparts who can seem overly cautious, uncommitted or anti-social.

When we're living or working with people whose natural tendencies are so different from our own, it's easy for misunderstandings and conflicts to occur. In those moments, if we swap judgment for an understanding of what drives each other's behaviour, we have a way to keep talking through the challenges to find a way forward together. It catalyzes rather than challenges trust.

Statistics vary widely as to how what percentage of the world's population is introverted vs. extroverted (apparently anywhere from 16% to 50% of us are introverted). The reality though is that most of us sit comfortably somewhere along the continuum, more extroverted than introverted in some scenarios and more introverted than extroverted in others. Where we sit affects how we relate to each other, how we create understanding between us and how we build trust.

Like all things related to personality, there is no 'right' or 'wrong' when it comes to which end of the spectrum feels most natural to you. We all have inherent preferences when it comes to how we think, socialize, work and participate in the world.

Both extroverts and introverts make remarkable leaders, invaluable team members and great friends. What is worth remembering, is that we don't have to be alike to bring out the best in each other, that sometimes our assumptions might mean we misinterpret other people's intent. And that even the most fundamental, immutable elements of our personalities can influence how quickly we offer, or embrace trust.

# Wired for Safety: Our Wiring for Threat is Acute and Constantly Alert

*"We need people in our lives with whom we can be as open as possible. To have real conversations with people may seem like such a simple, obvious suggestion, but it involves courage and risk."*

*Thomas Moore*

Our physical survival depends on our ability to identify, respond to and remember danger, not on our ability to recall and re-experience moments of happiness or joy.

Our responses are deep, rapid and the experience lasered onto our memory. It's the reason our responses to potential threat are more pronounced, and why they always seem so much more visceral than happy ones.

Thanks to this evolutionary brain wiring, mentally reframing and remaining positive in the face of adversity requires regular practice to convert into a habitual pattern.

Despite the fact that nature intended us to sense threats quickly and dramatically (as far as memory and emotion are concerned), our bodies were intended to respond swiftly and then return to a normal - calmer - state of being. Humans were never designed to survive prolonged and unrelenting worry, fear or insecurity.

However, for many of us juggling careers or businesses, families, extended family responsibilities and social lives, it can sometimes seem as though we're in a virtually constant state of sensing and reacting to threats or worries. It can be hard to ever really come back down to 'normal'. In fact, for many busy people, that sustained state of reactivity becomes the new normal. It's a new normal that we telegraph to each other in our rush, our easy distraction and poor attention, our always living in the future, kicking ourselves about the past, and never really being present in the now.

In short, it fosters behaviour which erodes trust.

It is behaviour which destabilizes our sense of self-and which rubs off on the people around us. In fact, our behaviour influences everyone who regularly shares our orbit, through the impact of our presence (stressed and distracted, or calm and attentive), our behaviour, and our conversations.

Even when we think we're being quiet and keeping ourselves to ourselves, we're telegraphing our moods to those around us. Whether they're strong or subtle, others can't help but pick up on how you're feeling. The more sensitive among us (which equates to approximately 15-20% of the population), will sense even subtle signals and their behaviour will shift slightly to accommodate you. If you're feeling low, you may see shades of compassion from them that indicate your emotions aren't quite as masked as you may think. Even the most insensitive will register moods at an unconscious level (such is the incredible strength of our biology).

What you may have noticed yourself, if you've ever had a great mood sunk by someone who's feeling particularly grumpy or aggressive, is that the strongest influence wins out. A single barb is sometimes all it takes to pierce a confident mood and leave you feeling totally deflated; especially if it's delivered by someone whose opinion you value.

But the opposite is also true. When we're busy and tense but we're with people who are calm and relaxed, if their calmness is grounded, solid and strong enough, their presence makes us feel better, simply through their way of 'being'.

It's an astonishing thought that we can all influence each

other to such a remarkable degree without realizing the lasting impact we're having on the people, the relationships and the culture around us. Although we all already know bad attitudes and low moods can spill over to others, we accept it too easily as something that just happens. A natural, if awkward part of modern life. It's not ideal, but it's life isn't it?

Yes, and no. Yes, because for many of us, life really is that way. And no, because in absolving ourselves of responsibility, we allow it to remain that way. We let ourselves be driven and influenced by our environments and excuse our behaviour as a passing moment. Rather than pausing to catch our breath and actively create environments that better meet our needs and expectations, and the aspirations we have for our closest relationships. We can be highly reactive parents, partners, siblings and friends, but most of us, only default to that because we are undermined by feeling 'less than' in the moment. If we had expert control of our emotions and behaviour we would choose something more worthy of those relationships. After all, none of us – when feeling happy and relaxed - actively chooses to inflict unhappiness on those we care most about.

If we accept the fact that our bodies are designed to scan for, respond to stress and then return to 'normal'. If we accept that our moods, whether openly communicated via language and behaviour, or simply intimated through the energy that we're creating around us can have a significant effect on others, then it's worth taking the next step. Understanding how to retune our thoughts, emotions and ultimately our behaviour means that these momentary slips remain just that - momentary.

# Energy is Contagious

We know what it feels like to be living or working alongside someone who is upbeat, downcast, pessimistic or optimistic. Without saying a word, their mood travels with them, casting light or shade wherever they go. It's a form of social contagion (truly) which has the potential to change the environment it inhabits.

It turns out, we pick up on those moods as soon as we're within a 10-foot radius of each other. Again, this is about our being able to read a situation accurately enough to judge whether it's safe for us to stay put.

And although science tells us upbeat moods are contagious (you can test this by smiling warmly at people – though I wouldn't recommend that if you're on public transport), the strongest mood is often the one that prevails. People who live with significant others' whose moods are constantly dark can find themselves resorting to self-preservation by retreating, disengaging, becoming defensive or becoming destructive themselves (all patterns of 'disconnecting').

No matter the path, each of those behaviours will test, and eventually erode trust. Even the heartiest of optimists will eventually concede defeat and seek to exit a relationship or environment that is so tense for so long that it seems to defy redemption. Our neurological and physiological make up may be complex and intelligent, but we are simply not designed to sustain negative, stressful environments indefinitely.

# The Role of Emotions

*"Emotions are real psychological events and they exist whether we recognize them or not."*

*Brown, Kingsley, Paterson (Fear Free Organisation, 2015)*

Our emotions are nature's way of helping us to regulate our behaviour so we know when to step back from risk and when to lean in. To use them as a precision instrument, rather than a blunt tool, requires us to understand what emotions look like and how to change the way we look at them.

There are eight universal emotions; fear, anger, disgust, shame, sadness, surprise, excitement/joy and trust/love. Each emotion triggers either a survival (protection) or an attachment (connection) response in us, which in turn releases a cascade of hormones and neurotransmitters that activate behaviour changes.

The first five emotions (everything from fear to sadness) are about survival. They result, albeit in varying degrees, in stress which activates cortisol (often referred to as the 'stress hormone'). Those chemicals are the ones which prompt a fight, flight or freeze response. When we experience those emotions in our relationships, our behaviour switches to protection, self-preservation, avoidance and escape. In that frame of mind, it can feel like a superhuman effort to even re-open lines of communication, let alone rebuild or restore trust.

The final two emotions result in attachment – a desire to connect with others – releasing the chemicals dopamine (which causes feelings of pleasure and reward), serotonin (which aids relaxation and appetite) and oxytocin (which promotes the desire to bond). Day to day, we can find ways of regularly sparking joy or excitement in others, or ways of reinforcing that they are loved and appreciated. When we focus on those attachment emotions (joy/excitement and love), we trigger that warm release of chemicals that relaxes their hearts and minds, making the desire and ability to connect possible.

The sixth emotion – surprise – sits in the middle and can rub both ways. A nice, welcome surprise results in attachment and bathes us in a cascade of feel good chemicals. An unwelcome surprise will do just the opposite, triggering stress.

In most relationships there are taboo topics – subjects we can't help but be triggered by. In the heat of an argument, we move into the emotional part of our brain, completely abandoning the part of our brain that thinks and reasons with logic and clarity. Sometimes we need a break to calm down and move from 'protect' to 'connect' mode where we can begin again from a calmer more thoughtful place.

There is real skill is in recognizing the signs that indicate we've set off the people that we love and live with. Yet when we know what triggers insecurity in the people we care about, we are infinitely better equipped to create environments that encourage and reinforce trust every day; and we can work towards creating safety in the situations where trust may be tested. With the right environment, their attention and energy will be working with you. They will be staying curious and open to understanding what's happening; rather than protecting themselves by creating arguments and counter defenses.

And, when we don't catch triggers in time, we can recognize the reactions for what they are. Vulnerability rather than aggression; and respond with thoughtfulness and compassion, redressing them before lasting damage is done.

We see untethered passion in others quite often; whether it's overexcitement, anger, or frustration. When we can see that behaviour through the lens of emotion - as someone who is passionate and wanting to be heard - the way we hear it, and how we respond naturally shifts. It converts difficult moments into trust building moments, where understanding and connection is built.

To build trust, we need to create safety. That means becoming aware of what we do that triggers fear, anger, shame and sadness in others, and what others do to trigger those responses in us.

# Social Pain: Does Losing Your Cool with Others Really Matter?

Science would offer you a resounding yes. Our memories of the social pain we experience at the hands of each other are much stronger than our memories of physical pain.

The brain registers both physical and social pain in the same place, yet when we remember a social hurt it elicits a memory that is often more visceral than any memory of physical pain.

Think back on a time when you were humiliated in front of a group. Or when your heart was first broken. Or the last time you felt foolish in public. It's bracing.

The things we feel most sensitive about hearing, reflect the doubts we have about ourselves. We are social beings who crave connection and who are innately conscious of our place in the world.

Our need to feel safe in a social context is so great that when we're feeling social pain, it can prevent us from focusing on anything else until our social need for connection and approval are restored.

Understanding the impact social distress has on us allows us to better navigate our own experience. It also helps us recognize how we may inadvertently influence and impact others, and inspires us to step in when we notice others experiencing distress.

# How 'Mindreading Misassumptions' Impact Trust

Unfortunately, because our evolutionary wiring is set for safety, our perceptions take shape at lightning speed. In less than a second, we have read, and begin responding to the signals we believe we're getting from the people around us.

Any sign of danger in another person's behaviour, irrespective of whether it is real or perceived, physical, emotional or psychological, triggers a series of reactions involving our brain, hormones, emotions, heart rate and breathing.

We know from personal experience that the most frequent and persistent threats we face begin at the psychological or emotional level before cascading into changes in our behaviour – whether toward ourselves or others.

Think back over the past twelve months. What were the biggest causes of worry or concern for you? What caused you the most stress? Most of us aren't living in fear for our lives (unless we have health concerns, or our choice of work puts us in harm's way). What most of us are frequently worried about, are the pressures we're facing in our professional and personal lives. And most of those centre around our relationships.

We worry about the quality of our relationships; is it ok to fall out with family? Should we make more time for our parents? Our partners? Our siblings? Our friends? Will our peers feel differently about us if we accept the promotion that makes us their manager? Do we have to take sides when our friends break up and if so, how do we choose? Which clients can we be totally transparent with? How can we be honest with our boss without losing credibility or being misunderstood? Does our significant other want the same things we want? We worry about our children; how safe are they at childcare, or in school. Are the changes in their behavior the start of something new, the sign of new influences from friends, the first hint that they're in trouble, or just a passing phase?

Luckily, we have evolved to guess the intentions and predict the behaviour of others to ensure we respond appropriately in any given situation. Our five senses absorb the information around us, send it deep into our brains for processing, sense making and pattern matching. From our vast stores of experience and intuition, we craft what we believe – or sometimes just hope – will be the right response.

That response takes one of two forms – we either move towards emotionally, physically or intellectually connecting with, or to protecting ourselves from the other party.

There's one - rather big - hitch. Now that we live in such a complex world, although we have the skills to predict and infer meaning from the behaviour of others, we're very rarely right. It is increasingly difficult to know what someone else is thinking or feeling, or how they might behave next. Especially when we – or they - are under pressure, or thrown into new, untested situations.

# Ideas to Begin With

### Create Safety in Conversations

While the physical environment is important (location, timing, privacy), language also goes a long way to foster or fracture trust. Before you talk, take a moment to think about what you want as a result of the conversation. For you, for them and for your relationship with each other. Open the conversation from that standpoint.

If there are things you don't understand and you're trying to get onto the same page, ask open ended vs. closed questions. It's innately human for first reactions to be reactive and defensive, even with our best intentions to create safe space for conversation. It's a sign that someone feels vulnerable. So, hold the faith, restore safety and keep asking questions, sense checking what you hear, until you feel there is no ambiguity left. You'll know you're there when you feel as though you're standing in their shoes, looking out at the world through their eyes.

### Unlock the Personality Difference Advantage

Catch each other in moments when those differences help you become stronger, happier and more aligned; acknowledge and appreciate those differences as those moments occur. Equally, when things get tense, as they inevitably will from time to time, isolate that tension to the ways in which your perspective differs. Hone in on the approach - the behaviour and the thinking - not the person themselves. Being clear that you're challenging the idea, or the behaviour, not the person, reinforces openness, honesty and security – every one of which is crucial to trust. It also gives you a foundation for understanding what the other person is attempting to achieve through what they're doing.

How do you do it? Simply avoid the accusations and blame and ask questions instead. Channel curiosity rather than judgement.

Appreciatively questioning the thinking and behaviour of ourselves and others, tests our thinking and teases out nascent resistance and problems before they happen. It enables us to think better together and to create outcomes that are more robust, fully formed and more openly committed to.

Our thinking and behaviour can and does change over time, but there are core aspects of our personality that will always be true for us, so feeling that we are taking a direct hit by being challenged on those can make us feel aggrieved and combative.

Ask questions that are clearly geared towards understanding the other person, rather than extracting the insights that will allow you to reshape and sharpen up your argument. You know they will feel the difference because you can sense the distinction yourself between genuine curiosity and the desire to sell an idea.

If you're struggling to get to the point of shared understanding, suggest you both take a step back and look at the situation purely as observers. Work together to separate the facts of what's happening, and where you need to get to, from the emotion surrounding it. Agree to park the emotions until the facts have been attended to. Focusing on facts is sometimes all it takes to create the emotional space and perspective needed to move forward together. You may even find that the emotions are replaced by relief by the time the conversation comes to a close.

Map out how your differences make you stronger together

and work out how you can discuss the difficult topics

When you know what drives and what triggers each other, you can frame conversations before you begin. Asking yourself what you want for them, what you want for yourself and what you want for the relationship clarifies your intentions and helps you to strike the right tone, find the right language and start from the right frame of mind.

Keeping those three thoughts in mind also helps to reframe conversations when you realize trust is on the ropes. Restoring safety by restating your intentions for them, yourself and the relationship is essential when they begin withholding, getting defensive or combative. Sometimes restoring safety can be done while talking and sometimes people need time to digest ideas before they can continue.

## Have Better Arguments

Know the difference between debating ideas and calling someone out on behaviour - agree ways (words, place, manner) in which both can be done constructively

If disagreements feel like negative and challenging events, it's probably because you've learned to associate them with discomfort, hurt feelings, lost opportunities and damaged relationships. They can lead to all of those things, but they can also lead to greater understanding, deeper clarity and to finding a way forward together.

Arguments are a natural way to express our concerns and differences of opinion and they can be the fastest way to raise concerns and clear the air. The trick to making them helpful rather than hurtful is to focus your thoughts as much as possible. Know each other's aspirations, strengths and challenges - talk about each other's blind spots with compassion rather than judgement

Identify the deal breakers in your relationships. What are the lines you don't cross? When might differing opinions or values mean you may need to choose to agree to disagree? Understand what triggers each other (words, experiences, people or specific behaviours) so you can recognize reactions for what they are - specific responses to a pressed button - and respond to them with care. Our emotional reactions to those deep-seated hot buttons can seem disproportionate but in the face of those flare ups, a compassionate, respectful and thoughtful response can deepen trust in a relationship.

Explore how your perspectives (using traits that are both complimentary and those that are contradictory) might be employed slightly differently to creatively resolve tensions.

## Don't Assume How to Treat Someone

Stop treating people the way you want to be treated - learn what they value instead. Relationships – particularly those closest to us – can be easy to take for granted. Too often it takes danger, illness or death to remind us how lucky we are to share our lives with the people we do. As unappealing as it may seem, in the same way that a strong organisation is clear on its vision and values and the behaviours that support both, great relationships often share a similar degree of clarity and focus of attention.

Being genuinely present with someone is becoming an incredibly rare and precious experience. Make time to listen - cut out the distractions and focus on each other. Acknowledge the people in your life the way they want to be acknowledged. Ask what makes them feel recognized and valued and then nurture what you want to retain. (Read 'What Does Love Have to Do With It?' in 'Social'). Whatever your 'love language' is, all of us love to be 'seen' for who we are and the occasions for that are increasingly rare.

## Find (and Cherish) Your Inner Circle

Who are the most important people in your work and life? The ones who, if they took their support, approval or love for you away, would make your work extremely difficult and your life very unhappy?

On a piece of paper, draw 4 concentric circles with yourself in the very centre. On the first circle out from you, write the headline 'critical' that's where your most important and treasured relationships go. The relationships which if you lost, you would feel keenly. On the second circle out, add the heading 'important'. Add the people whose relationships matter to you but who you could recover from or replace if you had to. On the third and final circle, add the word 'incidental' for the people you encounter who you like to have a good relationship with but who are on the fringes of your work or life (think extended Facebook friends).

## Notice Parallel Processes

What happens in one relationship is often playing out in other relationships too. Patterns repeat. Is there a relationship pattern that keeps surfacing which you would love to leave behind? How is it affecting you and your life? What would become possible for you if you were to shift that pattern? Redesign it? Upgrade it? How are you - maybe unintentionally - endorsing or reinforcing this pattern? What would you choose for yourself instead? How can you identify the moment of choice? The moment where you can catch - and correct - your behaviour to build a new pattern?

# SECTION FIVE:

ORGANISATIONAL

# Organisational Health

We know the difference that trusting someone makes in our personal lives – how we hold back or open up depending on how little or how much we trust. When you extend that to an organisational context the stakes are high.

| | | |
|---|---|---|
| Individual expertise | | Collective wisdom |
| Overwork & long hours | | Expanded capacity |
| Exhaustion | Becomes > | Energy |
| Judgement | | Understanding |
| Silos & withholding | | Collaboration & participation |

At every level - from the systems, to leaders, to managers, to teams – trust is about removing the barriers that prevent workplaces from tapping into the best contributions of individuals and teams; intellectually, physically and emotionally.

# What Does a Fear Free Workplace Look Like?

When you think about your best days at work, you're probably remembering the days when you felt on top of your game. Days when meetings were constructive, conversations flowed well, ideas came naturally and resolving conflicts and problems seemed relatively easy. In whatever way it happens in your work, you were 'in the zone'.

If you think about the days that just wouldn't end, or the weeks where you couldn't wait for the weekend, you're probably remembering the opposite. Wanting to avoid conversations, people, projects or work. You may have found yourself holding back, or maybe speaking up more sharply than you might usually. Or maybe feeling frustrated or digging your heels in in the face of problems.

We all want to exist in that first space. The place where our energy flows freely, where we're connecting with others to share our intellect, wisdom and experience to create unstoppable momentum and where we can always find solutions to the challenges that surface. That place - at least physically speaking - is your Executive Brain. It's a place that's only accessible to us when we trust the people we're with and the environment we're in. And ironically, it's a place most work environments prevent us from getting to, or staying in.

The opposite of trust is - naturally - fear. The challenge for manager's and leaders is to learn how to create fear free environments that allow their teams the psychological safety necessary to tap into the full extent of their potential.

We've felt the energy and enthusiasm of working with

people we admire and enjoy, and we've all experienced holding back when we've reluctantly had to work with people we distrust. It's the difference between connecting and protecting.

What neuroscience can now tell us is that those feelings – of connection and protection – exist in different regions of our brains and that trust is the lever that channels the energy. Critically, it shows us where that energy takes us. When we're connecting, we're working from our Executive Brain, our thinking and reasoning brain.

'Protect mode' shifts us into our Limbic Brain, our emotional centre which triggers a fight, flight or freeze response. It's the space dysfunctional relationships and toxic cultures come from.

Trust is the lever that pivots our energy. When people feel threatened at work, they may stay busy, but you can be sure they'll be spending more time focusing on their own survival than on working effectively. It's a natural human response. They may try to please their boss, but the act getting through their work will come at the expense of true performance, creativity and commitment.

When we trust each other, we connect. We open up the lines of communication and we invest in spending time and sharing ideas with each other. Success becomes a collective endeavour. When we don't trust each other, we play it safe, keep our thoughts and ideas to ourselves and refrain from sharing information that could help each other. In short, we switch from connecting to protecting. And when we do that, our energy and efforts are immediately and subconsciously redirected.

When you close off trust in an organisation, you immediately shut off access to the most natural and sustainable energy source within your enterprise.

What is most telling about modern working life, is that despite most of us having experiences of how fluid, seamless and ultimately effective high trust relationships are, we frequently expect and content ourselves with the exact opposite.

People's needs at work are simple. We need to feel valued and we need to have control, or at the least - choice. Feeling valued, knowing our role is relevant, feeling respected rather than judged and having good relationships all weigh heavily in allowing us to bring our full selves to work. With workplaces increasingly orienting toward becoming more human, allowing people to bring their full selves to work, feeling safe to just be you (though maybe a more 'socially aware' version) and to know that you are valued is a pivotal - and simple - first step.

A sense of control builds on this by allowing us the confidence to fully engage and express ourselves in that role. When we're unclear about how our role sits alongside others, or when there is uncertainty about our level of autonomy, insecurity is easily triggered. We can deal with occasions of being overarched, of duplicating work, of having decisions or changes imposed and of having decisions overturned. But the more consistent those occasions become, the more our insecurity turns to mistrust.

Trust is tested multiple times in business through changes (whether they are promotions, new teams or team members, new projects, new clients, mergers and acquisitions, or shifts in direction) or through high stakes conversations (reviews, negotiations, interviews, one to ones, presentations and meetings).

And day to day, it's easy to take shortcuts in favour of a quiet life, or to prioritise our own needs rather than being more socially aware. We check out of meetings through boredom, frustration or through pure mental distraction as we mentally juggle all the tasks that await us. We avoid sharing resources in case it's makes us or our team look as though we have excess capacity. We avoid working with others because we've heard them bad mouthing others and we don't want to be the next victim. We avoid calling people on their behaviour because we don't want to rock the boat or because we can't seem to find a simple and constructive way to do it. In multiple ways every day, we withhold information, support and insightful observations from the people we work with. And by doing that we keep the cycle of mistrust alive.

Highly successful professional relationships are the ones which develop our competence, test our thinking and which value and nurture connection. They allow us to collaborate in ways that leverage the skills and knowledge of others to bring our ideas to life. They keep our curiosity alive and our openness and desire to learn, strong in the face of mistakes and embarrassment.

Trust acts as a simple, effective and remarkably wide-ranging accelerator. Create trust between team members and information flows smoothly. Issues are raised quickly, debated openly and resolved with genuine buy in. Create systems for trust-based self-governance and peer accountability, and you replace cumbersome processes and bureaucracy with simple structures enacted by adults who self-manage and peer correct. Create trust between leadership and staff, and decisions become informed and bought into rather than challenged and derailed.

The bottom line is; if people lack psychological safety,

their energy will be directed at self-preservation, not performance.

# Is the Absence of Trust a Liability?

*"Smart organisations don't seem to have any greater chance of getting healthier by virtue of their intelligence. In fact, the reverse may actually be true because leaders who pride themselves on expertise and intelligence often struggle to acknowledge their flaws and learn from their peers. They aren't as easily open and transparent with one another, which delays recovery from mistakes and exacerbates politics and confusion."*

*Patrick Lencioni*

While we have advanced in leaps and strides economically, our work cultures in comparison have been slower to adapt. We still focus more on hours rather than output; on process, productivity and profit rather than the people who create them. Yet when we ignore how the 'people factor' influences engagement, capacity, productivity and creativity we create a tension that distracts and derails.

The industrial age gave us a great leap in advancement, but the information age is bringing change at a rapid rate and adjusting to it demands a different set of skills. Intellectual horsepower and functional expertise now takes us only part of the way to commercial or stakeholder success. The next test is how well humans can work together to build knowledge, capacity, adaptability and agility in the face of change and challenge. Our collective success depends on the degree to which we share our knowledge with each other, and our organisation, to grow our collective intelligence. We can co-operate without trust but we can't fully, or effectively, collaborate without it.

The behaviour that people bring to work, whether generative or dysfunctional creates and sustains a culture of trust or of distrust. Trust center's around the ability to be vulnerable. Something which isn't easy, nor often encouraged in organisational lives. In order to take advantage of the incredible upsides, we need to help people understand what vulnerability looks like and how and when to open up within the context of a relationship and a culture. If the vulnerability oversteps the bounds of safety or confidentiality, or it overwhelms the strength of the relationship, it will feel like an overshare to the receiver and a risk too far to the giver.

People are continually learning from, influencing and transforming the working relationships around them. The question is whether the changes and learnings are healthy and generative, or not. For companies and organisations to grow and thrive, people need to be able to share ideas freely, be open to learning from each other and be comfortable admitting when they unclear, have different opinions or need support.

Trust only becomes an asset when it is high and resilient. The absence of trust specific issues, is not the same as having high trust.

An investment in organisational health means investing in the welfare of the organisation and the people who work in it.

An intervention pyramid exists which is interesting when looked at in light of organisational health, rather than individual health. It has Prevention at its base, Proaction at its midsection and Remedial at its peak. The idea is that the majority of a person's wellbeing investment and activity takes place at the prevention level to keep risk and illness to a minimum so as few cases as possible make it to the 'Remedial' level.

I would argue that from an organisational health perspective, we have inverted that pyramid. The bulk of organisational development investments tend to be made at the proactive and remedial levels. Not because the people who decide are inhuman, but because we often wait for an alert before taking action, and those alerts by their very nature only happen once things have already begun to go wrong.

Preventative measures on the other hand are those factors we would normally consider 'best practice' or 'next practice'. In reality, they are well designed eco systems that support the generation and flow of energy through an organisation. Everything from workplace design, to the systems that gather, track and share information, to the behaviour of the people charged with bringing the organisations purpose and values to life.

Culture too sits at the preventative level. Similar to a weather system that guides the seasons, and gently nudges all the players into behaviours that enable them to shed old skin, generate new life, inspire stillness, or stimulate warmth and growth.

When we focus only on what we can see and measure on reports, we're missing the significant advantage that tapping into a vast eco system of trust can provide. We risk compromising the health of our organisation and we find ourselves plugging gaps – whackamole style - trying to restore health rather than taking a system wide view and creating health at the foundational (preventative level) across the organisation.

Organisational health relates not just to the sustainability of an organisation, but to its ability to be a generative force for the staff who work within it.

Using trust as the platform to re-evaluate organisational health means regularly asking:

*Which of our practices and processes are restricting our creative energy? (e.g. preventing open communication, information sharing, emergent goal achievement, flexible working, problem solving, initiative and innovation).*

*If fear and trust are two primary motivational forces - what is our current culture reflecting?*

Is there more to organisational health than trust alone? Absolutely. But starting with trust, when it's not already present, creates the intention of openness and collaboration, and gives you a strong foundation from which to move forward.

# Why Your Engagement is Often Highest on Day One

Think back to the last time you joined a new organisation and how you felt as you walked in on your first day. Were you feeling a little anxious, yet somehow still excited about the potential of your new role? Were you anticipating the people you'd meet, the new experiences and opportunities you'd be exposed to?

At that moment, despite the anticipation, you were likely feeling 100% engaged. Or at least, close to 100%. Fast forward to how you felt a year on. Were you still at 100%? Or did it feel more like 80%? Or even less?

In the process of starting a new job, it's not just the employment contract we're signing up to. There's another contract entirely that we (sometimes sub consciously) construct. When we accept a role, there are both explicit and implicit expectations that we are - in effect - agreeing to. The challenge is that it's easy for us to make assumptions about those unspoken areas, or to take for granted that some things are mutually accepted.

And that's where new starts can become more problematic than they need to be. Because trust doesn't just exist between us and others; it also exists in the relationship between us and the brands, cultures, teams and organisations we engage with.

When we join a company, we gift a degree of trustworthiness to our employer, our manager, our team and the wider organisational culture. Within that gift is a set of expectations about how the people we work alongside, the

154

leadership team, and the organisation itself will work. We have expectations about how we'll be treated and what we believe we can reasonably expect. When we join an organisation, we're often doing so with a sense of optimistic expectation.

It's those expectations that form the psychological contract we have with our employer. It sits alongside our formal employment contract; distinct from it, but no less powerful. In fact, after we sign our contract we often pay scant interest to it outside of our pay and incentives. Whereas, our psychological contract – our expectations of our roles, responsibilities and relationships, of fairness, equity and inclusion - is constantly being assessed and reassessed.

The day we begin a new role, marks the start of a relationship with the organisation we've joined. From that moment on, we become keenly aware of how our contributions will be recognized and rewarded by the organisation as our relationship develops.

Unfortunately, most of these expectations remain unspoken. And because it's hard to meet, let alone negotiate expectations you're unaware of, the risk of breaking trust without realizing you have, is high.

Relationships are so vital to the way we work, and trust so inherent in organisations, that it's also possible for people to elevate us to positions of power or influence without our knowledge. While that isn't necessarily an issue in and of itself, it does mean a fall from grace can be swift and surprising. We can misstep, and let people down, without even realising it.

Without frank, open, clear conversations, our workplaces are rich ground for stretching and breaching trust without us ever realizing. Our work lives are littered with opportunities to build or break trust. Everything from the degree of bureaucracy involved in decision making, hiring, or access to information, to the way promotions, pay reviews, meetings, poor performance, delegation and challenging conversations are handled, can impact the trust account of an organisation and a leader.

And because we tend to communicate in a style that works for us, we can fall into the trap of communicating with people the way we would like to be communicated with, rather than the way they need to be communicated to. Simple though it sounds, without checking everyone is clear can result in what feels like simple misunderstandings.

Psychological contracts - how we expect to engage with our employer, and they with us - can differ from employee to employee. Our expectations, and our triggers, can vary depending on what we've become used to - or wary about - elsewhere.

Understanding how the people you work with prefer to be engaged with, and what their expectations are, isn't just fundamental to rapport building, or delivering what's required - it's essential to building trust.

New beginnings can be disruptive - for the person joining a business and for the people in the teams they enter.

In our first 90 days, we're trying to make an impact but that means delivering fast while still getting to grips with the work, the people and the dynamics at play. All while we know people are watching us to see who we are, and how we do; which means in our first 90 days, we're also at our most vulnerable.

New people in a business is a great potential source of energy and presents an opportunity to reinforce who the organisation is, what it values and its commitment to a culture of connection. How on boarding - and the first 90 days - are navigated are one of the most frequent and powerful arbiters of positive change, and trust, that we could hope for. How we manage them matters.

# Trust, But Verify

For each of us, in our relationships with others and in an organisational context, there will be an acceptable margin of error on each of the Four C's (credibility and connection, competence and consistency) before someone's behaviour becomes a deal breaker. The point beyond which their trustworthiness is irreparable because we can no longer restore our faith in them. While we may not be aware of the boundaries those deal breakers create until someone crosses them, simply knowing how to have an open conversation about them when you feel the pressure building, can ease the tension and pivot you towards restoring trust.

Knowing what constitutes deal breakers to you, helps you understand your unique relationship with trust. The contextual aspects, and where and why your hot buttons may differ to someone else's.

Whether you vest trust easily or not, it's important to know that sometimes people want to earn trust, and for trust to be given, slowly over time. Too much trust placed in another person too soon can cut conversations short. It can leave people feeling uninformed or ill-equipped which can leave them at risk of proving themselves incompetent through no real fault of their own.

Every time a person is new to a situation, it is a perfect opportunity to communicate again – to make sure expectations are clear and that constraints and risks are understood. To gauge capability and resource requirements, and to make sure the channels and methods for delivering feedback are understood and agreed.

The challenge we have that we live in a world that is full and fast paced. And with our world evolving continuously and at ever increasing speeds, our ability to remain relevant relies on being tuned in, upskilled and competent at everything we turn our attention to. And therein lies the challenge.

Our attention, which has a finite bandwidth, has become splintered across many competing priorities, very few of which (unless we're intentional about it, or pressed by immediate need) focus on the health of our relationships.

Mastering the social skills needed to foster the Four C's of trust requires presence, awareness and the desire and patience to tune in to others. To listen, engage, reflect and respond with consideration and maturity. The demands of life – and our efforts to meet them – often redirect our energy away from people and towards outcomes. Trust requires us to embrace both.

# Enabling Agility in a Fast-Changing World

Though change has been a constant feature in our lives for decades, it's arguable that the pace and scale of change we experience and integrate on a frequent basis demands more of us now than ever before.

The Edelman Trust 2015 Barometer found that globally 51% of us feel that change in business and industry is happening too fast. While the prospect of change can be energizing and exhilarating for some, others find it disruptive and exhausting. Whether you find change exciting or daunting, the likelihood is that what comes next – the transition, the process of integrating the implications the change event has triggered – is a different proposition entirely.

Transitions can be open ended, uncertain and can push us into uncomfortable arenas that test our flexibility, our emotional stamina, our mental agility and our conversational maturity. That lack of certainty, combined with an expectation that we'll respond with resilience and flexibility, can be challenging at best and exhausting at worst.

Trust can be hard to win when it requires people to become vulnerable in uncertain circumstances. We're asking them to 'risk' a lot in anticipation of something worthwhile yet often feel we're unable to give them much to hold onto for security in the meantime. Yet vulnerability, navigated with care, is exactly when trust building is most powerful.

During times of change it's natural to seek stability to offset the ambiguity. Having some constants in life provides us a sense of groundedness and security while life shifts. Trust in those people leading the change acts like a gentle anchor – providing a sense of stability whilst also allowing flexibility.

Trust, in times of change, especially when people are being asked to do new things, or old things in new ways, or to simply hold the faith while the new path is made clear, can provide a much-needed sense of continuity and security.

# Why Work is Personal

*"Although we try to keep emotions out of it, in fact, the experience of work is saturated with feeling".*

*Ashforth and Humphrey (1995)*

In many workplaces, it isn't hard to see who is deeply engaged in their work, and who can't wait to get away at the end of the day. As I write this, I am a consultant with the luxury of subscribing to the school of thought that we all have the potential to do meaningful work that engages us; work which is valuable to the business or organisation. From that (somewhat idealistic and aspirational) viewpoint, disengagement is a sign of lost energy that either needs to be harnessed (assuming the person in question is in the right role and in the right workplace for them) or (if they're not) released to find a better fit for their aspirations. Disengagement is an avoidable elephant in the room, which ultimately serves no one. Acknowledging it and engaging with it transparently - and dignity - is the most human and respectful way to navigate it.

But there is one key thing to realize about humans and what distracts us. We all share a core set of needs, and if our most basic needs remain unmet, we will be needlessly distracted from giving our full potential.

## Simple Needs

In 1943, Abraham Maslow's submitted his Hierarchy of Needs model in a psychological paper titled 'A Theory of Human Motivation'. The central idea of the Heirarchy of

Needs is that we have a universal set of needs, each of which remains a focus, drawing our energy and attention, until they are met. There are five needs, which progress from essential to aspirational. As each need is satisfied, we naturally begin to seek out the next.

So, what does that have to do with trust? Or the workplace?

Of the five levels, the first three are 'deficiency needs'. They are the most basic requirements for our survival and if these remain unmet, they cause anxiety and stress. If our those most basic of needs aren't being met, fear takes hold, and it becomes harder to think clearly, work productively, or act collaboratively. Despite our best efforts, these needs - whether met or unmet - are fundamental enough to shift how we think and behave, no matter where we are.

When you link the model to engagement at work, it explains why our health can be compromised and our work and relationships can suffer when we don't get enough sleep or the right kind of nutrition. It also explains why we can be physically present at work, but totally disengaged because our mental and emotional energy is elsewhere.

It also goes some way to helping us understand how we can go from feeling safe and successful in our lives to directionless. Life isn't a static event, nor does life exist on a constant upward trajectory. Things happen. Life events, loss (of jobs, marriages, loved ones, health or property) and change can bounce us between the levels. Life is dynamic and uncertain and humans are complex and intricate. It can be hard to compartmentalize our private and our professional lives. What happens in one area of our life naturally casts shadow or light on others.

## The Hidden Link Between Our Needs & Engagement

| NEED | ENCOMPASSES OUR NEED FOR: | ENGAGEMENT LEVEL: | RESULT |
|------|---------------------------|-------------------|--------|
| **1** SURVIVAL | Nutrition, water, shelter, clothing, rest. | Actively disengaged. | Only working for the money; will leave when they can. |
| **2** SECURITY | Physical safety, financial security and to feel safe and secure in our home and our relationships. | Disengaged. | Open to doing overtime for the money; distracted at work; looking for other work. |
| **3** LOVE & BELONGING | Connection to others, friends, family; to give and receive love, and to have a sense of belonging at work. | Conditionally engaged. | Pride in workplace and a sense of being part of something bigger than themselves; may leave for greater development opportunities. |
| **4** ESTEEM | Status, recognition, appreciation, accomplishment, confidence, self-respect and to have the respect of others. | Engaged. | Feels valued and vital to the workplace; achieves and gets meaning from achievement; potential for stress. |
| **5** SELF ACTUALISATION | The opportunity to reach our full potential and to live with purpose and meaning. | Actively engaged. | Love their work; do their best; help others and inspire others to do their best. |

Over the years, the Heirarchy of Needs model has had additional needs incorporated:

- Cognitive: Curiosity, knowledge and predictability;
- Aesthetic: Balance and the search for and appreciation of beauty;
- Transcendence: Helping others to achieve self-actualization.

There have been questions about how well it stands up to cultural and generational nuances, which might result in elements within levels shifting, or levels rearranging in terms of perceived priority. There are people who also argue that it may have more contemporary relevance if it were inverted. Despite it all, the model still has an enduring place in psychology and in management training.

The model prevails because it's a simple way for us to understand fundamental enablers or barriers to our engagement at work. How things, which at one time may motivate us and drive us forward to such a strong degree, can suddenly cease to have power over us, or even to exert a negative stress rather than creative tension. It explains why, when there are deeper, more crucial needs that demand our attention, it's hard to divert our attention back to higher order needs.

The SCARF Model (David Rock 2008) adds to our understanding of how emotions can derail motivation by summarizing what people fear most at work. A loss of Status; the absence of Certainty, or of not being good enough; the Autonomy to control our own workload; a drop in Relatedness, or relationships becoming strained and difficult, judgmental or pivoting to where we may be taken advantage of; and the perceived absence of Fairness. These fears are especially heightened if they risk our credibility or our reputation.

Emotions can either increase or decrease our motivational energy. Attachment emotions increase it, avoidance emotions decrease it. Critically, threats don't need to be real to raise an emotional response in us.

Faced with fear, we're unlikely to admit, seek guidance about, or learn from our mistakes. When we're feeling stressed or under pressure, our mental energy gets diverted to stress management areas of the brain and away from motivational centres. We become less engaged, less resourceful and less responsive. Not because we choose to, but because that is how we are wired.

Eventually our performance, engagement, relationships and wellbeing will all suffer.

# Relationships and The Link to Motivation

*"It is unwise to confuse productivity with thriving and flourishing. Without thriving and flourishing, short term gains tend to turn into long-term opportunity losses'".*

*Susan Fowler*

Most leaders want to know how to facilitate engagement and motivation in their staff. The most human centred organisations want to understand how to sustain engagement and motivation for the duration of their employee's tenure with the company. They recognize that each person has a positive and generative effect both on the people they work with and the success of the organisation. To get there, most companies focus on promotion, rewards and remuneration, yet those only work to a point. In fact, one study found that improving trust in management by just 10% had the equivalent impact on staff of a raise of over 30%.

While there will always be an argument for paying people a fair and competitive wage, it's only one of the factors in people feeling 'rewarded' and it may be the factor with the least lasting intrinsic value. The satisfaction of the size of our salary can be disappointingly short lived and once it has faded, it can create a void which exacerbates the need for something more 'meaningful'.

Genuine motivation is ultimately an inside job. In reality, you can't motivate someone to do something. You can ask, tell, inspire, encourage, influence and incentivize people, but if the motivation remains external, it's easy to lose. That may be why there is so much focus on the why, the purpose, the values, bringing people together to understand how they contribute to those and aligning career aspirations to company outcomes. When people see that their commitment rewards them not just in remuneration, but in learning, connecting with great minds and doing meaningful work that makes a difference, the conversation stops being about pay alone. Motivation becomes a dynamic driver of energy, rather than a carrot or stick wielded by managers.

Susan Fowler, author of 'Why Motivating People Doesn't Work and What Does' has researched the science behind employee motivation and engagement and outlines three key and interrelated psychological needs which make up an employee's motivation; autonomy, relatedness and competence.

Autonomy relates to the belief that we have choices; control and the authority we need to make the decisions we need to. It's why we crave control during change, why we seek clarity about our role vs. the roles of others and why we need to definition around our decision-making authority so we're not overarched.

Relatedness tracks back to our inherent social wiring. It's about our need to have healthy, safe relationships and to feel part of something bigger than ourselves. It taps into fairness and equality, status and respect. It helps us understand our place and our value to others.

Competence is about both feeling equal to the challenges and opportunities we face, as well as having the freedom and support to grow and develop over time. It's why feedback that encourages and develops us are important and why we seek career conversations about our future with the company.

These needs are constantly in flux and inter-dependent. Sustainable motivation relies on all three needs being met. As soon as one need is in deficit, the others become weakened too. A baseline of trust underpins all three.

While meeting and maintaining those needs is the dual responsibility of both manager and employee, the manager may introduce the idea and initiate the conversations that make the practice a habit.

Ultimately, autonomy provides a 'safe' framework for delegation by clarifying both the expectations and boundaries of responsibility. Our need for competence creates the perfect opportunity to have conversations about where things are working well, where we need to improve and what getting to the next level looks like. But it's the strong relationships, underpinned by understanding, respect and care which means the conversations about autonomy and competence are possible. It's our relationships that allow us to have conversations that are clear, concise, constructive and compassionate.

Susan Fowler makes the point that while productivity will deliver results in the short term, creating a management relationship with your team enables healthy and generative levels of autonomy, relatedness and competence. Together, that dynamic deepens employee engagement, unlocks discretionary effort and ultimately delivers long lasting results.

# Nested Systems: The Systems That Bind

*"Trust is the lubrication that makes it possible
for organisations to work."*

*Warren Bennis*

We tend to think of trust as being a human quality. And it is. But is also exists in the culture, practices, processes, rules and regulations – the 'non-human' elements – of an organisation. It means that even when the people within an organisation have sharpened their interpersonal skills, trust may still be undermined by those artefacts. Ironically, mistrust can be the unintended consequence of compliance, quality, standardization, parity, efficiency and protocol.

Every organisation is a collection of systems that regulate how things work, both at a human level (like hierarchies in an organisational chart) and at a process level (like key performance indicators).

The systems that sit within an organisation can provide a clue as to how fear vs. trust based the organisation is. It's said that a system is operating perfectly to achieve the very results that it is getting. So, if the results your organisation is getting aren't what you want, it's time to step back and take a look at both the behavioural norms, and the processes which guide the business, to identify where negative tension, or bottlenecks, are occurring.

Performance and HR processes that aren't human centred or behaviour based, and rules or guidelines that border on excessive, are all clues that trust is being eroded. Systems can unintentionally inhibit trust by creating in and out groups, unhealthy competition, rigorous or unnecessary bureaucracy, and by fostering confusion about roles, decision making and purpose.

In fact, a highly bureaucratic environment is a sign of low trust. Irrespective of whether the bureaucracy was created to respond to possible risk or low trust in the staff, or whether the low trust is an unintended consequence of efforts to create efficient systems and processes.

Systems, no matter what their nature, either enable energy to flow freely, or they constrict it. In high trust organisations risk is mitigated, yet rules and structure exist only to provide safety. There are only as many, and as detailed or defined as they need to be, and no more. As soon as they become stifling or prevent the flow of information, resources and ideas between people, they should be health checked to ensure energy and progress is supported rather than stifled.

Enabling trust and connection throughout a system means stepping back at intervals, to understand the patterns which are occurring to sustain the status quo.

Every organisation is a series of nested systems whose interrelated parts, when individually changed, impact each other. It's the reason why positive changes can occur in one part of an organisation but create pressure in another. Or why changes are made, but don't stick (because other areas create a balancing effect which sustains the status quo of the system). Ultimately, whether your organisation is or isn't achieving the outcomes it should be; whether the culture is or isn't promoting health and performance, the system is delivering exactly what it is currently designed to achieve.

Sometimes though, the structures and processes we put in place with the intention of creating safe and legally compliant working environments, inhibit trust. They can result in homogeneity within leadership teams, siloed working, or people working at cross purposes to achieve success in their role. Or they can simply result in rules or procedures which feel oppressive, effort intensive, or borne out of mistrust of staff. All of which can be demoralizing for staff.

Once leaders and teams have embraced the skills of building and sustaining trust, and an organisation has committed to trust as a cultural imperative, it's time to review the processes that hire, fire and guide the day to day operations of the organisation to evaluate whether they are sabotaging or supporting that culture.

# Culture: What Your Culture Reflects About Trust

Culture is often described as 'the way things are done around here'. A state of being. But it's also dynamic. An organizations' culture is constantly being reshaped. Continually reinforced by the people and the processes within it, and the ways in which they respond to both their internal and external environment.

The culture of an organisation is built on organisational memories. They shape how decisions are made, how work is done, and how well - and quickly - both are executed.

In the past, fear has been used as the fastest way to motivate people, but it motivates people towards self-protection, not productive action. When our brains are in fear mode, they are on high alert for danger. All of our energy in those moments is being directed toward survival. Nothing else is possible. Fear kills energy and engagement at work. It creates silos and self-protection.

It's not just interpersonal factors that shape a culture of trust. Structural and operational factors play a part too; performance reviews/management, job processes, personal performance indicators, excessive rules and regulations.

Cultures high on performance driven objectives that rely on excessive and persistent fear, are unwittingly influencing the decision-making capacity of their staff short term through pressure and longer term through changes in their brain chemistry.

In some instances, trust can be more effective as a governance system than contracts; clear and candid communication results in faster and more effective conflict resolution, and trust and high regard often result in reciprocity. Trust creates trust.

That said, the kind of trust we foster matters. Too much predictive trust can be a bad thing for organisations. It can lead to poor management and oversight, delayed course correction, premature promotion, poor hiring decisions, weak team composition, a lack of learning and development and increased risk. Vulnerability based trust creates a mature mix of clarity of expectation, candid communication, constructive conflict and generative accountability.

Cultures adapt to reflect the way an organisation anticipates change, challenge, threats and opportunities both internally and externally. Healthy, high functioning cultures enable an organisation to actively seek and evaluate information and to generate insights that preserve or advance its success.

In many ways, high trust cultures echo the components of high trust teams; a shared purpose; collective awareness, appreciation and accountability; and norms and systems that free the members from distractions, so they can focus on delivering their best work in service of their core customers.

However, like people, cultures can become ambivalent. Lost in trading on historical success, or in big ideas that never quite convert to reality, or in false facts. They neglect to review - or may even fail to realize - that they're not as agile, adaptive or relevant as they need to be to remain successful.

Most often, cultures unwittingly become dysfunctional by falling back into 'power over' rather than 'power with' patterns. You will recognize dysfunctional cultures through behaviour as obvious as bullying, and as common as silos.

The challenge of the knowledge economy is that in a low trust environment, knowledge is power which has to be protected. Active 'patch protection' inhibits resource sharing and sees people jostling for status and profile. That sense of self-preservation entrenches silos, which erodes effectiveness and relationships. At a leadership level, it means teams never quite align to cohesively drive the organisation forward.

Humans are much the same. We adapt our behaviour to our environment to survive. In healthy environments, we open up and engage - our energy and attention are freely available to be invested in conversation, collaboration, and in doing our work well. When it comes to unhealthy workplaces, adapting can mean protecting ourselves to create the safety we all need to simply continue showing up. And the degree of discord doesn't need to be extreme to trigger our protective defaults. It can be as simple as working with someone you feel you can't trust, or something as obvious as working with someone who is aggressive or bullying.

Organisations socialize their leaders through their culture. Behaviour that goes unchecked by the Board and executive leaders, feeds into and perpetuates the culture. If people behave badly without consequences, our attitudes adjust to compensate. In the absence of the organisation creating a psychologically safe environment, we create it ourselves through self-protection. From that space we can survive, but thriving requires what can sometimes feel like a superhuman effort. The act of being constantly vigilant takes energy, so surviving becomes our default. Thriving becomes difficult to even access, let alone sustain.

Cultures are the ecosystem which - at an organisational level - blocks or enables the flow of energy and trust. Like any ecosystem, it needs to be health checked regularly for sustainability. As leadership changes, as businesses grow and as successful private enterprises are acquired and merged, cultures evolve. By design, or by default.

We each contribute to the culture we work in through the behaviours and patterns we endorse and those we discourage. There is sometimes little we can do from where we sit to influence an organisational wide culture, but leadership endorsement within a team can be powerful. It can create a culture within a culture - explaining how two people on different teams can have such a different experience of their organizations' culture.

Creating high trust organisational cultures is about releasing energy within an organisation both at a process and a people level. Internal processes that confuse, tie up time, add layers, or barriers without clear and necessary benefit or which prevent fast and effective information between teams should be evaluated and updated for appositeness.

Releasing energy at a human level is about understanding that people's identities are inevitably tied to who they are at work. What we do is - if we're lucky - an expression of what we're good at. Work is personal. For many of us, it's where we build confidence, make meaningful progress in our lives and build friendships. It's also how we benchmark our 'value' on the labour market. Work - for many of us - is incredibly personal. And we can do more to develop our competence and our confidence, not to mention the value of our contribution to the organisation, when the culture we're working within gives us the safety to contribute, learn and grow.

# Cultural Differences at Work: What Distinguishes Us?

*"Trust is like insurance – it's an investment you need to make up front, before the need arises."*

*Erin Meyer*

Cultural differences – while generalized – can be a good guide of how the environments we were raised in can influence the way we seek to build trust with our colleagues. It can also explain why sometimes we seem to be working at cross purposes with each other despite wanting the same outcomes.

Erin Meyer is a professor at INSEAD whose work focuses on how leaders can successfully navigate the complexities of cultural diversity. In her book The Culture Map, she outlines two different types of trust that exist and two differing approaches to building trust which are favoured by different cultures around the world. The two types of trust are cognitive trust and affective trust.

Cognitive trust is a form of predictive trust. It refers to how comfortably and confidently you can predict someone's reliability based on their skills and accomplishments. This is similar to how Patrick Lencioni defines predictive trust.

Affective trust is a result of empathy and a sense of connectedness. Like vulnerability-based trust, it relies on the ability to be completely open and candid within a relationship.

While we may form trust in one of those two ways, the culture that we operate in, or which we've come from, can affect which approach we default to as we build trust with others. Appreciating cultural differences towards trust building can avoid misunderstandings, wasted time and lost business.

When it comes to how our cultural preferences shape how we build trust at work, our approach can be either a blend of cognitive and affective, or can sit quite distinctly at one end of the spectrum depending on where we're from.

Task oriented cultures (such as the US, Australia, Denmark and Germany), tend to build trust through the process of doing business. It's through working with you that they gain experience of your reliability and consistency and can make reasonable predictions of your future behaviour. Relationships are more loosely held in these cultures. They're quickly built and quickly dropped.

In relationship-oriented cultures (such as Japan, Russia, China, India and Saudi Arabia) it is affective trust that counts. A sense of connection underpins the business relationship, business becomes social and time is taken to build a more personal connection. Once built, those relationships remain strong and loyal.

Many cultures sit somewhere in the middle, but knowing that there is a fundamental difference, and taking that difference into account when you're working with potential partners or bringing new team members on board, can save embarrassment on both sides of the relationship.

Professor Meyer recommends taking time to find common ground to build relationships and foster trust irrespective of who you are working with, and to follow the lead of the people you are working with if you're travelling. If they are all business, friendly but not social, don't force it and don't take it personally. If they work hard during the day and play just as hard after hours, don't be afraid to do the same.

Authors and researchers around the world point to the importance of relationships for working internationally. Especially in markets where contracts and regulations may be meaningless or non-existent. Affective trust provides reassurance in relationships; cultural digressions are more easily resolved, conversations about changes, risks or loss become less fraught. There is an expectation of goodwill and fairness in the relationship that provides a valuable safety net.

There are other areas of major difference that can influence how trust is built between cultures whose defaults are divergent:

### Decision Making:

In some cultures, consensual decision making is the norm. Ideas are discussed, refined together and then sanctioned (or not). Decisions are made with input from many, the conversations begin early and though they take time, once a decision has been made, progress is swift. Other cultures take a top-down approach where the leader makes a decision which becomes a mandate for the team below. While fast, it sometimes sacrifices the buy in of those who have to action it. When you're working across cultures and trying to get both buy in and action, it pays to understand both sides of the spectrum.

**Implication:** the way decisions are made may be different to what you're used to if you're working in a different culture, or with team members from different cultural backgrounds. Being aware of how to be involved in decisions, or how to get others involved so you can make an effective decision quickly can prevent confusion and frustration.

**Solution:** If consensual decision making is the norm, be patient and get involved in the discussion early; connect often to stay abreast of what's happening and to demonstrate your commitment. If top-down decision making is dominant, be aware of when decisions are made (prior to, or in meetings) and by whom and be ready to support the decisions made. In stalemates, work to understand the trade-offs, to prioritise, or suggest voting. If you're in the leadership role, and expected to make a clear decision, seek a diversity of opinions first, though be ready to act quickly and decisively.

## Timekeeping:

In much the same way as people can have very different approaches to time keeping, there can be big differences between cultures too.

When it comes to time, there are two opposite ends of the spectrum and while some cultures sit between the two, knowing the differences can make the way some cultures work and think, suddenly make much more sense.

Where linear time is characterized by reliability and precision, time feels concrete and brings a sense of order. We measure it, watch it. Conversely, flexible time is characterized by spontaneity and fluidity. Time has a looser quality, second to the people and the work which is being done.

**Implication:** When you're from a culture where deadlines, and time are prioritized and precious, working in more fluid cultures can feel disrespectful and frustrating. When your culture sees time as less important than the people or the work, a fixation on time can feel unnecessary, or petty and small minded.

**Solution:** Work with the cues you have. If your default is linear, yet you're working with people whose preference is flexible, factor in more time than usual to engage and complete the work, and allow time for human connection. If you default is flexible but you're working with people whose perspective is linear, be clear in your commitments about appointments and deadlines and precise in your time keeping.

### Performance Evaluations:

Some cultures are direct with negative feedback in appraising work and may be unlikely to give positive feedback at all. In those cultures, negative feedback is expected and seen as open, honest and candid by the receiver. Other cultures deliver negative feedback indirectly, softening the message but landing it with as much impact when speaking to a cultural counterpart.

**Implication:** indirect feedback to someone from a direct feedback culture may be lost on them. Direct feedback to someone from an indirect culture may feel overly harsh and imbalanced.

**Solution:** Be clear and specific and mix positive with negative feedback.

### Communicating:

Cultures can communicate in different ways too. Some cultures are 'low context' meaning they prefer communicating in a crisp, clear and specific style (e.g. US, Canada and Australia). On the other side of the continuum are high context cultures such as Japan, China, Indonesia, Korea and Saudi Arabia), where communication is nuanced and requires reading between the lines.

**Implication:** to high context cultures, the specificity of a low context culture can feel like a lack of trust. To a low context culture, the complexity and hidden meanings of high context communication can feel secretive or withholding.

**Solution:** Create low context communication and processes for teams that span multiple culture.

# Leadership: The Evolving Role of Leadership

*"Leadership requires five ingredients - brains, energy, determination, trust and ethics. The key challenges today are in terms of the last two; trust and ethics."*

*Fred Hilmer*

Much of our current modes of working in organisational life was founded on mechanistic ways of thinking and operating. They stem from a time when people were a resource to allocate and maximize, in pursuit of efficiency and profit. But what served us well in the past, is not what will help us adapt to rapid change or enable us to survive and thrive into the future.

Rapid change, increasing diversity in the workforce, and technological advances and access mean organisations today face greater demands than ever before. Where leaders and managers have historically been the stewards of the business, new practices are evolving to devolve the responsibility for meeting diverse customer needs, resolving complex and unexpected challenges and remaining relevant through the entire staff population.

It means the role of managers and leaders is evolving. Not only must they be strategic, innovative and adaptive, they must also be flexible in creating business models that deliver results for shareholders while meeting the needs of not just their customer base but their staff as well.

Meeting the needs of staff seems as complex as it is simple. Staff's needs are no longer satisfied through job security, salary or perks. Instead, people want the opportunity to feel competent and challenged in equal measure. With the fuzzy boundaries' technology creates around our accessibility, we also want - or expect - greater license to balance our work and home life. With the advent of new generations entering the workforce and approaching their careers as flexible and emergent; loyalty, commitment and the employee contract can be vastly different concepts to what they have been historically.

Organisations no longer have the luxury of control – or monopoly - over employees' job security or work choices. Growth is no longer available only through promotion, stretch assignments, secondments, contracting or sabbaticals, but through portfolio careers, side-gigging, blogging and advocacy. In fact, in smaller, or flatter organisations, career development isn't always possible through promotion. Instead, organisations are being challenged to think differently about how they provide development for staff in ways that both meets the aspirations of the staff member, while also unlocking the organisations ability to grow, innovate or disrupt the market.

The time is coming (though for many, it's already here) where people will no longer look for stable careers, but will develop the skill sets and seek opportunities to create the balance of work and life, of competence and challenge that fit them best at each stage of their life.

Across the world, employees are creating greater career agility by viewing their careers as professional journeys. Driven by the realization that their careers aren't as stable as they might have thought, they're approaching their careers as micro businesses, expecting a less hierarchical, more collaborative based approach to career development and growth.

For leaders and organisations looking to recruit and retain the best talent, they are no longer competing only with other employers, they are competing with the individual - the 'talent'. And with the alternative opportunities that person can create for themselves through the gig economy, executive contracting, freelancing, or entrepreneurship.

To lead this emerging workforce, managers and leaders need to know how to create a relationship with their staff which is mutually beneficial. Leaders need the skills to unlock motivation quickly, to keep that energy flowing through the business, and to quickly recognize and repair disconnects. It necessitates a shift in style from command and control, towards partnering for performance. And for leaders who have always found certainty in control, finding a more flexible, emergent style can be unsettling.

It's here that trust plays a key role in two ways. First, for the leader who needs to trust themselves to move into unchartered territory by letting go of what has made them successful in the past, in order to learn what will make them - and their teams and businesses - successful both now and in the future. Secondly, converting that trust into an environment which builds trustworthiness within the team; to enable people the safety to bring concerns to the surface, to fail and learn, and to experiment with new ways of working together.

At a time when most organisations are looking for ways to do more for less, or to deliver faster and with less cost and risk, or – increasingly often – all of the above, it's time to find new ways of working better together. When it comes to improving efficiency and effectiveness, whether it relates to people or processes, tension and bottlenecks create the friction that slows us down. Enabling both processes and patterns of behaviour that favour trust over constriction, unlocks time, energy and pace. Best of all, in the face of scarce resources, trust is one resource which can be generated simply through intent and integrity. A resource which is free, sustainable, universally recognized, craved and appreciated.

# Trust as a Leadership Advantage

*"Leaders need to focus on creating conditions that generate attachment emotions to ensure available energy is used in the pursuit of goals rather than survival".*

*Brown, Kingsley, Paterson*
*(Fear Free Organisation, 2015)*

The origins of trust in an organisation sits with its leadership team. Trust is the fastest way of unlocking energy, enthusiasm, focus and commitment because it calms our risk/threat seeking amygdala, and allows us to redirect our full attention towards working together. Trust destroys fear fast.

Organisations can become toxic when the relationships of the senior teams leading it are fractured, destructively competitive or antagonistic. Even if the team don't believe those behaviours are outwardly demonstrated, the atmosphere and fallout is noticed by the teams they lead.

Leadership teams can unintentionally undermine the health of their organisation in deceptively simple ways. By feeling a deeper affiliation to the teams they lead than the team they're a part of; by pursuing agendas that run contrary to the growth and sustenance of the organisation; and by holding onto outdated ways of leading to avoid perceived losses of control, expertise or status.

Leadership though, is evolving rapidly to face its own challenges. The divergent needs of more a diverse workforce, combined with the degree, speed and frequency of change is creating increasing levels of uncertainty. The access of customers to vocally - and visibly – vote for, or against brands or companies; and of technology enabling companies to develop both horizontally and vertically (and knocking out competition and intermediaries).

These factors and more mean demands on leaders are shifting faster than ever before. It's no longer about having all of the answers, being bullet proof, making concrete top down decisions and being able to make confident statements about what the future holds. It's about communication, authenticity, emotional maturity (though to be fair that has always been a feature of truly great leaders), comfort with ambiguity, open-mindedness, humility and connection.

What does it mean for leaders of the future? Status and leadership skills as we traditionally know them are no longer enough to create or sustain credibility - let alone create a cohesive and unified drive within an organisation. Credibility is one of the four interrelated foundations of trust, alongside connection, competence and consistency. Competence (how skilled we are) and consistency (how strong our track record is) have long been the most predominant measure of success, possibly because it is comparatively easy to track. It's about *what* we do, rather than *who* we are being.

As the world continues to adjust to political and economic changes, and to shifts in media access and consumption and influence clamour for share of mind; it is connection and credibility, those hard to measure 'soft' attributes which become a critical differentiator for both leaders and teams. It's those skills that broaden your leadership repertoire and which enable you to take your technical skills, and intelligence, to the next level.

How we relate to each other – the connections we build (whether in person, or remotely) is essential to transforming silos into collaboration; replacing presenteeism with engagement; and releasing leadership from a need to command and control to a focus instead on agility, adaptiveness, diversity and innovation.

Ultimately, it's about coming back to the realization that value and profit within an organisation is created by the people who staff it and determined by the ways in which they direct their energy and attention. Understanding what facilitates constructive energy flow in the service of value, profit, meaningful employment and constructive relationships, is paramount for leaders.

The pendulum is shifting from one where *employers* had all the power, to one where people can *choose*; between a full time role, contracting, or self-employment. The exchange of time for value is being viewed more flexibly than it has at any other point in our lifetimes. And for women or carers who have seen their earning potential sharply decline due to extended time out of paid employment, the tradeoffs are often more consciously weighed.

Trust in leadership has become a vital part of the employee contract. Not least because people have a stronger voice than ever before and they expect to use it at work. They want to be seen, heard and understood; they want their needs met. But also because without trust, you run the risk of fear blocking energy, preventing collaboration, shutting down contribution and fueling staff churn. The leader's new role is to create an environment of high expectation *and* high trust. With trust comes the ability to mutually explore and agree what defines success, how the team will achieve it, and the methods for holding each other accountable and celebrating wins as the journey unfolds.

Unfortunately, great performance isn't a set and forget

situation. It can take just one team member to unsettle and derail a whole team. We're wired to work well together, so when we don't it puts us all on alert. More than ever, our soft skills are playing a major role in unlocking and enabling the potential of team members and in managing the collaborative performance of a team - no matter how fluid the membership of that team, or the myriad challenges they face.

High trust teams rely on the stewardship of leaders to set the standard and light the way. By co-creating standards of performance, presencing those standards, and encouraging the team to live them too, leaders sustain the credibility to retain trust. Leaders must also demonstrate leadership credibility, connection, competence and capability with the team they are a part of, as well as the team they lead. It means leadership today is about practicing how you process your own worries, doubts and emotional responses before you engage in conversation with your team.

With consistent and credible leadership, challenges and difficulties become the learning platform for innovation and relevance. It takes a teams' competence, collaboration and comradery to the next level.

# Leadership Blind Spots

Blind spots can be hard to spot (hence the name) and even harder to admit to and address. They can stem from habit, conditioning or our own preferences. At the most elemental level of personality, it's worth considering how - if at all - your preferences for extroversion or introversion are impacting the team. E.g. Does extroversion stop you from listening to others?

Research indicates that extroversion in leadership can block participation; that it can lead people to feel, or assume, that their experiences or opinions don't matter. Leaders don't need to have all of the answers, in fact it's probably best if they don't! Introverts are more open to letting others speak, more likely to gather thoughts and facts before moving forward, yet that tendency can manifest as hesitation, caution or a lack of urgency. In what ways might your preferences we capping the performance or engagement of your team?

There are five leadership types, identified by Ryan and Oestrieich (1998) which generate fear in organisations. If you've worked with a difficult leader, you'll no doubt recognize them. They are:

- Absent leaders who… send mixed messages, make decisions covertly, use information as power, tolerate bad behaviour and avoid feedback.
- Ambiguous leaders who… are inconsistent, are unable to provide clarity and overreact to issues.
- Arrogant leaders who… are more interested in their own status and agenda.
- Abrasive and abusive leaders who… insult or ignore staff in public, shout or have outbursts, demonstrate

their distrust of staff.

Though easy for us to recognize, there are leaders who don't see themselves in this list, but who will complain about how their staff are often behaving. The bad news is how staff behaves is a reflection of how they are led.

- The staff of absent leaders avoid speaking up for fear of making mistakes.
- The staff of ambiguous leaders blame others instead of taking ownership.
- The staff of arrogant leaders will gossip and work to simply keep up appearances.
- The staff of abrasive and abusive leaders are the people who bully others.

When you reflect on the behaviours you see around you, it can be confronting to think about what that means for your leadership style. That's natural. Yet it's still better to know. Don't be tempted to let the vulnerability of owning up to your current leadership practice, prevent you from taking the next step in your leadership evolution.

After all, vulnerability-based trust requires the courage to go first in being open and honest. In being human. The anticipated reward (or avoidance of pain), simply needs to be greater than the perceived risk of failing. With trust, as with most things in relationships, we can't expect to receive from others what we aren't willing to give ourselves.

# Letting Go of Expertise to Embrace Emergence

Sometimes our desire to be the expert, or of having all of the answers, can stand in the way of building deep trust. After all, building deep trust requires vulnerability. It's only when we know we can absolutely admit to our concerns and our aspirations without fear, that we know trust genuinely exists.

But business life teaches us that our competence, our status, our standing is wrapped up in saying, doing and being 'the right things'.

Those 'right' moves we think we should all be making to maintain and promote our status depends on cultural, organisational and interpersonal influences. But it overshadows us with a sense of expectation that anything 'less than' may be career limiting.

Not everyone feels wary about openly expressing opinions. Some do it well, with confidence and gravitas. Some do it with gusto but without the maturity and tact for it to land well. And for everyone else, no matter where they are in their career, it can feel as though there are risks to speaking up, being open, challenging thinking, or admitting confusion or disagreement.

Yet the strongest trust is built in the face of risk; one (often tentative) step at a time. It's possible to overstep – to assume too much safety or to give too much trust - but finding the balance requires a leap of faith.

Because being frank and open can feel risky, creating enough safety to start experimenting with it means having a conversation where everyone has acknowledged the risks and rewards of building trust. Where everyone realizes they are in the same boat. Where a commitment to maintain confidentiality is given. And where team members endorse and appreciate the vulnerabilities they're witnessing.

# The Evolution of Leadership and the Trend Towards Teams

Change is happening at such speed that leaders are no longer required to have all the answers. Instead, what they need to do well is to anticipate and be adaptive to change. To create and propagate a culture where staff embrace the challenges and triumphs, and collectively draw strength, insights and resilience from the process.

Instead of controlling resources and output, leaders need to be increasingly focused on competitive edge and disruption, anticipating change, and accessing and developing collective intelligence. That in turn, means responsibility is being devolved to teams to create greater innovation, to work more smoothly and quickly together and to become increasingly self-managing in delivering business results.

Getting access to the best ideas means creating an environment where diversity is encouraged, valued *and* mined. Where ideas and input are drawn from members of the organisation that reflect the customer.

When we are tasked with working faster, covering larger workloads and continuing to stay sharp and relevant, time and energy fast become two of our greatest needs *and* our scarcest resources. And with that increasing responsibility comes increasing risk.

Building trust within (and between) teams can increase capacity on both fronts. When team members genuinely understand and appreciate each other's strengths and – more importantly – feel that they are understood and appreciated, the team dynamic shifts. When team members understand and appreciate their differences, diversity becomes a strength and a unifier. Especially in times of tension and challenge.

Trust allows people to comfortably ask for, and receive, help without embarrassment. It allows team members to call each other out early on non-productive, non-generative behaviour out of respect rather than criticism. It encourages people to raise concerns, ideas and observations because they know their perspective is different and that means they may see things their teammates cannot. Strengths are recognized, leveraged and encouraged rather than dismissed, judged or competed against. Blind spots are acknowledged and co-operatively managed, rather than hidden or avoided.

In reality, every member of a team is working to achieve the right balance of autonomy, relatedness and competence in every role they take on and every team they join, because that's what maintains our motivation and performance at work. But just what that looks like for each of us can be very different. It's that difference that can undermine a team or become its greatest asset.

A high functioning team, who understand and trust each other don't just appreciate their diversity, they actively use it. They know that through their diversity, the team accesses different perspectives on challenges, play to each other's strengths and support each other in bringing their blind spots into the open safely.

# Management: The Managers Mindset: Championing Trust

*"Few things help an individual more than to place responsibility upon him, and to let him know that you trust him."*

*Booker T.Washington*

There is a saying that people don't leave jobs, they leave managers. Add to that, that keeping staff engaged can feel like the holy grail and management can feel like a difficult gig. Especially when you consider that surveys worldwide consistently report a near even split of the workforce between engaged, disengaged (or ambivalent) and actively disengaged (you'll know who these people are if they're in your workplace).

Yet research has borne out the fact that where there are close relationships between managers and employees, trust deepens, the commitment is reciprocated and the employee will feel more committed to the organisation as a result. At its heart, all it takes is 'safe', simple conversations, held regularly. Individual and team meetings, which so frequently fall by the wayside, are vital for building the connections, competence and credibility that underpins trust.

A healthy relationship with our manager is critical to our success in an organisation. Yet the power dynamic can make trust a difficult quality to build and sustain. As managers, creating trust means enabling transparency, creating explicit expectations and championing both encouragement and accountability. It takes time and energy, but it sets the manager, team member and ultimately, the team, up for success. However, despite knowing people can thrive under one manager and wilt under another, we still habitually measure - rather than treasure - people. Ironically, it's distrust that robs managers of valuable time and energy from managers, by necessitating close (micro) management of staff.

If you're lucky enough to have worked with a manager who prioritized one to ones, you'll have experienced the value of being regularly coached and challenged in pursuit of bettering yourself and the performance of the team. Experience (and research) tells us that when we have those relationships of trust with our managers, we tend to return that trust. We feel more committed to the organisation too – the result being that we willingly invest more of our time and energy in our work.

Lack of trust in others can result in a lack of development, inertia in succession planning, delays, duplication of work efforts and lower morale and engagement. People want to be empowered, stretched and developed - not 'managed'. In order to unleash potential in individuals and teams, managers need to create stretch with a sense of safety rather than fear.

Ironically, one of the most common refrains of managers is that delegation is a challenge, even though through delegation, trust becomes reciprocal. For delegation to work, managers have to trust that the person they're delegating to has the desire and ability to do good work and that they'll ask for help if they encounter difficulty. The person being delegated to has to trust that they can flag issues without feeling, or being made to feel, inept.

Delegation means letting go while there is still a potential gap in competence. Both managers and team members feel that risk. When managers let go, they lose control of the process and exactly how the outcome will look. But it's that letting go which creates the vacuum for learning and competence – for both parties.

Without trust, feedback is a red flag. Without the proper set up of physical environment, context and delivery, it shifts from a great opportunity to reinforce connection and trust, and becomes instead an awkward exercise in critique and defense, or defeat. It can erode, rather than foster the engagement we're looking for from team members and the encouragement we seek from our managers.

The managers role in building a high trust environment is to create a structure of collective aspiration, and a dynamic within the team of mutual understanding, openness and accountability. Specifically, through fostering:

**Courage...** by helping staff identify the difference between parchad (an irrational fear of imagined things) and yirah (the fear of having more energy, or of being in the presence of something profound). By recognizing the difference when they're experiencing them, they can either let go of the imagined fear, or embrace the stretch opportunity ahead.

**Challenge...** by defining and understanding the roles of comfort, stretch and panic as staff develop, so they can self-manage the creative tension (and distinguish it from emotional tension) as they continue to build their skills and experience.

**Competence...** by helping them achieve clarity, embrace challenges, and seek feedback; so they sustain learning, energy and connection to their teammates – and the organisation.

**Choice...** in how they engage with and relate to others. To appreciate that through their work they are making choices whether active or passive, and creating consequences whether intended or unintended.

**Contribution...** to outcomes and culture. To understand that like voting, we all have a voice. Whether we are involved and active, or withdrawn and withholding, we each influence outcomes and culture.

Management is a central influence in shaping staff to access or nurture the resilience and resourcefulness to adapt to the changing world of work. Conversations where managers and employees can discuss what is going well, what needs to improve and what the career path and development plan looks like, is the difference between partnering in performance and leaving it to chance. It allows managers to advance each team members' skills by balancing the conversation between competence, and ongoing development. It offers managers the opportunity to bridge the aspirations of team members to the journey of the organisation, creating a developmental path that helps people to map the future they want to the value they can add.

Being a Manager also requires the willingness to meet each team member where they are in terms of both current competence and commitment, so they get the right level of support, encouragement and oversight to be able to express their strengths, and build skills and experience. A core function of a manager is to build the competence and cohesiveness within their team. Building trust with each team member is the first step.

# Teams: Why High Performers Aren't Always a High Performing Team

*"When a gifted team dedicates itself to unselfish trust and combines instinct with boldness and effort, it is ready to climb."*

*Patanjali*

Think about the work you do for a moment. How much can you complete (end to end) on your own? Most of us don't work in isolation - we don't usually have complete dominion over the work we do. Instead, there are elements that pass to, and from, teammates or colleagues. Our world - and especially our work - revolves around relationships. How enjoyably and effectively we are able to do our work, depends on the quality of those relationships. Take a moment to think about your work again. Is it easier, quicker, and more enjoyable to work with people you have a strong relationship with, or those you don't?

As luck would have it, humans are social creatures by nature; designed to live and work together. The caveat is to work well - or 'bring our full selves to work' - we need to feel psychologically safe in our workplace. It's only when we know we're part of a team that values us, that we're able to focus our thoughts and energy on the work, rather than on protecting ourselves.

It explains why teams can be full of high performers yet not be high performing as a team. High performance requires psychological safety and at the root of that is trust; between team members and between the team and their organisation. Within that context, challenges, change and ambiguity become an opportunity to build strength and capacity because energy is spent on solving problems and making progress, not on protecting positions, or hoarding resources. In teams where trust is expressed only as a predictor of behaviour, or where it's absent altogether, there remains a sense that at the end of the day, it's every person for themselves.

Because high performance is about discipline and ease across the team, sustaining its various dynamics means practice. It means holding the responsibility for being an advocate for healthy high performance, while also holding yourself and others accountable. That becomes tricky when we don't have the language for, or the agreed ways of, holding each other accountable. Or when new leaders or team members join who are unfamiliar with the dynamics, or who aren't onboarded effectively into the high-performance mindset and behaviours.

Some of the most common derailers of team performance occur for the simplest reasons. Most of our conflicts arise from shortcuts we take in how we communicate with, and relate to each other. We assume how things should be rather than being explicit about our expectations, concerns, aspirations, needs and preferences. We focus more (or only), on what we need to deliver rather than how we're doing it. We tend not to spend as much time thinking about what it takes to work together well when things are going smoothly as well as when they're not. Maybe most importantly, we stop - or don't begin by - assuming positive intent.

Yet teams are how we solve complex problems, resource big projects, and build and broaden out the knowledge and experience within a workplace. Teams allow us to network our knowledge, build on each other's insights and experience, and to contribute to deliver the things we each do better than our peers. It's how we each get to play to our strengths, while learning from others to stretch and develop a little further.

However, when we're under sustained pressure, or a pace which is unrelenting, our internal 'busyness' can ramp up, causing us to shortcut our behaviour. To act on impulse rather than taking a breath to choose our response. Under pressure, it's harder to access the part of our brain that enables us to think clearly. To be curious rather than judgmental; to entertain options rather than seeking to force an opinion simply to resolve an issue. We look to solve, rather than explore problems. And every time we do, we lose an opportunity to share, challenge and improve our thinking - as individuals and as a team.

Building vulnerability-based trust with each other means first peeling back the layers to really know yourself first. To not just be aware of our own strengths, our preferences at work, and our triggers and tendencies under pressure, but also to create an honest appreciation of who we are at our best. Our values, our innate value, and our humanity, so we have an organising principle to re-orient us when things get out of whack or feel too steep.

It's that sense of being able to be human, rather than having to be perfect, that not only level sets a team, but also enables us to swap the pressure of perfection with the rhythm of continual learning, improvement and development. As strange as it may sound, 'being human' makes us more relatable to others and makes us more forgiving of ourselves.

Default behaviours exist in almost any workplace where pressure exists. However, it's especially so in environments that regularly experience complexity, rapid change or regular uncertainty, complex stakeholder constellations, high scrutiny or where staff's conduct is held to a particularly high social standard (government, healthcare, education, clergy, charity).

One bad mood, or knee jerk reaction can derail a whole conversation - and with it the productivity of the team while they recover their calm. Our behaviour triggers the way others respond, altering not just our own state but the state of the team. It's why most teams get stuck in the 'norming' phase, rather than moving into 'performing' - even though many teams believe that's where they are.

The degree to which the people we work with influence our mood and our behaviour is dramatic. We are social creatures, who read our environment so we can adjust our behaviour to suit.

Team dynamics shift with every change or challenge a team encounters. Learning to anticipate (and prepare for) those, builds strength within a team. Being able to be resilient when they come, builds confidence and reassurance that the team have the resources they need to thrive no matter what they face.

In knowledge based organisations, agile and cohesive teams share wisdom and information to solve problems in innovative ways. Teams share a common purpose, or groups a clear commission, which aligns their effort. Giving them shared results to focus on and a clear reason to work together. When we view ourselves and each other as possessing a unique set of skills, strengths, experience and expertise - rather than being defined by job titles - how we collaborate, support each other and solve new problems changes. But unlocking that level of awareness means leaving the safety of our defined roles and being open to working together in new ways. And no, teams don't need to like each other, but they do need to find a basis of mutual respect and understanding in order to feel safe enough to trust.

# Accountability and Trust

Mutual accountability is one of the conditions for self-managing peak performance. Yet attempting to hold people accountable for delivering work without creating clear expectations and without providing the appropriate resources, leadership influence or support is a recipe for disengagement. It results in frustration, duplication of work, wasted effort, feelings of futility, stress and resentment. The expectation, or performance, gap may seem obvious to you as a leader, but if it's not clear to your team member, it's not clear full stop.

Trust enables productive conversations where there would otherwise be conflict; stronger, genuinely robust commitment to the decisions made by the team; and makes the usually uncomfortable feedback needed for accountability easier.

Trust also creates swifter and more transparent communication which speeds up delivery, reduces errors and directly improves the four key areas business leaders must focus on:

- Revenue gains
- Cost reductions
- Competitive advancement
- Attracting and retaining mission critical staff

Conversations are how we learn. It's how we learn to have constructive conflict; to hold each other accountable; to create a common set of results to aim for together; to make sound decisions. It's how we learn what each of us has to offer, how we learn to work together to bring out the best in each other and ourselves as teams. In short, it's how we learn to learn. The relationships we have with our team members – and the conversations we have within those relationships - can either stifle, or springboard, our success and our professional growth.

We often avoid having the conversations that feel awkward, when embracing them in effect, reduces the fear factor and makes the whole team stronger. Don't fear or resist conflict. Difficult conversations are how we surface and understand each other's diverse perspectives. Conflict is a prerequisite for gaining permission to hold a team accountable. Accountability requires engagement and commitment. And where adults are concerned, robust conversations, debate, conflict, are how you can ensure everyone's perspectives are heard, and that decisions have genuine buy in across the team.

The focus isn't on how to avoid conflict, it's on how to have *good* conflict. Conflict that builds trust, strengthens understanding, promotes ownership and permits accountability.

## Understanding the role of Trust in a Teams Development Journey

For leaders wanting to nurture mutual trust and respect in their teams, an understanding of the psychology of group development is a window into the fundamentals of how great team collaboration is built. Specifically, it enables leaders to recognize:

- Where their teams are on the journey;
- How to navigate to the next stage, and when the team are collectively ready to move further forward;
- What behaviours (of leaders and teams) are unintentionally keeping teams anchored in storming or norming, and prevent them from reaching true peak performance;
- How both leaders and team members can work together to create the conditions for learning and development;
- How to recognize and remedy slips to regain peak performance during times of pressure or change.

# The Integrated Model of Group Development

© Susan Wheelan

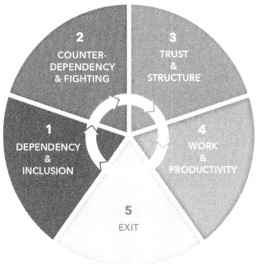

1    Characterised by:
- Dependence on leadership
- Desire to feel safe & included
- Shallow, surface conversations
- Artificial harmony

2    Characterised by:
- Team challenges leader
- Cliques and coalitions form
- Tension and conflicts emerging around goals, roles and values

3    Characterised by:
- Consultative vs. directive leadership
- High commitment to the group from individuals
- Increased collaboration and cohesion
- Increased satisfaction and welfare of team members

4    Characterised by:
- Intense productivity and effectiveness
- Delegation style leadership
- Clarity and acceptance of roles and status across team
- Feedback about effectiveness and productivity is openly given, received and used by team members

5    Characterised by:
- Completion of task, project or role
- Acknowledgement and appreciation of contribution and lessons
- Team member departure from the team or group

# Strategies for Facilitating Team Development

| STAGES | MANAGER STRATEGIES | PEER STRATEGIES |
|--------|--------------------|-----------------|
| **1**<br><br>DEPENDENCY & INCLUSION (FORMING) | • Be explicit with directions and expectations.<br>• Be clear and transparent about goals, constraints and challenges.<br>• Help team members feel safe and included – encourage questions to clarify understanding.<br>• Provide a safe space for experimentation.<br>• Give positive and constructive feedback often. | • Ask questions to clarify and understand.<br>• Double check assumptions.<br>• Engage with peers with positive regard. |
| **2**<br><br>COUNTER-DEPENDENCY & FIGHTING (STORMING) | • Further refine role responsibilities and overall goals.<br>• Recognise and resolve confusion or conflicts around task ownership quickly.<br>• Enable team members to take ownership and responsibility for their work and commitments.<br>• Help the team understand the difference between productive conflict or creative tension and personal conflict or emotional tension to ensure passion is being harnessed in constructive ways. | • Work to understand both the similarities and the differences in personalities, and working preferences between team members to create respect for diversity.<br>• Recognise the difference between emotional tension and creative tension, and work to break emotional tension and pivot towards creative tension instead. |
| **3**<br><br>TRUST & STRUCTURE (NORMING) | • Agree processes and autonomy for decision making.<br>• Reinforce clarity with regards to roles and responsibilities.<br>• Catch good and bad behaviour often – especially during peak pressure periods.<br>• Create awareness and ownership of how the team are expected to work together to sustain effectiveness, relationships and welfare. | • Learn how to value and leverage the differences between team members to build the competence and skill of the team.<br>• Practice stepping into greater responsibility with confidence, and failing and learning quickly with humility. |

# ORGANISATIONAL

| STAGES | MANAGER STRATEGIES | PEER STRATEGIES |
|---|---|---|
| **3** *Cont...* **TRUST & STRUCTURE (NORMING)** | • Facilitate conversations between team members, supporting and encouraging new ideas, ownership and collaboration and acknowledging productivity and progress. | • Agree how you want to work together to maximise effectiveness, relationships and welfare; especially when pressure is high.<br>• Agree ways of holding each other accountable, and accept mutual responsibility for encouraging each other to succeed in following through on those intentions. |
| **4** **WORK & PRODUCTIVITY (PERFORMING)** | • Step back to enable the team to fully and effectively self-manage; act as an expert and mentor rather than 'manager'.<br>• Participate without controlling or leading team conversations.<br>• Watch for signs of tension or regression and coach team members (with open questions) to jog awareness and challenge thinking and behaviour.<br>• Encourage the team to self evaluate and manage progress effectively. | • Prioritise the priorities.<br>• Recognise the difference between 'busy' and 'effective' and practice discipline.<br>• Be crystal clear on deliverables.<br>• Address tension quickly.<br>• Proactively support team members in the pursuit of team goals. |
| **5** **EXIT (ADJOURING)** | • Facilitate the team in saying goodbye well.<br>• Recognise team members may feel sadness, loss or confusion.<br>• Manage logistics so each person's farewell is handled with appreciation and dignity. | • Acknowledge the contribution your team members made, what you liked and what you learned from them.<br>• Recognise people may respond differently and practice compassion.<br>• Give yourself and team members space and time to process their emotions. |

By being honest - and candid - in recognizing where your team is on the journey of development, you can engage the right strategies for co-creating the move to the next stage.

Each stage of a team's development is essential to creating a fully formed, mutually respectful, self-aware team who are genuinely – and sustainably – capable of generative self-management. No single stage is better, or worse than another. All are necessary, and if rushed, will draw you back through the stages by virtue of the behaviours of your team or group members.

Working together to understand not only the behaviours that keep you tethered to early stages of working, but also what it takes to get – and imbed - the thinking and behaviour required to develop cohesively as a team. This practice imparts skills your team members can deploy over their career. Simple disciplines they can use to swiftly regain high performance during times of pressure and change.

**Points to Note:**
- You can locate the stage you're in by identifying the behaviour of your team. If some of your team are operating with a degree of trust and structure, yet you have some team members jostling for status or stepping on each other's toes, the team is still in Stage 2.
- Changes to the team membership, promotions, new leaders and changes within the wider organisation may temporarily pull the team back to Stage 1 or Stage 2. What matters is not the temporary changes, but that the team and leader recognize and acknowledge the shift and work together to restore, or redefine, the conditions of peak performance so they can find their way back. Learning is fundamental to performance

agility.

- Onboarding of new team members is an opportunity for the leader and team members to work together to move from Stage 1, back through to Stage 3 or Stage 4 together, educating their new team member as they go so the knowledge of group development becomes shared wisdom and skill.

- These behaviours and stages relate to both 'intact' teams who always work together, to groups and to project teams. Whenever a group of humans are required to work together to achieve an outcome, these stages are in play.

# Change as a Catalyst

*"When the trust account is high, communication is easy, instant and effective."*

*Stephen R.Covey*

Change brings with it a degree of vulnerability. In that moment, the way an organisation and its leaders respond can determine how well people embrace the change and how swiftly, constructively and effectively the change can occur. Vulnerability is a precursor to deep trust.

Trust is a necessary component of change – at some point, people need to choose to trust in order to move on.

There are different kinds of change: imposed (those we feel are forced on us with minimal input or consultation from us; intentional (those we initiate ourselves, or which we take an active role in initiating and planning); incremental (small and/or staggered changes that happen slowly over time); and transformational (large scale changes that fundamentally shift our experience day to day). Change that is imposed or transformational can feel like a threat or a risk and if it does, it can breach the safety and trust of others.

One of the earliest considerations of a change or transformation programme is how to maintain safety and engagement by avoiding the perception of threat.

Trust is tested during times of change because change naturally creates uncertainty, drawing people into a more aware state.

We are hard wired to minimize danger, and as one scientist puts it - we are descended from people who survived *because* they paid attention when the bushes rustled, so it doesn't take much for us to be on alert.

Yet change also provides a remarkable opportunity to deepen trust and commitment within a team or organisation when it's handled well. Unfortunately, it's also very easy to get wrong.

Change is frequently planned when it feels urgent, and often at the highest level of an organisation, before plans are communicated downwards and rolled out with a greater focus on the process than the people. The speed, and the focus on making it happen, can threaten the engagement and action leaders are hoping for.

There has been a general rule of thumb in business for decades that 70% of all change initiatives fail. With change a frequent factor in organisations, that fail rate doesn't just impair organisational agility, it strains employee engagement and team collaboration.

While the process of change may look watertight, it's the human element where initiatives come unstuck. Those responsible for leading the change often aren't prepared for the realities of engaging their teams in the process of transition, so resistance replaces engagement, and the job gets harder as managers and leaders find themselves confronting people's fears as well as attempting to progress change at a practical, operational level.

For leaders and managers to effectively engage and navigate their teams through change, they need to understand the human dynamics of change. Most people dislike disruption. Unless it's our idea, or unless it's clear that the change will improve our lives.

Though it may sound excessive, being mindful of how differently we approach change can affect how well we navigate it collectively. Ultimately, if we're embarking in change, and need to enroll others, we need to know what's going to prevent them from taking part.

There are a few factors that play into how we see change. Where personalities are concerned, there's a scale of being open to experience that we all inhabit - a gauge of the degree to which we willingly embrace new things. Where we find ourselves is often a matter of the context surrounding the change. What matters is that some people require more information, more time, or more consultation to build the desire to engage. Creating the space for people to take the time they need, to ask the questions that bring them greater context and security saves time later in the transition.

Our experience of change can also depend on our position of relative 'control'. We share a basic need to control the circumstances of our own lives and while that's not always entirely possible, it doesn't diminish that desire. The degree of agency we believe we have in a change event can dramatically shift us from 'toward' behaviours where we'll engage with change, to 'away' behaviours where we'll avoid, resist or argue against it.

Some of us also see danger in change, whether others see opportunity. That can be as a result of our natural disposition (whether we see the world as a safe, or a dangerous place. It can also come down to our assessment of whether we have had a hand in creating the change, or not; the perceived scale and impact of the change; and our perceived ability to adapt to the change based on our current levels of knowledge, ability and resourcefulness.

Essentially though, change at work presents itself in four different ways:

| INCREMENTAL | TRANSFORMATIONAL |
|---|---|
| Small tweaks or modifications (small updates to process, environment)<br><br>Often feels like a natural progression. | Big changes to direction or the status quo (mergers, restructures, changes in senior leadership).<br><br>Often feels uncertain and ambiguous. |
| IMPOSED | INTENTIONAL |
| Change which feels as though it has been forced upon you.<br><br>Often feels sudden, disruptive and arbitrary. | Change you initiate or are involved in.<br><br>Often feels like a conscious, considered decisions to solve problems or improve situations. |

When change feels imposed or significant, it can create a sense of risk; yet alongside that risk is an opportunity to knit teams together. The inherent vulnerability in change, and how managers and leaders respond to it creates the conditions that build resilience and bring staff closer together.

For organisations, the challenge is with imposed and transformational change, where it can be easy for people to feel vulnerable because of their relative lack of control or clarity about how things may change for them. When we're under pressure, our perspective shifts. We become more sensitized to information (both the content and the tone) and we expect more immediate answers (as we seek to assuage the uncertainty and still our anxiety). While people are in this mindset, their energy is being absorbed by the uncertainty and productivity and communication will dip.

Because control over our own experience is so central to our sense of safety, organisational change that feels transformative or imposed can be disruptive and create significant performance lags while we acclimatize to the shift. Because change feels different depending on how much control you have, the degree to which people feel vulnerable during change can surprise leaders. While a sense of vulnerability is natural, normal and can be worked with, the fear that can result from unchecked levels of worry can be harder to dial back.

The truth is, the less control you have, the less certainty you have, and the more vulnerable you're likely to feel. We're being asked to let go of what we know, and embrace the unknown instead. Maybe it's one of the reasons why our experience of change mirrors the grief cycle. Take a moment to think about that; change mirrors the grief cycle.

We understand that grief is a visceral experience. We know it affects everyone differently, that some people need longer to recover than others. When people we know are in the throes of grief, we give them time and compassion. Compare that with how we engage people in times of change. We jostle them along; we rationalize instead of empathizing; we listen to counter an argument, rather than to understand; we sell or tell, rather than ask or explore.

When we begin working on change processes, we tend to

focus on the process side of change (making sure everything is well planned and scheduled), and largely neglect – or underestimate - the human aspect. How the change will impact the people involved.

Given it is people who implement the change process (or 'transformation' process), overlooking how people are engaging with change undermines the entire initiative and can result in unnecessarily slow, or stalled change programmes. The high failure rate of change programmes is due predominantly to the people factor; in terms of both how the change is managed and how well (or not) staff are engaged in the journey.

There are several change models available, but the simplest to remember may be the ADKAR model. The acronym highlights key steps to actively engaging people in change: Awareness, Desire, Knowledge, Ability and Reinforcement.

Essentially, people must be ready, willing and able to understand and implement change. The desired behaviours and outcomes must also be reinforced often and clearly for change to be effective and enduring.

The questions to ask are:

- How will I create awareness about the need for change?
- How will I build peoples' intrinsic desire for change?
- How will we share, or develop, the knowledge about how to map and navigate the transformation process?
- How can I best encourage the people I work with and lead as we practice and refine the new skills and behaviours that are required?
- How could we celebrate and reinforce the desired

behaviours and outcomes to ensure change sticks?

Before you embark on change, there are two human responses worth reflecting on…

First is people's need to clarify their role - and degree of control - within the change. Second, is how the tension created both by the announcement and the process of change, will affect both yourself and the team as you implement the changes and navigate the transformation together.

The uncertainty and ambiguity that often accompanies transformation creates a tension that heightens our sensitivity to trust. As humans, we sometimes try to minimize the tension and look for harmony instead. But tension is necessary and harmony - when it is artificial - can be more damaging over time.

Artificial harmony is present when people profess to agree decisions which they later resist behind closed doors, or through inaction or sabotage. Or where people say all is on track and they're working together well, while in reality, they're not collaborating or progressing towards their commitments. In those situations, trust begins to break down. It can feel safer for teams to tell managers what they believe they want to hear, rather than convey the uncertainty or vulnerability they are really feeling.

Tension, when understood and harnessed well, catalyzes transformation and brings difficult conversations to the surface so the team can share the vulnerability change often creates. That shared experience 'level sets' the emotional tone of a team, by reminding people that part of growing as a human is learning how to navigate change. Acknowledging the tension - and determining whether it is emotional or creative - is a powerful first step that determines the next steps to take as you work together on building resilience and resourcefulness.

Emotional tension feels personal, heavy, unproductive. It comes from personal discomfort and can define the space where a person, or people, need to develop their own self-belief, competence, emotional maturity, or interpersonal skills.

Creative tension is the tension which propels you forward, triggering the curiosity and motivation to explore and solve challenges. It's ideological rather than personal, it feels as though it sits outside of you. It can help you move beyond ego to the greater good for the team or organisation.

Most important, is for the manager or leader to understand the nature, and source of their own tension first. In doing so, you convert your tension from a gnawing distraction into an identified gap you can begin to address practically. You'll also feel the difference between leaning into the tension and becoming stronger through it, rather than letting it take over and derail you. When you manage your own tension, or distress first, it creates the space, understanding and credibility to ask the team to face theirs.

When it comes to role clarity and perceived control, working with team members as they find ways to engage with the change from a place of opportunity rather than danger helps them to embrace the journey by feeling involved in what may have previously felt imposed upon them.

In times of change, confidence, productivity and results go through an inverted bell curve over time as people traverse the three stages of 'letting go', 'uncertainty' and 'new beginnings'. To let go, we need to release the things we've relied on to be successful and the ways of doing things that we've become used to. In uncertainty, we need to trust our leaders have the best interests of the organisation, and its people, at heart. We need to manage our tension so it works for, rather than against us, and we must learn how to be flexible and open to begin practicing that adaptability. In finding new beginnings, we need to be open to learning new ways in which we can add value to the organisation. We need to celebrate what was good before, while being optimistic about the future vision for the organisation.

Each place can feel bewildering, frustrating and uncomfortable. When people resist, often they aren't resisting the change itself, but rather reacting to the fear of letting go of what they know, or the risk of having to reinvent themselves to remain relevant. Change is often more personal than you realize. But, helping people to find their feet by leaning in, rather than backing away, builds strength, confidence and leads to great conversations that can move the entire team forward. Heightened reactions are a sign of vulnerability. How you respond to them will unlock or block trustworthiness in your ability to lead through change.

Treating change with the same compassion and partnership as grief, odd though is sounds, helps you view it through a new lens. That new lens is necessary to appreciate the fact that people will need to find their way with it, and that everyone will embrace it at a slightly different speed. As a manager, meet them where you can, whenever you can. Creating space for staff to digest and reflect, while also discovering and acclimating to their role in the transition is a fundamental step in engaging people in change.

To enable people to embrace change fully (or at least as fully as they're able to) you have to get them to a place where they can balance the risk of making themselves vulnerable, with the faith that their vulnerability won't be taken advantage of.

## Sustaining Trust While Leading a Team Through Change

- Realize others may not be as immersed in the change as you are, so will be seeing and hearing less than you think they are. Communicate until it feels like you're over-communicating. At least 10x more than you think is necessary. Even when there are no updates. Even when there are some things you can share and some you can't - be explicit about what that is. Honesty supports connection and credibility.
- Listen. To what you hear *and* what you don't.
- Encourage questions, ask for feedback and check, never assume, whether messages are understood and whether anything else is sitting unresolved.
- Allow time for people to process the changes and what it means for them.
- Be alert to changes in behaviour and performance that may signal someone is feeling unsafe.
- Don't judge someone for needing a different kind - or level - of information than you do; remember, they are seeking safety. Help them find it so they don't arrive at their own (often incorrect) assumptions.
- Be transparent - open about what you can share, what you can't, and when that might change. Admit mistakes when you make them, with plans for rectifying; humanize yourself without lowering your status or credibility.
- Help people to understand the stages of change, what to

expect, what it means for them, and how they can engage with it at each stage. Frame it as an opportunity to learn and grow. No matter what the outcome, change gives us all the opportunity to build strength and resilience that can we can draw on no matter where we eventually land.

# Constant Change vs. VUCA Environments

We know that change is a constant, but rather than acclimating to the shift in the frequency of change, a recent study shows that globally, 51% of employees feel change is happening too fast. Worse, the general rule of thumb for the last couple of decades has been that we can expect almost 70% of all change initiatives to fail. The largest single factor influencing that is poor training for managers around how to effectively lead their teams through change. A skills gap which leads to ineffective communication from managers which then creates greater uncertainty, insecurity and resistance from staff.

Yet the pressure to navigate change well, and to create resilience and agility around the process of transformation, is also gaining speed and becoming business critical. Internationally, 94% of companies now say 'agility and collaboration' are key to their organisations success, yet only 6% say they are highly agile (Deloitte Global HC Trends Report 2017).

The stakes get higher when that change is not only constant, but also volatile, uncertain, complex and ambiguous, creating an environmental dynamic known as VUCA. And it's that changing context of work, which is putting unprecedented pressure on teams, while at the same time creating an urgency for those teams to work more effectively together.

# What is VUCA?

The term VUCA migrated from the military to the business world in the 1990's and refers to landscapes which can be defined as volatile, uncertain, complex and ambiguous. Collectively, it's a set of circumstances that challenges the agility, adaptiveness, resilience and competence of both leaders and teams as they navigate new ways of operating successfully in uncharted waters. The ability to anticipate change, and to prepare by realigning thinking and resources to embrace and positively adapt to change at pace, is a skill that is already a prerequisite for leadership and management in many digital, media, entertainment and political organisations.

Each of the factors which define VUCA is enough individually to throw enterprises into a tailspin of fear, rumour and self-protectionism. For organisations to thrive in the face of a VUCA environment requires a culture of trust and emergence which is actively cultivated and reinforced through both behaviours and systems. It requires leaders to redefine how they view leadership, risk and delivery, and challenges them to open up communication, ownership and contribution to everyone in the organisation.

The shift begins at the leadership level and often requires setting aside many of the management and leadership strategies which may have led to success in the past.

VUCA environments test senior leadership to trust each other enough to have the types of robust debate about the potential opportunities and threats which ensures solutions are well considered and carefully crafted. There are several shifts leaders and leaders can make to actively embrace, manage and lead their teams and organisation through VUCA environments. Each are outlined below.

But the key change leaders need to make is around their mindset. They need to be open to emergent strategy, rather than having the answers and being certain. They need to engage differently with their leadership peer team members, and the teams they lead. They need to trust themselves and their peers enough to be open, to navigate tension constructively, to remain observant enough to intuit shifts. They need to develop the confidence, and collaboration, to pivot with grace and agility. And they need to be sufficiently mature and nuanced in their leadership and communication style to maintain just enough pressure to sustain the desire for, and support of, change by the organisation.

Ultimately, two of the biggest challenges for leaders in a VUCA environment sit with the leader.

How can you navigate the delicate balance of maintaining tension *and* engagement?

How can you create sufficient transparency to foster credibility throughout the organisation *without* triggering fear?

While staff want to know the truth (in the hope that it's not as bad as they might imagine), building trust in times of rapid change means sharing often, and with candour, while reconfirming confidence that the organisation, the team that lead it, and the body of staff are equal to the challenge of navigating the change.

# Ideas to Begin With

## On-boarding: Building Credibility, Connection and Consistency with Future Staff

- Check that the hiring processes and behaviour throughout the recruitment phase mirrors your employment brand in language, tone and behaviour. Give new, or future, staff members a consistent experience of what they can expect when they join you.
- Refine induction processes to create a complete on-boarding experience that combines induction on systems and processes, with cultural and human connection to enable new staff to acclimate quickly during their crucial first 90 days. Give new hires an opportunity to build connections – and their understanding - across the business.
- Work with hiring managers to enable them to actively partner in the performance of new team members by:
    - Creating a plan that includes time with peers and other key stakeholders in their first four weeks;
    - Clarifying key focuses and outcomes for their first 90 days, with regular contact points for review, guidance and support;
    - Being explicit about how you'll communicate with each other, especially when it comes to raising questions and concerns;
    - Pointing them toward trusted resources for company and industry insights.

## Systems: Creating Ease of Connection Throughout the Organisation

Review the systems at work in your business. Begin by looking for the bottlenecks in the organisation where progress slows, or tension builds. Consider how you could alter the design of the systems in play to create feedback loops that are generative and constructive.

When you find yourself fighting a problem multiple different ways, or too frequently, you know you're attempting to fix the end result, not the cause. When you find persistent problems, look beneath them to find their source. You'll know you've identified the source when resolving it closes off numerous problems.

Before acting, play out possible impact scenarios for each potential solution. So you know what challenges you may face, who will be impacted (directly and indirectly) and how, as well as how best to communicate changes.

### Leading: Building Trust as a Leadership Advantage

Clarify how your membership in the team you lead, and the team you're a part of, differs. Consider what that means for how best to build trust and trustworthiness with both your peer group and your direct reports.

Build an awareness of the trust touch points that exist within your organisation day to day. The moments that allow trust to reinforced, extended, withheld or broken; and actively work to trigger attachment - not avoidance - emotions to foster trust.

Champion trust through leading by example with emotional maturity, behaviour regulation and admitting when things go wrong. Share your values, experiences, aspirations and learnings.

Become familiar with group dynamics (covered in 'Teams'), to fine tune your awareness of the conditions which build and break a team. Normalize healthy competition, conflict and accountability; appreciate how times of high pressure, or high stakes, changes people's behaviour, and acknowledge slips as a natural part of being human, and learning.

Avoid the temptation of taking decisions - or creating systems - that prioritise short term gains over longer term sustainability and impact.

## Managing for Trust: Championing Trust as a Manager

Make expectations explicit - encourage candid conversations where every question is worth asking.

Meet each team member where they are in terms of competence and development. Scope their levels of comfort, stretch and panic on each new significant piece of work. Use stretch experiences to help them develop by providing increased touchpoints or support.

Be prepared to tackle hard conversations early when things go wrong. Conflict and accountability are ok - dysfunction is not. Surface the patterns you're observing with team members. Explore what's happening for them and what they'd like to do about it. Help them solve the problem - solving it for them will erode their agency and personal commitment.

Consider how to help your team differentiate between the two types of fear which can stifle progress. Old Jewish texts refer to them as pachad (the sense of dread about imagined or projected things) and yirah (the sense of finding ourselves in a space larger than we are used to living in). One fear isn't real, and the other is – at its core – a reverence and awe in the face of great stretch, which can literally be breathtaking. When do they show up at work? How can they use these moments to foster and strengthen trust rather than weaken it?

Nurture greatness - be as specific with positive feedback as you are with constructive feedback. Help people to identify and develop their strengths, then give them opportunities to keep learning and developing.

## Tight Teams: Developing Trust Within a Team

Create opportunities for the team to meet, and to understand their own - and each other's - personalities and working styles.

Lay the foundations for everyone to contribute to shaping the culture of the team. Discuss how diverse and remote teams require clarity and understanding about how to work well together. Teams need to balance flexibility in meeting individual needs, while working effectively together as a team. Explain that in order to understand and adapt to each other, those differences need to be expressed, perspectives need to be heard and expectations collectively agreed.

Create a team playbook that captures team generated agreements on communicating with each other effectively, making decisions, managing time and deadlines, resolving conflict, and holding each other accountable. Co-creating is central to supporting agency and building trust within a team.

## International Trust: Being Attuned to Cultural Difference

Allow time to both do business *and* to get to know each other. If your counterparts are from relationship-based cultures, allow more time for socializing and don't rush it.

If your counterparts are task oriented, don't forgo the socializing, but make sure there are clear boundaries around it. Appreciate that the degree to which we socialize is a cultural artefact, not necessarily a personal one.

Tune into the communication styles of the people you're working with so you can adapt to - or match - their approach to show respect and build rapport.

Be prepared to spend time over several calls or emails getting to know someone before getting down to business.

# Leadership Pivots for VUCA Environments

| STATE | EXPERIENCED AS: | PIVOT | STRATEGIES: |
|---|---|---|---|
| VOLATILITY | Change which occurs at speed, at scale and with unpredictable dynamics | VISION | • Communicate the purpose or vision often to focus energy on the bigger picture, and to provide overarching direction to guide decision making and action day to day.<br>• Communicate often, with clarity and openness to foster trust and transparency.<br>• Continue to work towards the vision and to be committed to a positive future outcomes |
| UNCERTAINTY | Unfamiliar territory and outcomes that are unpredictable or unknown. | UNDERSTANDING | • Construct possible scenarios and map out potential strategies for the next six months for each of them to develop awareness, thinking and agility.<br>• Prioritise trust, respect and psychological safety to encourage people to continue communicating and collaborating.<br>• Use the context as a challenge to rethink new ways of doing old things. |
| COMPLEXITY | Multiple issues and factors, which are sometimes intricately interrelated. | CLARITY | • Be prepared to keep navigating through the chaos and confusion – focus on the information you have and on solving problems and testing solutions.<br>• Identify the nested systems at play and look for the levers which will enable the most effective change with the most palatable trade-offs.<br>• Continue to enable trust and collaboration by communicating frequently, clearly and with transparency. |
| AMBIGUITY | Unknown causes or effects, lack of clarity about the status quo and multiple interpretations of possible outcomes. | AGILITY | • Engage as many diverse insights, opinions and feedback as possible in problem solving, decision making and innovation.<br>• Encourage experimentation to keep teams executing – failing and learning fast to build resilience and capability.<br>• Foster change-ability by creating working environments that support innovation, contribution and ownership. |

# What to Look Out For

### Using overly 'directive' leadership styles:

Leaders are, by definition, people who stand up, verbally or physically, and initiate, then facilitate change. They're people who influence and inspire groups to get things done. It's those behaviours which we rely on for momentum and delivery, but which, on overdrive, can mean we test the engagement, commitment and trust of our team members. Excessive speed or unfettered 'overreaching' can see us talking more than listening, selling our ideas vs. canvassing input, and assuming understanding and support, rather than inviting and assessing it.

The days of leaders being experts, the source of creativity, initiators of change, and the final point of authority, are numbered. The pace of change, and scope of specialisms, has escalated to such a degree that knowing how to access and leverage collective wisdom has taken over as the fastest way to access relevant, timely expertise.

Organisations who open themselves up to collective wisdom will find the journey of remaining relevant and viable (socially and commercially) more fluid, energizing and engaging for their workforce.

### Change Mismanagement

Encourage people to have input; *but* only in areas where there is a possibility of responding to and integrating contributions. Otherwise it will exacerbate a sense of disconnection and powerlessness. Encourage people to find ways to contribute and bring their skills into the transition; encourage teams to find ways of adapting to the new order.

Seek to regulate the distress, rather than remove it. You can't remove all of the uncertainty, but you can ease it to a degree by giving clarity about what is and isn't known, (timelines, expected decision points etc.).

Never assume people know about – or are up to date with the latest information. You will likely be closer to the source of information than they are. So communicate significantly more than you would usually; approximately 10x more. Remember Barbara Fredrickson's ratio of positive to negative statements 5:1 as one way of sustaining morale and psychological safety. Acknowledge the pressure and discomfort people are facing and use the experience as a learning curve that provides an opportunity for everyone to build change-ability.

## Not Allowing Time for Teams to Become Teams

It's rare to hear a team or group say they have ample time for getting together; for thinking and planning, for exploration and discovery. Yet it's that time and space – whether micro or macro in nature – that provides an opportunity for open conversation. For surfacing viewpoints, testing thinking, exploring imaginations, sharing mental models. For hearing each other, understanding perspectives, and yes, building trust. Allow time to meet as a team and have the conversations that make attending those meetings a no-brainer.

## Micromanagement

It's easy to confuse management with control, and to get more involved than we need to, stealing autonomy from the people we want most to step up, engage and deliver.

Micromanagement has the often-unintended consequence of signaling distrust. If you can't trust someone with the appropriate level of autonomy to execute their role, amend your management style and follow up process with them until their competence and consistency is where it needs to be for them to run at full speed.

## Focusing on Expertise Rather Than Growth Mindsets

Rather than allowing expertise to be harboured in silos, encourage staff to have conversations where they can share their knowledge, discuss projects and cross pollinate ideas. Though there may be resistance at first (and some people take longer than others to join in), over time natural curiosity will take over and, as ideas are shared and spread, the value and joy of collaboration, and of being valued, will slowly bring people together.

## Creating (or Inherited) Reward Structures That Discourage Collaboration

One of the biggest structural challenges to creating a foundation of trust in an organisation is personal performance objectives. Often the key performance indicators designed to incentivize individuals and teams, work against collaboration by effectively pitting people and teams against each other.

To weed out offending performance indicators, review how success is measured in each area of the organisation. Where does one party's success impede or impact on another's? How can those objectives be redefined to achieve success and collaboration?

If it seems there is no obvious way around having competing objectives, ask: What do we risk losing by having teams, or individuals, incentivized in ways which are directly competitive with each other? There are alternative ways to focus someone's efforts and energy. And sometimes, what you're incentivizing isn't what you really want people focusing on at all.

# SECTION SIX:

CONVERSATIONS
ABOUT TRUST -
THROUGH A LEADERS LENS

*"Trust is the energy of the connection between each of us. Whether that's one to one, or across 1,000 people in a company. Because as soon as distrust becomes a thing, it's the switching off of the lights."*
**Dominic - CEO SaaS Start Up**

## Caroline - Head of People & Talent, Tourism

### On building - or rebuilding - trust...

I entered one role with a very entrepreneurial company; I was the first HR Director and I was seen as an overhead. Three weeks in, the President essentially said to me "you're a waste of space, you haven't done anything" and I said the usual HR thing - I'd been listening to people and working out where the pressure points are. That was a pivotal moment because I said, "you can either work with me or not, and if that's really the way you feel and you don't feel any trust towards me, we could just leave it here and that's fine".

Then I worked with him little by little. It took about a month, but I didn't push it. If you're gaining people's trust, you don't force them into a corner with things and you don't force decisions. You give them support from the start. I ended up having a really close relationship with this President and we're still in touch. But for him, trusting people was really important. To do great things you've got to be able to trust people. And no matter how many management workshops you go to where they say, 'fall back into my arms', you can learn it. Trust is sometimes very subtle and it's not something that's just taught like that.

### The point you realized you'd gained his trust...

He started to seek me out and then he would talk about things that made him vulnerable. He would trust me to have a go and do something rather than just immediately saying no. Clearly, trust was so important for him, and working with a CEO later on who didn't trust any of his staff at all - the polar opposite - that was something that ultimately, I found impossible to work with. It's not just misanthropic, he didn't even trust people he could see working in front of him.

## On what leaders will look back on in five years and realize was unintentionally limiting trust...

The quick buck. I've seen it in different industries, be it in private equity or privately held companies, where they care so little for the company that they would do anything. That can lead to some really short-term decision making.

## On the conversation's leaders need to start having now to cultures of trust...

There is a thing about showing vulnerability through conversations. And not treating staff like they're stupid - e.g. with pay; people understand if there's not much in the budget. As soon as leaders say we haven't got any money at all and yet they're taking full bonuses when they're not giving anybody else a bonus, it's an issue of fairness. So, it's not so much what they're saying as what they're doing. People notice if you're honourable.

## On how trust - or its absence - influences an organisation...

I think the impossible becomes possible with trust. For me personally, because it's such a deeply held value, I could never be satisfied in a role where I'm not trusted and where there isn't trust in the whole organisation.

#

## Chris - Managing Director, Consumer Goods

### On trust and being trusted...

I think through a career, trust probably comes out in two core ways. One is through progression, so through promotion and recognition, where I think you get feedback around how you've been performing, whether it's on track, off track, again allows a conversation of trust to develop.

Something someone said to me a little while ago, was, in a corporate environment, dress and act two levels up. That's again putting into someone's mind that you're considering your working environment. I look around the environment we work in at the moment, young vibrant team, sometimes they'll be dressed like they are going to a concert, for a workday. That's ok, I get that. If I'm looking for someone that's going to do an executive job of leading the team and building a strategy, part of the persona, part of that trust that I'm trying to see in them is that they understand the game that they have to play.

### On building trust in a new role...

The role I'm in now, there was no strategy, no direction, so the first thing was to understand the business, understand the key points, build a direction. Not just build a direction, but build the story behind why we need to do something, so that everyone in the organisation knows their part. We have one specific key action right now, and I'm just watching it unfold because everyone gets it. When you've got everyone in the organisation that gets what that key one thing is, it's really golden to stand back and just watch. My analogy is the rowing eight. When you get eight people on a boat and you get one person microscopically out of sync, the boat does get maximum speed. When everyone is totally in sync, doing their job - and that includes rhythm and pace - that's where the optimal power going forward occurs. Anything out of sync it doesn't go optimally.

## On being trusted to take a leap of faith...

I've come into this role relativity new, and I think I've built trust just by being authentic, by being open and respectful and by trying to anticipate what my manager needs from me and playing that back to him without him having to ask. I stood in front of our group the first day I started here and I just try and build a story around most things and I was saying to them, "I've walked into the place and I'm like a jar of marbles that is half full. The marbles in the jar that's half full represent the trust that you put in me just because I've been appointed into a position of authority. Every day I'll work with you so that you can put more trust marbles into that jar. Also realize that at some point in the future, that jar may fully tip out and empty, or some of it may leak, and we'll have to rebuild."

## On the conversation's leaders need to be having now to build cultures of trust...

Be real. So, if something deep and meaningful is happening in your life - as it is with me as you know right now - I told my team. I hadn't told them every detail, but I've told them that I may arrive at work in a different state than what you normally expect me. When I do that, either give me some space or give me some support. Every person arrives at this place with something in their background that either promotes or erodes their ability to be productive.

I think as a business if you can understand what makes people tick, you can get a lot of support and productivity out. I'm really interested in mental health in the workplace because it's a topic that I think is real, but largely unspoken about.

I think authenticity and openness - those are bullshit words if you can't follow them up. So, I know the power of the rowing skiff, if everyone is doing their job. If I tell everyone what's going on, maybe it helps them do their job. If I get people to believe in the way we are going, maybe it helps them do their job. If I try and fill the marble jar with trust, maybe it helps them do their job. It helps the business move in the right direction, a faster pace, a better pace than it would have otherwise. An organisation is an entity that people move. Businesses don't achieve things, people do.

What I see is that there are a whole bunch of businesses that have a great vision. I think it's marrying - in a business context - your vision and your purpose to the actions that get you there, and providing a story around the why. Many businesses are good at seeing where they want to go, getting action plans in place, but real lousy at saying 'here's why'. People invest emotionally in the why. Storytelling, bringing emotional connectivity, everyone knowing their part to play. You employ someone at some point in time to do something and over time that changes. Like the waves coming into the shore change dependent on the weather. I don't think we tend as businesses as leaders to react to the weather change sometimes overly well. Some obviously do, some don't.

There is only a handful that are able to effectively communicate the vision and purpose of the way forward and match it to the lowest common denominator in the business so that they come to work rewarded. So, people come to work, knowing exactly how they contribute.

Where a business can achieve a zen of flow, of business purpose, not just throughout its business but also with its consumers, stakeholders, shareholders and the greater public, then I think you almost reach this state of perfection. Or this state of beautiful rhythm. And that rhythm may only be moments - it may be long moments or short moments. But if you can find that, then where you align individuals knowing - how they contribute - they do contribute. They build a story, or a platform, consumers trust and buy into.

In the big bad world, I think one of the most remarkable things that happens in the corporate world, is that Apple can keep a secret until the day they decide to say something with so many people that must touch that. In this world of connectivity, that is remarkable. And that's because they must have some kind of business rhythm that synchronizes people's activities, the information they share, the product development process, the manufacturing. All parts of that business must be incredibly aligned around that one key thing which is no one knows until we decide to tell them. Incredible.

#

## Chris - CEO Consumer Goods Retail

### On the first time he remembers being trusted…

When you're given a leadership role. All your personal interactions have such an impact on outcome. Before that it's very logical or work based, but then, you start to be trusted to hire people to manage their performance, to grow them, to coach them. Because its more variable engagement, it has all those human factors in it, the trust is quite different.

One of the first early realizations that you have is – why aren't all these people thinking the same way I think? You go, "of course I want to get that done to a high standard, of course I want to work hard", and not everyone was the same. And it's not saying that they weren't good people, it's just saying that they weren't the same. You hit that moment where you go – "right, I'm going to have to think about this". About how to engage and how to manage.

In those first six to 12 months you get your first poor performer issue. This first team was six to eight people from memory and you must have a range of performance within that and you start to get that awareness of that range and how you work with that. And also, that awareness that there's a ratio that's against you. It's eight to one or six to one. Everything you do is amplified by that, so it makes you think much more about your own behaviours and your own reactions to everything and your own example setting. It's much more exposed I think.

I think you become aware of the leadership halo – that you have a shadow, good or bad.

## On how that first leadership role influenced his leadership style…

If you're ambitious and determined and want to do good, you can work very hard and achieve a lot that way - but as soon as you hit more than three, four or five people in your responsibility, the only way you can deliver is through a team.

You hit that moment where you realize actually it's all about that now and you move from "if I just do a lot of work", to "what I've got to do, is do a lot of good" in terms of leadership. That these people are trusting me - or not trusting me, in some cases – but they're looking to you for support, for clear definition of what good looks like, how they're going, and what's next for them. And so, you start to get those feelings of responsibility build in you. And your choices about what style of leader you want to be, start from there.

It evolves a lot over time, it doesn't stay static, you learn a lot over time but I think in those early days you're learning. You also learn the power of recognition, so actually stopping and genuinely telling someone you thought what they're doing is great and how powerful that is so all of that is part of those early messy days of leadership.

Most leadership mistakes are sins of omission. Very few leaders do brutally the wrong thing, I think most of us just don't do the right things often enough.

## On what the 'right' things are…

It's people skills, ability to lead change, a focus on results. The focus on the basics, does everyone know what good looks like, how they're going and what's next for them? That structure. Setting direction, being connected, being clear and being able to generate action and have things occur.

The fatal flaws are – not being accountable; zero people skills. Today, you have to have people skills of some description. It doesn't mean everyone needs to be gregarious or massively extrovert. And then any dishonesty or lack of trustworthiness doesn't work as a leader, because in the end that 'ratio against you thing' finds you out.

### On building, or rebuilding trust...

One of the things you learn early as a leader, that balance of seeking to please, by making an optimistic commitment vs. I deliver what I said I would.

You start with optimism because you'd like to be liked and then you work out later that actually being respected is more important than being liked. So that power of saying "sorry, that's not going to happen in the timeframe, or in the way you would like it to, but this is what will happen". And then doing it; that's in the end, much more powerful over time for trust. But I think, in the early days of leadership you often want to be liked. You've got to resist that and live with the heat that comes with not giving people exactly what they wanted.

### On the insights gained from building trust across different levels...

My observation I that it goes a lot to people's own sense of confidence and power as a person. So, people who had a good sense of confidence in themselves and a good feeling of "I have some power as a person" gave trust quite easily because they weren't living in a constant  everybody's against me' mind state.

I find people who've got their own self-confidence right, very easily trust. People who have not, kind of assume that someone is doing something to them and then don't trust as a result.

What's getting some conversation and some engagement is "can we move from allegations to questions?" So, whenever you see something that you don't like the look of, or that you don't think is right, don't make an allegation, start with a question.

And I think it comes back to the ones who are more self-empowered and more above the line in general, start with questions. The others are generally lower performing, more 'victim like' in all conversations, and generally not at ease in their organisations. And you see the differences.

## On the moment you know people have crossed from mistrust to trust…

The questions they ask change because they tend to be questions that are 'above the line'. They're questions for outcomes and solutions rather than "how could you do this to me?". Their question style shifts.

They go to questions, not statements. They don't assume badness; they assume misunderstanding and try to qualify and then make a call.

## On the degree to which people skills, an understanding of relationships and trust is factored into the business…

Quite high. It's probably not called trust as bluntly as that, but we talk about the culture, our values and our style. Trust is really strong throughout

With co-ops you don't influence through power, you influence through excellence. The key here is agility of decision-making; "where should I just be making decisions and leading us forward?" vs. deep consultation; "where should I probably go and listen and get opinion?". Just putting the initiatives in the right camp is critical. You have to have a good sense of judgement yourself you need to check with your board if you've got your board in the right place. Using words like; is this consult, inform, or decision? What am I talking to you about? And having no one offended by the fact they're not getting to make the decision. Sometimes the committees get a bit 'we should approve that'. But we're clear – that's a management decision.

## On managing big personalities while maintaining respect...

The really professional use of 'consult'. It's a subtle and tricky thing. Saying "I'm not asking you to say yes or no, I'm asking you to understand it, ask me questions, give me views on how to make it work. Give me warnings about the pitfalls but I'm not asking you to say yes or no". It's a fascinating thing to watch unfold.

We work on "what do we mean by 'consult?'". Because when you sit down and talk about it and say, 'hey guys, you know we can't vote on every issue', they say 'of course not – but this one'. So, you just have to keep coming back to principles; that's how we run an organisation with good trust and setting out parameters and saying we'll always behave like this, and consistently doing that.

My issue to managers, is making sure that every part of the business is doing it the way we said we would, because then you keep trust, and people get used to consistency. That really matters. We forget because we come from a faster moving corporate world, that for these guys, whatever we do has to work half a million times a day. We say you're slow – they say they're being appropriately guarded. So, it's the right balance.

## On what leaders will look back on in five years and realize was unintentionally limiting trust...

I think if there's anywhere that leaders aren't sharing the commercial reality of the business. There's a great line about "culture without strategy is aimless, strategy without culture is powerless". The way strategy is meant is as commercial reality. If teams aren't aware of where profitability or cost, or the pressures are.

I think leaders have to be connecting people to initiatives. We have 22 initiatives over five years. I want to be in a position where every team member knows whether they fit, and in which initiatives, and how their work delivers to that initiative. If they don't know that, they can't make the right decisions.

Thinking about diversity, and true diversity. There are three levels; there are the people who are ignoring it as a business performance driver; there are people who are paying lip service to the popular thing - gender is probably the one that fits in that list – and then there are people who genuinely go, "in principle my business needs to look like our customers to understand them". Leaders who are only doing the first two will look back and say that's a mistake. You cannot ignore diversity and I think its diversity of style and thought and skills and experience and happens to be driven by gender and culture, but isn't necessarily about gender and culture.

If people are ignoring the value of high performing teams, and facing up to people who are not team people, and saying "it's just not going to work". Because in the world we're in – and going to be in – the pace of change is enormous. We're not in jobs, we're in current assignments. And our current assignment will shift and our ability to de-form and re-form around what the priorities are will be critical. So, I think if leaders are not doing that, you're going to regret that. Rigid power structures that are about control won't work.

Communication – open, straight communication, that's regular, that's engaged, and that's two way. We say we need to be innovative and so we go outside. And you think "why aren't I assuming that if I want to know something about shopping, we should ask here first?". Everybody in this building shops and the difference is they care about shopping more because we're a business that does it. Our natural bias is to go to a global expert, an advisor. And sometimes you think "no, I just need to listen".

## On getting communication, and high performing teams, right…

Any feedback you ask for, you have to show that you heard. You need to go back and say, "thanks for the feedback, this is what we've taken from it, this is what we might do immediately, and we're going to keep thinking about these things", because that's just true.

(In a previous role), we launched a new network – got 100,000 customers on it and it stopped working. For days. Not minutes, days. It was TV cameras in the building, it was all on. I ran the corporate business at the time and the PR people were advising not to set expectations. I said "I'm going to ignore all of you, because if I put myself in the shoes of the tech leader in each of these businesses, what they need to know from us is 'do I need to make other arrangements now to keep my business going?'".

So I ended up doing two or three emails a day to a set of

4,000-5,000 contacts saying, "this is where we are, this is where we're going next, this is what we know right now and here are alternatives to keep your business running and what you can do, and I'll update you". And saying, "right now, I can commit this, or I cannot commit this, and if not being able to commit this means you need to make another move, then this is what we'll do to help".

We did that for weeks, daily at least. What happened as a result of that is that during that time is that we grew our connection base – which was weird on a network that didn't work. It was a really good lesson in trust for a lot of communicators. A lot of the PR people were horrified because normally PR is about hiding the bad stuff and this was just going 'no, that is broken and no, we don't know right now what's broken, and how long it's going to take to fix but I'll tell you when we do'. It was quite 'relationshippy' for a few days and then it switched to technical because there were technical people in the customers who understood. And what we were trying to do was earn their confidence by explaining the process we were going through, and they looked at it and went "that's probably what I'd do".

You got credibility for moving from sales and business, to technical, at the right time. But also, what I used to think about at the time was "what would I need to know as a CEO? What would I need to know as a CIO?" And, it was bad that it happened, but we learned a lot around open honest communication, and the trust it builds, and the business that comes off the back of it.

So, if you come back to that and change…. People probably aren't asking enough questions. So, what's the message for people? Be ready to change.

## On the conversation's leaders need to be having today to create cultures of trust…

I think first it's about being clear about the drivers or the strategies. Being clear that these are the things that make me decide what we're going to do, so if you understand those things, then when we make decisions, they line up.

Two things are really important to communicate; the <u>why</u> we're doing what we're doing, because if you just say "we're doing this" then people have to make up their own mind about where it came from. And then secondly, communicating the <u>impact</u> of the initiative, or the change. Because if you show you know the impact, then I think you get trust because people can see you understand what happens when you do something.

Something I've been drilling in here is that any communication we send out to our members or the business, has to have <u>why</u> and <u>impact</u>. I think if we get that over time, we'll build a more trusted environment. Then there needs to be a "this is what we think is important, you need to trust us to make decisions in that frame of reference with those drivers".

'Say/do' is really important.

The other thing I think is really important is that your internal story and your external story have to be the same.

Communication is a massive part of building trust followed by doing what you said. I think trust also comes from taking a genuine interest in people. But it has to be genuine.

I think if you get those basics right – and not being guarded - we live in such an open world you've just got to be good every day. Don't spend any time trying to work out how to hide a bad thing, just don't do a bad thing

#

## Dee - Senior Director HR, Not for Profit

### On what you remember most about your first experience of being rested at work...

The fact I was given real responsibility rather quickly and it was almost based on my potential, rather than my performance.

It made me feel "wow, you value me and you clearly think that I'm good enough" because at that age, I was definitely new to the world of work, so my confidence was building but it was "you think I'm good at what I do, you think I can do this". It's an investment of trust to not screw it up. I'm not going to screw this up, I'm going to show you why it was absolutely the right decision to give me that trust and to give me this work. I want to do it to the best of my ability.

It was interesting the motivation it inspired, but also a new level of work ethic that I'd never come across before. That was when I learned I'm willing to work hard. It fires something up in me when I'm trusted to do something that's bigger and boy, will I want to succeed at it. It helped me tap into ambition.

### On how that has influenced your leadership style...

Now, at my most recent roles, I'm leading teams and I'm having to lead through teams so I've had to make that switch, and boy is it a lifelong learning experience. But I would say that the one thing that I've taken is that I think about "how do I make sure that my team know that I have their back, that

I support them and most importantly that I trust them?". I've hired them, they're in those seats because I believe in their ability and I trust in their ability to do great work. How can I then be an enabler of that great work rather than trying to do the great work myself?

I'm explicit about these things, I will say "I've got your back on this, I trust you, I trust your judgement. Help me understand. I will always be curious, so my questions will always come from a place of curiosity. This is your work, this is your patch, you've got this".

I don't think those things were explicitly said to me at the time and I think with the young team I'm working with; they need to hear feedback much more explicitly.

### On building - or rebuilding - trust...

I remember a situation where I'd been told I was a high performer. They'd done the nine-box grid, apparently, I was top right, and I was told I was on a path to progression, and the next level up would have been a Head of HR. I was given all the right signals so I was excited by the trust they'd placed in me and while it was never explicitly said, I had understood that when the next opportunity came up, that would be the one I would be moved into.

The next opportunity came up, and someone else was placed in the role. I remember thinking at the time that it was a serious breach of the psychological contract we had. I'd been working hard over the previous year to do all of the things they had asked me to do. I'd jumped higher than they'd asked me to jump, so how had we got to a place where, now their side of the bargain was on the table, it had been taken away? What it came down to was that it was the right decision, but the biggest thing that broke the trust was the lack of communication or explanation as to why.

The decision would have been painful, but in that moment, and for the six-month period that followed until everything came good, the breach of trust for me was in the lack of explanation. Because there was a lack of explanation, there was a void. I filled it with a story that was self-critical, based on hearsay, became based on quite toxic behaviour. I saw that if I was looking at myself as a third person, I'd been this model person and then I'd turned into this person on the bottom left of the grid.

There was barely an explanation, despite me asking - so I realized that I had an active role to play to seek the truth. But it was also important that the truth came back to me in order to continue a trusting relationship. It happened, but it happened really late, and I was soured. I felt I lost trust in the organisation. In particular, my manager at the time.

What rebuilt trust was one of managers' peers who took me out for a coffee, gave me a bit of tough - honest - love and gave me a level of transparency into the decision that my manager probably felt unable to give me which gave me a little bit of hope. And when that hope converted to my own movement and my progression there, while the trust wasn't completely re-established, I was back to being valued again and the 'deal' had been fulfilled.

It changed the loyalty I had to the organisation. After the experience, I thought, they're going to get something out of me, how will I use this to take me further? Maybe it's a healthy thing to do, but I wasn't thinking that way before that experience.

**On the key insights from that experience...**

Communication. There's something about congruence in the way that we perceive other people. So, when someone is saying and doing something that feels out of whack based on your experience of them, immediately trust is shaken, or you question that trust. There's a suspicion that brings into the system.

How I felt after that experience is that it's my accountability as a leader to be crystal clear on the decisions I take, why I'm taking them, and to explain them. Such is the trust economy in my mind; my units of trust will keep building with the team if I remain open and transparent. For me, a key part of that is being held to scrutiny, explaining my decisions, being open to the challenge of those decisions and ultimately that centres around having communication and feedback.

I say, "you might not like the clarity that I give you, I hope you respect it as much as I'll respect the clarity you give me, even if I don't like it".

What I really enjoy about the team is there's this real hunger and energy to do more, and that has to come from a place of feeling "I have got the space in which to do this. I feel trusted to do this. This is my hope". And I think also being really clear on what we don't do vs. what we <u>will</u> do in order to help our organisation succeed. That comes from tough conversations, tough decisions on "that project is not going to happen and these are the reasons why; or I really support this, and I'm finding it hard to support this". Those types of conversations I'm trying to make normal.

In order to have these types of conversations, I have to spend time with my team. They can't be deprioritized on our to-do list. And that's everything from the 'all team' meetings through to the meetings I have with my direct reports, which are franker and more direct.

I make sure that we don't shy away from the uncomfortable stuff. If I feel something doesn't feel right in the room, I'll raise it. I have two reflectors on my team, so I try to create space to say 'look, I know that right now may not be the time to have the conversation, but clearly something is happening here, I want us to get to a place where we can deal with these things more in the moment, but I also want to give you a bit of space as we learn to use this new muscle in a different way'. I try to be the champion of it. I think, if I don't role model it, the team won't then do the same things.

## On a significant break in trust...

In a previous role, I had been hired to do a job that didn't exist before. What that led to, was me joining and having a big part of my role that overlapped with (one of) my peers. She didn't know that I was coming in, or coming in with that particular mandate. So, what initially happened was a desire to collaborate and trying to be very polite to one another, because it was about working with our most senior stakeholders on quite critical change projects.

It soon started to become competitive - who would get to that meeting first, who would keep the other one out. I'm sure I played my part, but at the time I thought "I am the victim in this situation, it's not my fault, I'm new, I've been brought in". My boss wasn't willing to sort it out, so it was left to the two of us and ultimately it led to a breakdown of trust.

She clearly didn't trust me, because there was a moment where I'd sent a note to our joint respective teams based on a discussion we had had about how we were going to roll out a management development programme. I remember sending this email, and she said, "can I have a chat with you?". We went into a room and she said, "I was really unhappy with the note you sent for all of these reasons". I remember asking her specifically "based on what you've said to me, you've assumed negative intent. You've assumed I wrote that note to make you unhappy and create a conflict". I remember at that time, she said to me "yeah, actually I think that's exactly what I thought". So clearly trust had broken down. I didn't trust her, and she was the first one to articulate "actually I now assume negative intent in our interactions".

I remember that was the first time I'd ever experienced a breakdown of trust at work. And I realized I didn't want to fight for the role, that I could dust myself off and start again. That's when I went to my boss and said, "look, you've got conflict in your team (we were about to go through a merger), you're going to lose some heads in HR anyway, I'm happy to be one of those heads that leaves. There's a brewing conflict - I don't have the energy to resolve it, and I don't think you do either". We had a really frank conversation about it.

That breakdown of trust came from a lack of role clarity which then became a turf war and competition and ultimately, there were clearly things I - and she – did, that unfortunately got us to a place of assumed negative intent and which lead me to eventually leave.

### On the insights from that experience…

It made me think about new roles - is there role clarity - understanding the structure better. That's a very tactical thing. I'm never going to walk into a job again where the lines are so blurred that I find myself in the same position.

From a life and leadership perspective, I wish I'd had more

empathy for her. She was going through a number of different things and I knew that. She clearly felt threatened by me, I don't think I ever tried to minimize that and, in my mind, you can be stronger together. I wish I'd angled more on that. I wish I'd appreciated the differences between us and been explicit about them and talked them through.

I probably put up with that situation for a little bit longer where it started to affect my own morale and confidence, so getting out was a huge relief and then I felt confident again because I owned my destiny. It made me think about don't wait for situations to fester, have the guts to go in and have the difficult conversation, you often get to a better outcome quicker.

## On being trusted to take a leap of faith...

My current boss is fantastic at that. She's someone I've learnt from - being really explicit about the space in which I play, and saying, 'go play' and literally the word 'play' - have fun with it.

Sometimes she would say, "why are you asking me, because it's your decision" and that was powerful because I'd realize I was the decision maker, she's giving me autonomy which is great.

She said something to me in our most recent one to one after I was promoted. She said "I want to give you some feedback, there are a couple of watch-outs that I've seen happen since you've taken on this new role. I say it to you with love, because on my watch you won't be failing". And that was lovely to know that I had her as a backstop, that she trusted me so much that she was saying, "I'm here, go do - go work on some things, but I'm here. On my watch you're going to succeed, you're not going to fail".

We're having some conflict at the moment, which is good because I don't agree with her, but I know it's not personal. She's short with me at the moment but I know she's not going to hold it against me. We're just going through some professional conflict. I feel that's happened a couple of times, which has reinforced trust. You start to feel, actually - this is ok. The first time, you wobble; you wonder what it means for your career. But it's reinforced really good, open dialogue between us, which ultimately leads to better outcomes.

### On what leaders will look back on in five years and realize was unintentionally limiting trust…

I think it's as simple as being visible and present. When we're talking about trust both at an organisational but also a team level, I think little time is given to those things. To me, it speaks to the culture. How do you reinforce trust into the system? How do you make sure trust is present in the system? I think all the meetings we're constantly in, thinking about who you spend face time with, I would put money on it that we are in a number of ineffective meetings. We're probably wasting time in the right places, and probably not spending enough time with our teams to inspire them, give them trust, empower them.

Delegate effectively with purpose so it's an exciting thing, it's something that motivates and stretches someone.

There is something about the way we use time because I think trust comes from spending time with people. It's about relationships ultimately. Recognizing that maybe we focus on other relationships, like shareholders, investors and so on, all of which is important, but your people are a segment of your audience that you also need to spend more time with

Communication. So often really valid decisions are made, but we're moving so quickly that we don't slow down to explain our thinking, our ambition, our hope, our fear around a particular decision. What that means is that people then fill in the void. How can we stop people filling in the gaps themselves? How can we make sure we give them the truth? How do we make sure we give them authenticity in the way that we communicate with them? How do we make things more human and more dynamic in the way we communicate? I think we don't do that well now. I think most organisations undervalue internal communications. I don't mean the function - I mean just communicating internally. I think leaders will look back and think 'It was so easy; it was within our control'.

## On the conversation's leaders need to begin having to create cultures of trust…

There has to be honesty. I think a leader that's able to be honest about both the good and the bad. Not in a way to destabilize the organisation and create panic because there's this real balance. People look to leaders to be strong, therefore sometimes I think leaders sometimes find it hard to show vulnerability which is different to weakness. Sometimes I think vulnerability is equated to weakness. I think vulnerable, open, conversations which show authenticity will inspire trust.

I think being explicit about your intention and your trust in your team, reinforces trust. I think then that your actions have to follow through on those words. That means, don't micromanage, don't wade in when you don't need to. If you said you're not there as the decision maker, you're just there as a sounding board, restrain yourself. Play the role that you've committed to play. Unless something is going completely off course, or is going to create significant risk. Of course, then as a leader, you step in. But if you really are going to play that role of side coach, on the benches, helping your team play the field, then live up to that promise. There has to be congruence between the conversation and the action that follows.

## On how trust or its absence influences an organisation…

When trust is present, there's all the obvious things that research tells us. You have an engaged workforce, it improves performance, it leads to employee retention, culture, brand advocacy, employer brand - all of that is banked in my mind. I'm thinking about what I personally see. I think it shapes relationships, community, bonding; things that are quite inherent and intrinsic to an organisation's competitive success.

When trust is in the system, you ultimately get better results and that comes through better relationships. Better relationships in my mind are absolutely the unspoken, below the surface, part of competitive advantage that in my mind every CEO should be thinking of. They think about their product portfolio, they think about their investment, they think about their returns.

But as a currency, quality of relationships is something that enables an organisation to flourish. It helps information move quickly through an organisation; it helps you move from thought to action quicker. But more importantly in my mind, in the world of matrix organisations, where people are having to work to this relationship and that relationship, I think trust reinforces strong relationships. Strong relationships in these highly networked organisations, where you have the org chart, but then real work takes place outside of it, if those relationships are strong, you get other gains such as new ideas, innovation, speed to market. I think that's the type of thing that trust can really breed.

#

## Dominic - CEO SaaS Start Up

### On creating a culture of trust in a small organisation…

The culture in smaller organisations is not something that can be created, it's something that 'is'. And it is on the basis of how the founders, or the people who lead those organisations behave. And it doesn't really matter how many times you go through a culture definition process, ultimately, the way the founders behave is the culture of the business.

In a case where we have challenges with performance and things haven't gone well, the founders may feel unable to speak up and so bulldoze through an optimistic vision without acknowledging reality. Leadership coaching enables them to draw out why they can't acknowledge the reality people are in, allow everyone else to acknowledge that reality and then forge forward a position of optimism and how we're going to resolve it as opposed to glossing over it and not actually addressing it.

And that's a key element of trust. It's very much about the ability of people to be able to show vulnerability and explain they don't know the answers and that the reason there is a group of people is because that group of people working together is much better than just one founder. Ultimately, if they didn't need others, the founders would just get on and do it. It's alright in a small business – in any business – to say, 'I don't know; let's try to figure it out'.

There is something about genuine authenticity that comes from leadership that builds trust. It's the ability to be able to acknowledge your human side through every interaction you have with everybody throughout the business. Not just one to one, but in everything that you do.

When I think about the cultural elements that preclude the way through to trust, it definitely comes from arrogance, ego and an inability to acknowledge that it's ok to not know.

### On encouraging people to speak up in a founder-led environment...

We've created a way for the next tier of management to ask their teams about how they're feeling and what it means and for that to be surfaced up. The challenge we have is that that can get stuck because some managers are good and are able to turn around to the founders and talk about risks. Others aren't so good at doing that because they aren't – or don't feel equipped – to have challenging conversations with people who pay their salaries.

The difficulty is the dissonance between words and behaviour. For example, a founder would say "I really want to be challenged" and then when they're challenged, that challenge is shut down. So, what that does is it shuts people down from challenging; they say "really? What's the point in putting my vulnerability out there?"

What I've been trying to do is help them have those conversations where they're able to say to the founders "this is how I feel". That then comes through the leadership coaching element where those conversations are being facilitated by a third party so it's less constrained around the worker, employer/employee relationship which is a power dynamic that stops the ability for people to work in an honest way.

It's about empowering people who are 25, 26, 27 to have difficult conversations and not feel like they're going to lose their job.

That point of when you get into work – mid 20's to late 20's where there's almost a lifting of the veil where you go into work and you think that the world is a relatively orderly place, that people know what they're doing. That these people have been doing these things for a really long time, and clearly, these are big functioning organisations so everyone must know what they're doing that's why they're so successful. And of course, what you recognize over time is that that's not true and the only thing that makes them successful is a group of people figuring out new things and trying to work through problems as they become visible.

In all that period of time, what you're demystifying is this nature of certainty that when you enter the workforce is that "oh, I just do these things and I get paid", or "I just do these things and everyone's going to be happy with me". And the reality is, that as you get through your 30's and into your 40's you recognize that actually nobody really knows what they're doing and that's all the more reason why you should be speaking up because there isn't a right way. There isn't a right way, that's always a tried and tested route.

We've just taken on a student and it's mystifying to him when he says to me "hey, what do you think about this" and I'll say, "I'm not sure, what do you think?" and he says "what? You've been doing this a really long time" and I say "yeah, but I've never seen that problem before. What do you think

I'm going to do?", "I don't know – ask some people?"; "Yeah, I'm going to pick up the phone and talk to some people". "Well, I can do that". "Yeah, you can!"

## On how high trust cultures can support the transition from the way we work now to the way we need to be working in the future…

It's challenging because everything is built around the perception of certainty that comes with experience. It becomes even less relevant in the future if you take the 4th Revolution, the things we've done in before in terms of division of labour and ways of working – all of those things that have come before aren't a crutch to lean on for the future and that requires an entirely different thought process about what it is to be organized around a purpose of achieving things. And the reason why that purpose exists also changes, which is less about income necessarily and more about trying to find what you might call 'good work'. So, the conversations that need to happen, the experience we've had for the last four or five years is not going to help us for the next four or five years. The nature of the value of experience becomes more challenging. Experience is largely thought of as a hard skill, which you become expert in, but the nature of experience will become about how well you are able to interact and have good conversations with people and to have critical thinking.

A real change in the definition of what experience is for and that experience is about. Allowing young people to express themselves; to recognize that whatever they're thinking is probably just as valid as what I'm thinking because I've not experienced what we're about to experience any more than somebody who is 18. And it's those challenging conversations – that idea that just because you've lived a long time does not mean you're necessarily equipped to be able to deal with the new. Those conversations are really difficult because everything we've learnt about the way society is organized right now is that fundamentally, experience and power is what makes success happen. What we'll see increasingly is that the effort that people put into the production of things will be considerably lower from a human perspective, than the end of the $21^{st}$ century; and the preparation for that has to start now. The conversations with senior leaders need to be about how you help young people coming through the education system to be those expressive people. To not think there's a wrong way. We need to find a way of being able to help society recognize that just because $2+2=4$ on the form it may not necessarily mean that that's the answer you need to bring at that point in time when you're experiencing whatever it is you're trying to solve.

### On how trust touches the subject of our identity...

The ability to build trust within groups of people who are trying to achieve things is so important. You need to be truth-telling all of the time because as soon as you have a group of people who believe they have all of the information and are making decisions on that basis, and when it's proven that there are a whole series of extra data points that help to change the direction, those people who originally came up with the idea need to be able to accept that there's a new direction that everything needs to go in. And that's a massive test to ego; it's a massive test to the ideas around what it is to be a leader. So, this nature of truth-telling becomes even more important, particularly when we're seeing this very basic challenge to the nature of "What is fact? And what is narrative?".

When you put those things together at the moment – stories are so powerful that people will believe stories more than they will believe facts. "We can excuse the way Donald Trump behaves because it's just the way the media portrays him".

I see the future of work being governed not by the need to earn income, but through the provision of control to the individual to make decisions about what they want to do. If you think about it from the perspective of the idea that one day, we'll stop working because we'll have enough money. But what we mean is that one day I'll choose the work that I want to do; without the restriction of circumstance. There's a big challenge there that's coming. Vocation and identity are so closely tied, that when vocation changes so frequently, what does that do to identity?

The things I think will help in terms of conversations – and trust specifically – is how do you help young people to not be at school having conversations about being one single thing rather than whatever they want to be at the time.

It's those old perceptions of what it is to contribute and to be a citizen that needs to be peeled away as things change. And that has to happen through leaders being trustworthy, by being truth tellers, by showing that they're vulnerable, by allowing people to ask questions and taking questions that are hard. And that acknowledgement that there isn't a 'right' way.

## On leadership and organisational adaptability...

I think they all get it. I think equally they're all scared of not being seen to be the leader they've been conditioned to expect that they should be. They're fearful of being able to expose themselves in a way that's not expected because there's a perception of what leadership should be.

It's not that they don't get it, it's that making those changes is really hard. It takes a lot of effort. And in many cases, what you're doing is peeling away the very fabric of the identity of a person.

It's a crushing blow to your ego to realize that the misfortune of your business at the moment is actually being caused by yourself. But equally, finding the right time and space to figure out what you can do to change your behaviour is a very intensive exercise and if you don't dedicate the time to it, you don't get the value from it. At the same time, you have a business that needs to perform and do well and you have investors and a Board to report to. The challenge that people have is that they recognize the problem, they also have a challenge in finding the time to focus on it.

I think people are stuck in the motion of trying to make the businesses work, without recognizing that what they probably need to do is look more carefully at the organisation and at where and how the money is being spent and recognize that if you spent less in some areas and more looking at how to build trusting relationships, particularly within the groups of people who are interacting at the senior level all the time. If you don't do those things, you have a high chance of your business failing. And that might not be immediate, but over the course of five to six years, I've seen businesses begin to fail as a result of it.

The future of work is going to be based on continually reinventing and creating new business and so the more people who are skilled in thinking about how to build trust within their organisations, the more likely it is that those businesses will succeed, which means the more likely it is that people will be employed. And when those businesses are then no longer required, that same entrepreneur will jump into the next thing and then have the same ability to create those trustworthy organisations that people enjoy working in and are successful.

### On rebuilding trust...

Not delivering on time for projects. Typical of working in IT. The issues are all about cadence of communication and being clear when things are going wrong, even if you know that people will be pissed off. Trying to cover it up and fix it without help is a natural thing to try, but always ends in failure. To fix it, I acknowledged I had gone wrong and that I didn't highlight this early enough. I explained how we could fix it but also talked about what help I needed to get things back on track. There is a degree of vulnerability that people shy away from, but I've found that when I say I don't know, let's figure it out together, or this is going wrong and I need your help, that vulnerability really helps to get trust back on track. Bring your human to the issue, not the corporate professional.

### On a significant break in trust...

In this instance it is a behavior similar to the above but in reverse. Caused by an inability to show vulnerability and project strength when totally unsure or don't have all the facts. Consistently not telling the truth to the team, but not maliciously, but because of delusion. Thinking everything is known and it's weak to admit things aren't known. This break of trust means nothing stated as fact is taken at face value, so people discount those statements and search for the reality. It slows you down, constantly checking. Creates frustration and cynicism within a team.

## On the conversation's leaders need to begin having today to create a culture of trust...

Any conversation that allows them to show they are people and not automaton robots. Embracing opportunities to show vulnerability and to know that this builds trust, strong bonds and connections. The "I'll go into bat for that person, because they would for me" not just because of a tribal 'team' perspective, but because of the human connection. Vulnerability and expressing it is a route to creating a culture of trust. It brings truth telling in an environment that is there to solve and not blame.

## On how trust - and distrust - shapes or impacts an organisation...

Trust is the energy of the connection between each of us. Whether that's one to one, or across 1,000 people in a company. Because as soon as distrust becomes a thing it's the switching off of the lights. They may be switched off one at a time and it takes a little time for them all to go out, but fundamentally, that nature of distrust is an absolute killer to organisations.

When a senior leader sets a direction but it's a direction based on falsity or on incomplete information, people don't believe it and because they don't believe it, they don't trust that individual, and because they don't trust them, they spend more time bitching and moaning about the person, or they spend a lot of time trying to uncover what's really going on so they can help fix it.

What that does, is it creates inertia in an organisation because you have people who are either not engaged, don't care, don't believe that there's something worthwhile working on, or you have another group of people who are creating a huge amount of work within the business which is actually only about trying to disprove a leader or to try and help that leader make a better decision about the direction and build that level of authenticity.

Just telling the truth and sharing vulnerability is like putting petrol in the car, because it allows people to focus on what they're good at and not on things that are peripheral or distracting because you don't really know what you're trying to accomplish anymore.

If there's one thing to really emphasize around trust and what it does it's that ability to be able to truly focus an organisation. When you have a whole bunch of distrust, what it does is it creates fiefdoms, it creates the ability to antagonize and create discord between people, and those very behaviours are the things that impact productivity and allowing people to be the best that they can be.

#

## Eleni - Managing Partner, Advertising

**On the first time you remember being trusted in your career...**

The very first time I was so explicitly trusted was working for my first boss at Grey who I followed and am working with now at Hummer.

His approach was: "I'm hiring you because I trust you – I'm hiring you because I want to set a vision and I just want to hand you the keys and go, here you go - drive". That real sense of "if we don't trust our people, what have we got? We don't have anything else in our business".

He spoke about that so openly and so explicitly and so overtly. I remember it from the very first interview I had with him, because I was a little bit cynical going into the interview and wasn't as open to the opportunity as I could have been. I remember walking out and thinking "I'm going to have to think about this quite seriously now – I've never met a guy like him before." He made such an impact on me – I didn't know people like that existed, it was quite a profound moment.

## On how that shaped your career or your leadership style...

It made me very confident as far as my career was concerned, in being able to articulate to the business what I was looking for. I started as a freelancer – doing an eight-day fortnight. I started trusting in myself, and my own abilities more as a result of someone else trusting me; and it made me incredibly valuable. And I started believing how valuable I really was.

In the past maybe I'd been a little bit more humble or shy in pushing my agenda – you always sort of wanted someone to do that for you - and it really flipped at that point. I started being more overt and expressive at that point. About how important it was for me to be in a position where they did just trust me to get on and do what I needed to do. It made me understand how valuable my skills and experience and past achievements were. I started to realize my own worth.

It was so important to me witnessing someone behaving in that way to me. I think I'd always been that way with other people – with colleagues and members of my team – but I think I became more explicit in saying to them "you're good, you've got this, I trust you, go for it, push your own agenda, back yourself" that sort of thing. I really started encouraging people to leap a little bit more rather than holding back, because he helped me take such leaps. Particularly with women. I hadn't really worked with an employer before – particularly a male employer – that had been so transparent and so vocal. I felt like a valued member of the team, that there was no discrepancy between men and women.

### On being trusted to take a leap of faith…

(My boss) had a unique style and I make it sound like he's quite paternal or there's some nurturing going on, and there's not. It's anchored in a business sense, it's a rational thing – I don't think it's an emotional thing.

I think he said "well I don't want to get dragged down doing that stuff, I need to focus on much bigger picture things and in order to do that, I need to free myself, and in order to free myself, I need to raise smart people into positions where they're making smart decisions".

### On building or rebuilding trust…

There was an instance when I found it really hard to build trust. I think in hindsight that a lot of that came from the fact I was in a really vulnerable position personally, due to changes in my personal life. I wasn't feeling very good in myself and I think that manifested itself in all sorts of ways, where I felt nervous, where nothing I was doing was good enough.

I delivered as well as I had in any other job, with the same commitment, energy and passion, but I think because of my own vulnerability I was questioning whether that was enough. As a result, I think that put up some real barriers between me and some of the senior management that I was working with, and with a tricky client. But I can't say with any confidence that that client relationship was any different to any other; I think it was the energy that I was bringing to the situation that was creating a real barrier to building trust with that person.

I wasn't able to build trust with that person, and I remember expressing to the business that I didn't feel that they had my back. There were a number of instances where I asked for help in trying to manage this particular relationship and I communicated it quite openly and clearly and I don't feel that there was reciprocation there. And so, I didn't trust that they were looking after my interests as well, so we agreed to part ways.

Again, I can't help but think that that was partly me recognizing that I wasn't in the right frame of mind for that. I didn't believe at the time that I could build a trusting relationship either with my employers or with my client.

## Your insights from that experience…

We sometimes have an overactive mind when it comes to analyzing what may or may not be going on in a situation, rather than just being able to take it at face value. I can be quite hypercritical of myself, and therefore the situation.

I do believe that trust is something that has to start from within. You do have to trust yourself a little bit in order to be able to have the confidence in what you're doing, such that you can then have confidence in engaging with others about the things that are working and the things that are not, or about the road you're trying to go down.

People feed off the energy you project, so if you're not trusting yourself and backing yourself, and going in with a point of view, then it's hard to get other people to do the heavy lifting for you. Trust isn't something where you just have to get one person saying, "I implicitly trust you", they have to be sensing, or hearing or seeing something in you.

Trust is definitely a two-way street. A meeting of energy, and thoughts, and values, and contributions.

The other thing I've realized is that – because I'm quite an emotional person – I think in the past I've found it hard to separate personal agendas from business agendas. So that if I didn't gel with someone on a personal level, maybe I couldn't trust them on a business level. And I don't believe that's the case anymore. I believe you can trust someone in a business sense and not necessarily be similar types of people. As long as there's clarity on the shared agenda and you're both able to contribute to that in the ways that mean that agenda can happen.

I always thought I was a little bit of an outsider, particularly in the advertising industry. A little bit more conservative, stoic, less casual, not in the drug scene, not a drinker. So as someone who didn't necessarily play the ad game as much as others did, I was concerned that I needed people to like me in some way and that if they didn't (and I didn't think this enough to compromise my values - I was still unapologetically who I was) but I still felt this inherent need to make sure people liked me rather than just respect what I did. I got to a point where I realized it wasn't important that everybody liked you.

It wasn't a shift of a moment – it happened over a period of time, where I relied on myself more. I assessed different interactions with people – personal and professional - and determined what made a good interaction. That's when I realized, particularly professionally, I didn't have to have common values with someone to trust that we could deliver on something from a business point of view. And realising that personal interactions were different and that trust works differently on that level.

When I realized that people didn't need to like me to respect me, I realized "well I don't need to like you to respect what you do and whatever it is you bring to the table."

## On a significant break in trust….

I can think of two examples and both were clients that tried to run their businesses through a culture of fear, and that was the corporate culture. People felt afraid to manoeuvre, or afraid to move fast, or afraid to try something different, for fear that they were going to get dumped on and potentially lose their jobs.

What it bred was paint by numbers, and it didn't allow for good outputs. It also meant that whatever fear they were feeling from their internal organisations, they then cascaded to their partnerships and that included their agency relationships. And so, on any number of occasions, we would feel that our trust was broken. In fact, it just became part of the relationship, we just operated in an environment where we just knew that what was said one minute wasn't going to be the case the next.

My job then became trying to protect my team from that. Trying to make them feel good about what they did day in and day out, knowing that they were going to be disappointed, or that their expectations weren't going to be met time and time and again.

It's an interesting role to have as a manager, trying to keep a team of people motivated, when you know that the relationship that they deal with day in and day out is one of mistrust and fear.

#

## Fiona - Head of Marketing Communications, Tertiary Education

### On the first time you were trusted...

I was in my 20's with a few years post grad experience, living in a country on the other side of the world and got handed the opportunity for a key secondment role by the then CEO of the organisation to work with the receivers of a company that my organisation had a very high media profile vested interest in (running to hundreds of millions of $'s) let alone risk to reputation.

It was a life changing experience as it initially 'scared the shit' out of me as I was reporting to board and ministerial level and I was picking up the reins of a very publicly perceived mess with media eyes all over it and I really had very little support.

I dug deep, I put in the hours, I built relationships with staff where I was seen as the 'big public service spy' and with the existing team I learned that working together even when realistically you are on opposing sides with high emotions and stress running through everyone's veins you can still confidently with the right attitude and development of competence return on your KPI's, encourage, motivate and coach others and deliver an outstanding result.

What stands out – it was a hell of a ride and the adrenaline was intoxicating. It influenced me by giving me the confidence to be able to do whatever I set my mind to and I was able to really develop my relationship building skills and stakeholder management to the highest of levels internally and externally. The role set me up for the next step in my career which took me to yet another new country, a new type of opportunity that I would possibly not have considered and yet another new sector. It made me appreciate that many of the skills we have as individuals are transferable into any environment

## On a breach of trust...

I worked on building trust of a very damaged and broken client relationship that had cost the organisation I worked with one of their highest profile accounts many years prior to me joining that particular employer. I set about re-building the relationship with soft introductory calls, they were met with little enthusiasm, I continued and persevered with my calls and eventually 'for my sheer cheek', I got the opportunity to meet with the client.

The meeting started out with a full run down on why they would never work with my organisation again. I listened, I countered and I offered to deliver a piece of work at no charge. I left the meeting on good terms having found common ground with the client on a family matter and was told they would think about it but it was highly unlikely they would indeed engage with my organisation ever again but they 'enjoyed meeting me'.

Undeterred, I continued to gently coax the client and follow up with regular but not overbearing communication.

My manager was unimpressed with my offer of 'free work' but I told him I would, if necessary do the work in my own time but we had to give something up to repair the damage to the relationship and be seen by that client to genuinely want to work with them and work on the damaged relationship positively and with the right intent.

Fast forward six weeks later and I was provided a consulting opportunity that can only be described as a 'hospital pass'. I took it! I worked my tail off, putting in many hours outside of the normal working day and I delivered what the client said was an 'incredible turn around and result'. Two weeks later I landed a high value consulting project and within a year this client had become my own highest value client and within a very short space of time was in our organisation's top three client set and number one in their sector.

The key insights to this example - relationships are crucial, find common ground, gain trust, use your personal brand when the organisational brand is seen as a derailer, act with courage, authenticity and most of all trust your instincts and make courageous and bold and sometimes unpopular decisions when your gut (and logic) give you the confidence to accurately predict that you can and will succeed.

### On being trusted to take a leap of faith...

Working in an organisation for only four weeks in my first job after moving to the other side of the world I was approached by the head of marketing who was going on leave. I barely knew the manager, but she had been made aware of my quick integration into the organisation. I was taken into a meeting and asked by her to look after a suite of clients.

Firstly, I knew very little about the business, secondly, I had never met her clients and thirdly she was on the senior leadership team and I was three tiers below and extremely green and inexperienced. I thought 'what the hell' – we did a brief handover, I met her clients, I moved to her office and she took off to the States for three weeks and literally left me holding the baby!

I felt like I was on some kind of theme park ride without a buckle! It was high adrenaline, I made amazing relationships with the management team, I worked my tail off and made sure that when she returned, she would be vindicated in her decision which I knew from 'office talk' had been questioned. She was wrapped, she employed me as her second in command, and we have now had a 22+ year friendship which is deeply precious to me.

### On what leaders will look back on in five years and realize was unintentionally limiting trust...

I believe they get too into the detail, there isn't enough trust or autonomy in roles. Sure, you have to be careful how much rope you give but certainly trusting, encouraging and sometimes really pushing people out of their comfort zones will build their confidence as long as they know the support is in the background. It grows people, it develops the skills they need to go on to lead and trust others.

Micromanagement or being pedantic or over controlling situations / work / output / decisions leaves organisations open to limited innovation and not enough space to grow and develop those that will take businesses forward as individuals naturally progress their desire to move forward.

## On the conversations could leaders begin having now to build cultures of trust...

They need to start being more open on strategy, direction and issues that they themselves as leaders face in the climate they operate in. They need to involve their future leaders, managers and indeed core staff so that there is a greater feeling of ownership on organisational performance; and as such that ownership will, by default, engender trust.

Leaders need to be visible and be seen to lead with open communication and be prepared to front up to the hard questions.

## On how trust - and distrust - shapes an organisation...

Trust invariably creates cultures in organisations that are enjoyable, empowering and motivational. Employees feel part of something bigger than a pay cheque, they feel the gains and the pains and they walk in the shoes of the organisational journey through good and bad performance (for example in terms of revenue) times.

It creates higher degrees of motivation and it energizes and invigorates people to strive as hard as they can to deliver what they have been entrusted to do.

Distrust creates disharmony, negativity, derailing behaviours, fear, rumourmongering, a 'them and us' mentality and a feeling that there's something more going on behind the scenes.

It causes people to feel disengaged and they do not feel empowered and it can leave them feeling like their current role is just a bus stop ride for them as opposed to what could be a real career trip!

#

## Helen - COO Government

**On the first time you remember being trusted in your career...**

Being put in charge of the largest shop in a chain of bakers with a staff of nine just before my 18th birthday. They left me alone to run the shop; they decided I was somebody they could trust and that I would handle things.

**Key things that stood out from that experience...**

Reflecting on it from this distance, it was a bigger thing for them than I realized at the time. The risk wasn't that I was going to run away with their money. The obvious risks aren't the risks – the risks were about the staff walking away or customers dropping off. Those things were their business risks, not the obvious things that you would think about. So it's about what you're trusting people to do.

The big stuff is relatively easy to make decisions about; if I turn my back, will that person going to walk off with my purse? That's a simple question to ask yourself and mostly quite an easy one to answer. But the questions we ask about trust at work are; "Do they care about this as much as I do? Do they see the thing in the same way that I do? The kinds of things that they escalate, will they be the kinds of things that I would escalate? Will they anticipate the sorts of problems that I would anticipate?" It's tied in with a whole load of other things which you wouldn't actually call trust, but how far you trust people, there are a lot of fine line judgements in there.

## On building - or rebuilding - trust...

Right at the beginning of my career, I was a management consultant and early in that, what you realize is that you are constantly walking into organisations where people distrust you. Particularly public sector organisations which are the ones I was walking into. Every time I walked in the door, the staff would look at me and think – you're here and I'm going to lose my job. Because that's the mental construct: consultants come in and they will be here to take money out of the business. So there's a complete disconnect between your personal relationships and whether or not they trust and like you, and you can use your experience and your sense of empathy, you can build personal trust and empathy.

As a consultant, I remember walking into a room and facilitating a session and a group of mid-career social workers turning on me and saying, "and when have you ever taken a child into care?". So you say, "Ok, I know that's what you're thinking. Of course, I haven't. You guys are the experts and you do this really tough stuff. I don't do what you do, I do something else and if we work together, we can pool your experience and mine and solve the problem here, or we can fight each other."

And when I first became a Chief Executive at a London Council, we had been judged by the regulator to be poor – the bottom rank. Staff just felt "what's the point?". I remember walking into a group of social workers and asking to see a file and them saying that it was confidential. So I said that whatever duty of confidentiality applies to you as a colleague, applies to me. They didn't buy that. I remember eventually saying to them, "look guys, imagine I've left the council, stopped being Chief Executive, walked down the road, signed up with a temp agency and you've got me in as a team clerk. Will I, or will I not be walking around the office clutching this file?" And they said, "well, you probably would, yes". So I said, "well let's imagine we've done that shall we?"

You've got to not take it personally. You've got to try and understand where the logic is in what people are doing. Because to be fair to my social work colleagues, they weren't just being difficult, they were trying to say something about their concerns about their professional status and responsibilities, which you have to be seen to understand. And they were also explaining something about how they felt about how more senior people in other organisations had treated them.

I suppose what I keep doing is to separate trust in me as a person, from trust in my role. Because as a public sector leader, there are times when people say "can I tell you something in confidence?" and the only honest answer is "I will respect whatever you tell me, but I cannot promise until I know what it is, that I won't share it with it with anyone else because you might tell me something I have to share with someone else. The only thing I can promise is that if you do tell me something I have to share with someone else that I will tell you what I'm going to do with that something before I do it." That's a difficult thing when you want to gain someone's trust.

## On a significant break in trust….

It happens a lot in small ways. In the past, working with politicians – as the senior intermediary I would have conversations with police officers about what the Mayor intends and then sometimes you'd say "but remember I work in a political organisation and it's possible that I could be overruled and all I can promise you is that if I think that's likely, I'll tell you. I might not see it coming either!"

So you're also building a personal and an organisational trust. You're trying to share with people that sense of how the organisation works, what is it that matters around here. If a politician changes his mind and what I told you was the case is not the case, it's not because he's being arbitrary, it will be because, in the mind of that politician, something else is a bigger prize. I'm trying to explain that and I'm also trying to build a personal relationship of trust that goes "Helen, you're straight with us and we believe you'll tell us the truth as you see it and understand it; and our experience of you is that what you tell us is mostly the case."

In the work context, I never think trust is an absolute thing, I think you trust people as far as they can be trusted and that's not about personal intent, it's about recognizing what they can do. For example; in a previous role, if a senior police officer said I 100% promise you I'll be at this meeting, you put that in a context in your head that says, that means you almost certainly will be there, but you work in a hierarchical organisation, and what you've said to me is you'll do your damnedest to override any interruptions by the hierarchy with what you plan to do with yourself. But it isn't impossible that you will ring me up and say you can't come, and it won't be because you're being untrustworthy or loose with our relationship. It'll be because there will be a force majeure there. You have to have trust the other way too, to believe that there really has been something that has happened.

## On being trusted to take a leap of faith…

I used to be involved in a couple of organisations that

promoted women in the workplace and I did a number of speeches about great feminists that I'd known in that context. They all looked like unlikely middle-aged men. People who saw something in you and said "ok, go for it. You may or may not get it, but go for it" and "I think you can". And also helping you get through that bit of - it looks bad if I simply put myself forward for it, but if I ring up the next person and say "Fred says why don't you go for this?", suddenly I feel that there's a legitimacy about it. If I ring you up and say I've seen this fabulous job and I'm really interested in it, you might think, oh who are you? You're being really presumptuous thinking that's something you can do. Whereas if I ring you up and say, "I wanted your opinion because I've had a call from Fred and he really thinks I should do this", then you're in a different place. Because then I'm putting you in a position of a third party where you can say "yeah, well Fred's always been a bit over-ambitious about that sort of thing you know", without insulting me.

Also, that's about trusting yourself. What other people are also allowing you to do is to trust yourself. They're saying to you "you may think it's a really big deal", or "you may think you have a capacity for failure here, but actually, I think and therefore, other people think, that you will be fine – this is something where you should trust yourself". The two things are quite bound up together.

Women in my generation, brought up in the UK were brought up to not be too forward. The thing I was always told as a kid was not to be too bossy, not to be too pushy. And therefore, if you can use someone else as the excuse to push yourself forward, it gets you past that. Sometimes, outsourcing it to someone else first allows you to test the reaction without it being such a personal put down if someone else has a different view.

I employ that approach even now. If I ring someone now, I say "I've been approached about this and it has many interesting aspects as far as I'm concerned but I wondered what you thought?". What I'm testing out is, would people whose opinions I value think I'm a being a complete idiot if I go for this? And if they do, I need to think about that.

## On what leaders will look back on in five years and realize was unintentionally limiting trust...

The thing that leaders are tempted to do in my world which is the public sector world is the 'never again' thing. In the short term that's designed to build trust and in the long term it completely destroys it.

For instance, when there is (an incident and a senior leader states 'this must never happen again' ) this is where,  in my world, trust goes completely. We are, as a country, spending a lot of money saying, "this must never happen again", without saying what the 'this' is. Usually, something very specific goes wrong and we must make sure that specific thing never goes wrong again. But what we do is panic and that destroys trust in the long term. What is the 'is'? We can't stop all things, but we also know that sometimes mistakes are made that can be as a result of a failure of good practice and pressure on time. We rarely get down to the degree of sophistication that tells us specifically which piece the 'is' is. Instead, the public narrative is "it must never happen again" so the next time a similar case is reported, the level of trust in public authorities go down. Because what the public heard is "this must never happen again" and it's happened again.

One of the risky behaviours around trust is to make those

kinds of pronouncements and yet of course, what leaders are always advised is that the more honest stuff "we will do whatever we can to make sure…" isn't heard as being definite enough. It doesn't sound 'active' enough.

Also, there is a dialogue that we don't have about the individual and society. What is it that society stops? If you have 10 children and neglect them, you will expect - it will be expected - that society will get involved in that and stop those children from suffering at your hands. But at what point is that some of your responsibility?

If you neglect them because you've been run over by a bus then that seems pretty clear-cut. but if you neglect them because you've got a shopping habit, and you've spent the family money then that feels clear cut. But there's a lot of quite complicated stuff in between. At what point does society say - actually, there's an abuse of trust happening here.

The honest conversation, because the preoccupation with leaders in this sector is about how do we carry on? There is an expectation that hangs over them that undermines trust which is that services will continue to be at a level people expect which is not always easy to describe, but we're spending less and less money on them.

You create distrust in a lot of organisations because your public narrative says, "we're getting more efficient, we're doing more with less", and yet the people who are driving those services on the front line are giving a very different story. So, you're creating an expectation of duality and distrust. So I think in my world, leaders who spend too much time talking about what's been lost, lose trust because people don't trust them to have a forward vision. If they never acknowledge it, then it feels to the people they're leading, that they live in a completely different world. So the hardest thing is to find the language that expresses "I know that those of you who work here feel that we have less to offer than we did, and I know that you are all working very very hard to deliver stuff, and I know that we are all pretending to the world that we are all providing as good a service as we ever did. But nonetheless, we have to be positive about the future". I think you have to acknowledge the circumstances you are in and you have to tell the truth about how it looks from the position you're in. I personally find that works well, whether you're talking to one person or the whole organisation - although you may use different words.

If I think about some of the more difficult things I've done, it's talking to people about pay. When people bring the research they've done and you say, here is what the budget is and here are my options. We can engage together - the Trade Unions and I - about how we spend that bit of budget or we can fight about whether or not that budget should be bigger; but actually, that's not in my control. Here are the things I can do something about and here are the things I can do nothing about. I'm happy to have a conversation on two levels; a conversation about the world as it ought to be, but we also need to solve the problem about the world as it is.

If you don't acknowledge people's anxiety and what they see, then you lose their trust. I think you diminish everybody if you don't say "I understand what you're saying, and in your position, I might be saying something similar, but this the room to manoeuvre that I have on this issue. This is what I can, and cannot do, and this is what I'm willing to do. You think I can do X and Y, but for me the consequences of doing that knock into other parts of the organisation and sometimes I can't tell you what those consequences are because it means sharing information that I can't share."

I think that's the other bit about trust, particularly in public organisations where freedom of information means people have access to information. In order for you to understand how I'm thinking I would have to tell you somebody else's secrets and I can't do that. I can tell you what I can't tell you, but I can't always tell you why I can't tell you it.

## On the conversations could leaders begin having now to build cultures of trust...

I think there's a listening issue. I think we've substituted transparency for trust in a lot of instances. For example; freedom of information and those kinds of bits of legislation were designed because people felt that public authorities weren't being honest with them. What we've done is say "you can see the decision making". What we haven't done is to say, "there are a lot of complex, multi-faceted decisions going on here and therefore it isn't simply x is right and y is wrong". We live in a world where people want to believe it's quite simple, but because of the complexity of decision making, it's really hard to lay out and explain.

We are very nervous in the public sector of trusting people which is why we have procurement processes and tendering processes. In fact, we enshrine the opposite. It is possible to know that company A is a bad company that has done shoddy work, but to recognize that you can't prove that in a court of law. Therefore you still have to let them tender for work, and still have to give them work if they offer you the cheapest price for it, despite feeling that you can't trust them. Because all of our law around procurement is designed to stop you from working with people you trust. Because if I have a relationship of trust with you, then we might have a collusive relationship. And we don't know how to describe the difference between a collusive relationship and trust, so we do all sorts of other things instead.

I think the shared morale of that is that we have to be aware of putting proxy's into trust, because trust is a personal thing. You trust people, and you trust institutions because you think you have some idea about the people in them. And I think trust is - at its most sophisticated - understanding based. I trust you to do this because I know that it's in our shared interest that you do, and I understand where your interests and mine coincide. I will lose my trust in you if I trust you to do things that are beyond your competence or likely intent. But people do that a lot in our world - they want to know why public authorities 'let it happen'. They're disappointed because they've never really thought about what the trust is, what it means, what is within our capability and what isn't. And they don't distinguish between the individual and the organisation. So you will also find that because there is a huge amount of duality with it, they have a sense of having the measure of an individual and what they can trust them to do, and not do. And I think that's true for organisations as well.

There is a lack of clarity about where boundaries start and stop. This is where I find trust a difficult word. If you think trust is absolute, if I trust you in the way that a small child has to trust its parents, I'm going to be disappointed. But if I trust you to do the things I think you're going to do, and I know you to be capable of doing; and I fulfil my half of the bargain by being honest about what I'm expecting and what I'm trusting you to do, and I understand in the circumstances when I can expect you to fulfil my trust and when that is going to be tough, so that we can have conversations before you let me down, chances are, you never will.

We spent a lot of time working out how to build better relationships between public institutions, but in fact, institutions don't have relationships, people do. What it means is having an honest conversation about "You're running a hospital, I'm running a bit of the police force, you're running a local authority, where is our flexibility to make a difference to these circumstances, that matters enough for us, that we will put the energy in to actually making sure our staff do it?" Because nothing will change if we agree to do a new bit of practice around childcare really well, if we then just send out a note to our staff saying we've all agreed to do this differently. It will change if, in each of our organisations, we are willing to put the time and energy in to find the right people to talk to them, to explain why this has to change, to introduce them to the people in the other organisations who are committed to making that same change. That we report back on it, that we tell people that it's serious. That we make demonstrations of its seriousness. It takes time and energy and if I'm sitting across from somebody who is running a hospital which is in big financial difficulties, where A&E is its major problem, then without distressing them, I shouldn't anticipate they are going to do it. Or at least I should have the conversation that says, "is this something that you're able to put time and energy into now?" They need to feel free enough to say no.

## On how trust or mistrust shapes an organisation…

I think that in the organisations I've worked in, trust is bound in with consistency and with the behaviour of senior people. We know that in this organisation, these behaviours will be supported, rewarded, appraised, these will not be. And we see a consistency about that and we see leaders who care about what goes on in the organisation, who are interested in it, who don't disregard it as some kind of dull job and we see a shared sense of purpose with the leaders who are leading us.

I think distrust is where people are feeling that what they're doing matters to them, but not to anybody else. If you don't think you matter to the organisation at all, you will either just get on selfishly with what you're doing in your own way, or you will start gaming the system and not think about the organisation.

The thing that most breeds distrust is a perception of uncertainty and randomness. I don't know how the organisation will behave if I do X. I don't know if I go out and talk to someone at my level in another organisation, will I get support or will I be undermined? That comes from uncertainty. Because if I know broadly what we're trying to achieve, and how senior people behave when they're told I've gone slightly beyond my brief, I know that broadly speaking people will understand that what I've been trying to achieve is in line with the common goals. If people feel like that, then they can trust the organisation to support them even when times are difficult or when they've done something slightly stupid.

If their experience is that they really don't know how anybody is going to react to anything that happens, everything feels random, crazy and arbitrary. If the sense of the organisation is that you feel you are operating in an environment of arbitrariness and uncertainty, then you will end up with an 'every man for themselves' lack of trust in an organisation.

So for me, it's about consistency, behaviour, values and explaining - being willing to enter into dialogue - when some of those things have to change. Explaining why.

## On building trust across complex stakeholder groups in a public sector organisation...

You can't do anything without having relationships of trust with people who run the other organisations in your sector. I think it's one of the things that is time-consuming and not recognized. If people see you sitting having a coffee with a colleague, what they think is that it's social, not work. But it's probably the most important thing you do.

I think it comes back also to the honesty bit. Not to promise what you can't deliver, but to recognize where you are, where they perceive you to be (what is it people believe about what you can and can't deliver?) and to work in an honest and open way with that.

It's as simple on one level, as when to challenge people's perceptions. Being consistently honest and open both about your own motives, about the performance of the organisation and about the capacity of the organisation.

#

## Jason - Director, Technology

### On the first time being trusted...

I'd been working in retail for six months and I went overseas to work in Camp America. I came back and the company gave me the job back again and within two or three months there was an opening in the corporate sales team, which they offered to me. The role was the top corporate account management position responsible for managing the largest and most critical corporate and enterprise accounts. Councils, banks and the like, worth millions of dollars a year in revenue. It was significant, particularly as I was still relatively early in my career. I was 22 at the time.

### On the insights gained from that experience...

The first feeling was being overwhelmed. It was a massive job, it was a massive opportunity, it was a massive budget, none of which I'd had to contend with before. I was dealing with corporate and enterprise level CIOs, whom I hadn't had to deal with before. Very senior people. So that first feeling was one of being overwhelmed. After that, it quickly became a case of just getting on with it. I was going to either sink or swim, but I was determined to swim. I was determined to put my best foot forward and do the very best job that I could, which I did and I was successful. I managed to hit my budgets and win new business, respond to RFPs and win some sizeable deals. I really enjoyed that feeling of being out of control and a bit overwhelmed with that sink or swim mentality, but it worked well. I stayed in that role for about five years.

### On how that shaped your career...

One of the things I took away is that it doesn't matter how old you are, if you've got the aptitude, the capability, the mindset that you can do this sort of stuff, if you've got the maturity to do it, you can take on anything you want, which has kind of led me full circle. I had an interview about four years ago with an IT magazine that asked that sort of question, "what's one of your hiring processes or mentalities?", I said, "I don't care about age, I don't look for age as a validator, but I look at capability, aptitude and attitude". Get those right and I'll hire someone that's 20 years old for a role that I've typically got much more senior people doing.

## On a significant break in trust…

I've had a couple at different stages in my career. One example was very early on and it was with a new sales manager who came in at the time to manage me and the team that I worked with. I went out within a couple of weeks of this person joining the company and found a new BIG fish. Out of courtesy to her, I took her along to my second meeting with customer and immediately after that, the rug was pulled from under me. The sales manager took the deal, which was for a major enterprise, enjoyed all the sales, the kudos, the commission, the whole lot. Simply blindsided me.

I was gobsmacked and ropable. Trust had been eroded, to the extent that I closed off from the manager completely. I didn't share. I didn't provide visibility of pipeline. I treated this person with a degree of hostility "I'm only going to give you what I need to give you to tick the boxes." That was incredibly disappointing. It was an unfortunate error of judgement on the manager's part, which really contributed to the rest of our working relationship from that point forward. We worked together for another two years after that incident, which wasn't ideal. The outcome of that experience now? I see the person socially from time to time, but would I trust her in business? Probably not.

Another good example was a direct report of my own,

who wasn't performing, wasn't hitting his numbers, was never visible and was out of the office a lot, to the extent that I thought, "what's this guy doing?". Over a period of months, I discovered he wasn't likely doing what he was supposed to be doing and was about to kick off a performance management process with him.

One Friday afternoon, he had taken off at about 2pm and I knew that he had a holiday home and figured he'd probably skipped up there early to beat the traffic, which if he'd been open about it and had a solid performance record, wouldn't have been a problem. But if you sneak off and then say you were out doing what you were supposed to be doing for the business, it's different story. So, I asked him about it and he said he was visiting a specific customer. Little did he know that I know the customer he mentioned very well, so I picked up the phone and asked, "when was the last time you saw this guy?" The customer replied, "about six weeks ago".

Long story short, trust had already been broken with that guy. He'd already been in the spotlight and that was the final straw. I was fortunate that his particular contract had an honesty clause in it, which he'd clearly breached, so I terminated him that day. There wasn't any coming back from that. It was a massive integrity issue and I dealt with it firmly and finally.

**On trusting someone to take a leap of faith…**

Someone had his hand out saying "can I, can I?". The business hadn't backed the person. It put him in a comparatively junior role to what he thought he was capable of. He wasn't enjoying the role; he was treated like a doormat and was given all the menial work to do because he was the junior of the team. I had an opportunity that came up, for a particular line in our business that hadn't had a lot of attention and I suggested that we put him in on that particular line of business. I got it across the line, got it endorsed and he grabbed it with both hands, ran with it and absolutely owned it. Smashed all his targets the following year and made a lot of money, both personally and for the business.

The people leading that particular business line were hugely thankful for the focus and the effort we had put into growing it. It went absolutely gangbusters. It come down to spotting that capability, spotting the potential in in the individual and providing them the opportunity to unleash that potential.

### On what leaders will look back on in five years and realize was unintentionally limiting trust…

Where you might portray your management as open and communicative, having a door always open policy, which you would argue creates an air of trust, then there's a lot of activity going on behind closed doors, which people become aware of and then they become suspicious. All of a sudden, you erode the trust you've built up, because while you've said one thing, you haven't necessarily followed through. I think we've got to do more to 'walk the talk'.

As manager, how we treat our people, how we coach them, is important in terms of building that trust.

### On the conversation's leaders need to start having now to build cultures of trust…

I borrowed this from a friend. It resonated with me five or six years ago and I've used it since. That is "ask me any question and I'll tell you the answer. If I don't know the answer, I'll tell you that I don't know the answer. If can't tell you the answer, I'll tell you that I can't tell you the answer. What I won't ever do is make things up, tell you lies or direct you down the wrong path".

I tend to do that with each new team, each new person that joins my team, to emphasize that the door is always open and certainly as much as I can share with you, I will. If I can't because I'm under NDA then that's something you have to be mature enough to accept. Outside that I'll be as open as I possibly can be. I think, by and large, a healthy degree of trust flows from that sort of approach.

Constantly learning from mistakes and improving our own interpersonal interaction as a result of learning from those mistakes. I think as a leader you've got to be open to being fallible. But also taking input and constructive feedback and actually looking at yourself and being a bit introspective at times and saying, "I'm not always right, I've not always got the answers", and learn, develop and improve from that. I've got leaders on my team that do a great job of taking feedback on and adjust course as a result of that feedback. I've got others that are not sufficiently self-aware that they can take that feedback and struggle to progress as a result.

We need the ability to learn and gauge from people's reactions how they are actually taking what you are saying, and the adjust our approach accordingly. If you're a salesperson, you must be very good at that. A good salesperson will talk to you, watch for when you are starting to close down, and adjust his/her approach as necessary. It comes down to that whole human interaction and learning, if you can see someone is starting to close up and fold their arms during a conversation, then clearly they are starting to feel defensive, or insecure, and you've got to rebuild that trust on the spot and get them to a more comfortable place.

There's a lot that we can all learn and it's a daily challenge. You might read a book today and think, "great I know the answers now", but you've got to put that into context and into your daily life and still be able to have the thousands of other tools in your kit bag, which you can draw upon when you're having those daily interactions.

If you are an insecure leader, then you've got to be the boss, you've got to have all the right answers, you've got to be leading your team by telling them what the best way of doing something is. Whereas if you take it from the other angle and say, I've employed experts that are very good at what they do, all I need to do is empower them and take the hurdles and barriers away, so that they can be the very best that they can be. Ask them for their feedback and their input. It's not easy to do and it's a reasonably hard bridge to cross, particularly as a young or reasonably new people manager, particularly where promotion has come as a result of experience and expertise. But things change, and you've got to take on other people's viewpoints and ideas to get the growth that you need out of your business.

## On how trust or its absence influences an organisation…

Trust frees us to get on with the job at hand. If I build an air of trust, an environment of trust within the business, then my team is going to be free to do what they are paid to do and I'm going to be free to do what I get paid to do, which is be strategic, look to the future with growth aspects in mind.

As soon as we get involved in an air of mistrust, we find

ourselves second-guessing, we are putting people under a microscope, we get stuck in quagmire of "how do we fix that particular problem?" and people are always looking over their shoulder. It creates are more closed environment, rather than a free, open, and get-the-job-done environment.

It's important that we work towards a trusting environment. We would get a lot further if we did. It's one of the things that I strive to achieve. Do I succeed? Not every day, but as long as I'm succeeding more days than I'm failing, I'm happy.

What is different (with trust) is that you get a higher degree of energy and people just getting on with their jobs and actually succeeding.

Trust is important, and when you give it freely, you get the value back in spades.

#

## Jim - Managing Director, Entertainment

**On what leaders will look back on in five years and realize was unintentionally limiting trust...**

Having a level of trust in your workforce – you can't walk around the office at 9am and see who's late. You have to trust that the people that come in at 10am are going to do their days work or that the people who are going to work from home are genuinely working from home. There'll always be 5-10% of people who are going to take advantage, but you probably don't want those people in your organisation anyway and you probably know who those people are.

I think leaders need to trust their workforces a little bit more, and be progressive and brave in embracing what will have to become a more flexible working environment.

For us – allowing people to leave early, or to come in late – you can just see has made a big difference to people's work-life balance. When we announced it, you could just see how happy people were. The question for me is what's happening to productivity? It's very difficult to measure, but the happier people are at work the more productive they're going to be. You have to trust and believe that. You have to take a leap of faith and monitor it.

## On the conversation's leaders need to begin having today to create a culture of trust...

Trying to understand your people as people – what motivates them, what's their ambition? And not doing it once a year in a formal appraisal but understanding who's just bought a house? If somebody's just bought a house for the first time, that's going to put pressure on them, may make them feel different about their finances, may make salary more important than stability. So for me, anyone that manages a team needs to get to know their people – not prying, just understanding a little bit about what's going on in people's worlds outside of work. What the highs and lows, and the pressures might be. Just being aware so you can help and support people. Being more authentic as a leader. It's about talking to people.

## On how trust - and mistrust - shapes an organisation...

For an organisation to be successful, you need to trust and respect your work colleagues. That means that not doing your job correctly has an impact further down the line. We have our vision and values as a business and one of our values is

'Trusted'. We do what we say we will do and we act with openness. And I think that's really important. Don't tell your team you're going to look at something or change something and then not do it. Because if you don't do it, they'll never believe you again.

We encourage people to take responsibility for their actions. You're trusted to do a job and all we ask of people is that if you fail or if something goes wrong, put your hand up and put your hand up quickly because then we can help. Don't try and cover things up, don't try to justify the unjustifiable. You won't get in trouble for failing, you'll only get in trouble if you're not honest about it.

The business needs to trust its leaders. To be doing the right things, to be progressive, to be looking to the future and building the right strategy. That's becoming more important. Increasingly, when people are looking to join a business, they're looking far more at who the leader is and what the culture is than just how big the business is or what the turnover is. That's important - you want to join a successful business, but you want to understand what the culture is like, what the values are like in the business. That particularly comes down to the leadership team in the business.

If there's distrust within an org what typically happens is that your retention becomes an issue, you start to lose good people but the workplace also starts to become dysfunctional because you get into blame culture, you get people focusing just on their job and becoming protective and insular rather than working as a team.

It becomes much more siloed. People don't want to get in trouble. People don't want to be seen to be taking risks. People's energy goes into the wrong things and you get a poisonous workplace,

You need healthy tension and challenge because you'll probably make the right decision or a better decision when you have that. When it becomes personal, poisonous, and there's a breakdown of trust, that's when things go wrong. The best resource we have, and the only way to be successful, is to have a successful team. And you need to create the right environment and the right culture for that team to flourish.

My role is to try and create that right environment and create some direction and make sure all the parts are moving in the right direction and in the right harmonious way. You need to have a good team and good people to make the business successful. And they must trust you as a leader to do the right thing.

#

## Katie - Head of HR Centre of Expertise, Telecommunications

### On the first time you remember being trusted...

It was something really simple. I started off working as a graduate for a professional service consultancy firm in the organisational development space. One of the things I did a lot of was psychometric testing, so I'd do psychometric tests, but of course as a graduate you are administering the tests rather than playing back any feedback. So you would administer the test, and then you would go to the next level which is interpreting the tests, and the next level which is giving feedback. And I remember one of the partners of the business said to me, I'm doing a feedback session with a CEO candidate, you've administered the tests, you've interpreted the tests, I want you to come and do the feedback session.

I would have been 22 at the time I think. So it was something really simple but the sense of confidence and validation that that gave me was quite remarkable in terms of "wow, he thinks I'm good enough, he thinks I'm ok to do this", so I remember going into the room, and to be fair I did a really bad job, but it was an incredible confidence boost and that was feedback, that was that sense of "hey, he thinks I'm good". Which was fantastic, it's a really simple example but remarkably vivid.

## On how that has influenced your leadership style and your career…

One of the things that I do with my guys is that I do stretch and challenge them. It was interesting, at the time I felt young. I didn't feel supersonic. I was like, this is really serious, so I did feel like there was a major differential between what I thought I could do and what I was being asked to do.

And the lesson that it's taught me, often interestingly, particularly working with women - and I know I'm generalizing - but in my experience, people can do much more than they think that they can do. And I say particularly with woman, because I think women on average, are socialized to have less advocacy than men I think, but people can do more than they think they can do. So what I find is that you kind of lend people your confidence, you kind of go, "I know you can do it", and then they stand up and go, "well if she thinks I can do it, then maybe I can!". And then they do it and then they go, "oh, she was right, I could do it!", and then they go on from there.

## On supporting someone during stretch assignments…

I think the foundation of leadership is trust and I'm not

saying that because you and I are having this conversation, I do think that is the core. And trust is built through a strong relationship, and time in that relationship I believe, and consistency. So you are always the same person and so on and so on.

So when you have trusting relationships, you create a sense of security and safety, and from that platform of security and safety, people will go further and travel higher than they ever thought that they could before. But you must have that sense of safety which I think is generated out of a strong sense of "you believe in me, you're on my side and so as a result, I will go with you, I trust that you're going somewhere that I want to go".

It's very interesting that when I talk to my guys and say, "hey, help me be the best leader I can be for you, what do you need? What do you want me to do more of, less of" etc., the most powerfully positive piece of feedback that I get from people is two things. One is "I find you inspiring", which is what I go after as a leader. I'd like to be an inspirational leader, but the second piece that they find is sort of the apex of positive feedback is that "you've got my back Katie. You've always got my back", which is something that I wouldn't articulate as being what great leadership is about.

When I think about what that means, it's trust. You're on my side, you're with me. I know that you have my best interests at heart, whether you're pushing me hard, or asking me not to get involved in something, I know that it's about me and my wellbeing and my career and my achievement and my successes, rather than your successes.

Clearly I'm looking for a win/win on an ongoing basis, and the team also knows that, so I will always put the business first. But there are plenty of times – in fact most times - you can find a win/win scenario. When people know that you've got their back, which is the language that they have used with me, and people know that maybe I don't trust myself to do this, but you do, and you wouldn't let me fail, you will put supports around me, then people do amazing things that surprise themselves. And to be completely frank often surprise me!

Often, I'm going "you've got this". I'm not sure that they necessarily have got it, but I'm always going to be there to help them. The other trick I use is a really strong safety net. Someone on my team was reflecting on the year and said, "there have been moments of panic in the year because it's felt really stretchy and challenging, but I know that you're there if I need you and I know that you won't let me fail". And that's true. I won't let them fail dramatically. I will let them fail in a different way. You learn a lot from failure, you learn from success but you learn a lot from failing, so failing is fine. What I won't let people do is limit their careers, so I won't let people go to a place where they say, "actually that was such a disaster…" Failing fast is fantastic, fail fast, learn, move on. Fail fast, learn, move on.

### On the insights from that experience…

What I try with my guys is challenge and support. So going, "hey I'm going to really push you forward", otherwise, why are we here right? People want to be great; they want to do really well, they want to be seen to be doing really well, and they want to grow and develop. It's one of those fundamental philosophies that I have.

Spending time with teams that I've worked with over the years, I think that holds true for most. Now I work in HR.

people want to be great, better than they were yesterday, so our job is to go, "let me create you a safe environment in which to play and experiment and to better than you were yesterday". And you know that's the gig of the leader, right? How do I help you be better than you were when I first started working with you?

## On building - or rebuilding - trust...

I was consulting in Europe, working with client in a global entity engagement and I went to work inside the European cluster - the European region. It was headquartered in Switzerland, so reasonably laissez faire model; it wasn't a UK or US type model of command and control.

We, the consultancy, had broken our trust with the leadership team of Europe. We had done some things which made the European cluster, particularly the CEO of Europe decide that we weren't on his side. That we were working on behalf of 'Group', which was true. We were working for 'Group'. We were trying to put into place a different business model globally. I turned up and he was really cynical, really like, "who are you?" And I was the only consultant in the region because they had shipped out all the other consultants back, so I went in and it was very much, "Why are you here? What are you doing? What's your agenda?" and so on.

Because of my role, I was the only consultant in there, and my stream of work was the change management stream of work, it was the people stuff. You can't do anything if you don't have the people on board right? It wasn't like I could rock in and go, "let me show you my competence", because I'm putting in an IT system, it was, "how do I build

313

a relationship with you through talking, and showing my competence through what I'm doing, through a reasonably ephemeral kind of a project?" That took a lot of patience, a lot of time, a lot of really simple messaging.

## On the key steps to restoring trust in that situation…

I didn't go to the CEO; I went to his direct reports. There was one person in particular who I knew was a key influencer. I spent a lot of time with him, understanding who he was, what he wanted, what success looked like for him. Finding a way to help them be successful and trying to add value in that way. What I didn't do was any selling. I took up his agenda, the regional agenda, and started to drive that work. I demonstrated competence, demonstrated, "I am with you. I have your interest. We are on the same team ultimately". And then very gradually began to introduce the broader agenda that we were going after. Eventually we managed to get a team back in there and the engagement was back on track, but that took six to nine months of being fully embedded in that team, rebuilding relationships. It takes a long time.

## On the point where you realized you'd regained trust…

There were three key behaviour changes. One was an increase in staff disclosure and vulnerability. If I'm on the change side, I'm on the people side, which means trust in that environment looks like, "let me tell you my worries, let me tell you what keeps me awake at night. Let's talk about that individual over there. You know what, I'm not feeling like I'm doing a brilliant job". So self-disclosure and being prepared to be vulnerable is one indication of trust in my world.

The second piece was being invited to meetings. "Hey, you

should come to this, why don't you come into this conversation." Again, being let into the inner circle. Which is the same thing, but it's self-disclosure on a collective level, rather than individual level.

And the last one, was being asked for advice and opinion. "What do you think? We are thinking about this, and this, what are your thoughts? " Being invited to the table was the other indication that you are on the team.

## Your insights from that experience...

In my world, a big part of what I do is influencing at senior levels - the people who have the real decision making. I am that person in HR, but of course HR touches every function. So a lot of the time I'm influencing decision makers to do something that I want them to do. It's like any function in a corporate, we all have to influence each other to get stuff done because we all need the top table to be in alignment, otherwise nothing is going to work.

And so, those lessons are lessons that I use now to build those relationships with my directors to influence them, and my CEO. It's about how do you get a sense of, "I'm your friend, I know you, I believe that you're doing some great stuff". All of the work that I did way back then, was probably over 10 years ago now. But those techniques, getting alongside what's important to you and how do I help you achieve your own agenda, and then only when I've done that, and we are on the same team and you see me as being one of your guys, then we start talking about how else I can help you, which is me bringing in the things that I think can help them. It is all about people understanding, or believing, that your motivations are the right motivations and additive to them, and additive to the business.

The other technique I use a lot is feedback. Both positive feedback and constructive feedback. Of the two, the one that creates the most trust is constructive feedback.

Let me give you a story… Many years ago, I had just moved to London, and I was working for the consultancy that I mentioned earlier. When you turned up to the consultancy, you did like a week of orientation in Paris. It was very glamourous for a New Zealander. I was like WOW. They said, "one of the themes of what we do around here is a lot of feedback". I said, "I can do that".

The following week, I went out on a client engagement in London to do a brief with one of the senior partners with the firm. We got back in the black cab driving back towards the office and he turned to me and said, "how do you think that went?" And I remember my stomach hit the floor and I thought I might actually vomit. That sense of, we are really doing this, this really happens all the time! It was evident that he was looking for my own self-assessment. So I had to give him feedback and there was like five layers between the two of us; he was a really senior guy. I had to say what should I have done better, what should I have done differently. And then of course he gave me feedback. That happened all the time, so every time you did something, ok cool, feedback, what have you got for me, what have I got for you. You got really used to it. It created an incredible sense of safety. Because you knew exactly where you were. There were no surprises, there were no secrets, there was no sense of "I think I'm doing ok, but I'm not entirely sure" I knew exactly what people thought about me because they told me all the time. It's a fast way to create trust.

## On how long it took to actively invite feedback...

It would have been months rather than weeks. Even now, I am a zealot for feedback. All my team know it. They get feedback all the time and I ask them for feedback all the time, because I do really believe in the power of feedback to support performance and create a sense of relationship and trust. So I do it a lot, and even now when I'm thinking, I need to give you come clear and constructive feedback, I still feel it's scary for me to give this to you.

## On a significant break in trust...

This is an example that has played out a number of times, it's quite common. I was working with an individual on a companywide transformation project; he was leading the project and I was his second in command. He was the figurehead, and I was going to work with him on the people side. We had streams working, it was a really big project, we were working really closely and spending a lot of time working together.

We were doing a lot of work together and I thought we were doing some really great work together; then he took the work we had been doing and represented it as his own work to the CEO. I had no time for that at all. I would never do that to any of my peers, let alone my team. I just find that completely unacceptable. I say that as an example, it doesn't happen a lot, but it's happened a number of times, particularly in a corporate environment. That was one of those times were your self-interest supersedes even the business interest, because I'm not going to work with you, to give more than I need to. I'm not going to go out of my way, I'm not going to help you be successful, if your self-interest overrides even what the business requires and the business requires us to work together. It broke the relationship reasonably successfully.

He had a very short-term view. It's a pattern that he has. He's been given a lot of coaching feedback around that, but has never learnt the lesson. But you start wondering what else he's saying that I don't know about. I fundamentally don't believe that we are on the same side anymore. The whole project became tainted. It went from being a really fun piece of work to a drag. What was interesting was it was one piece of behaviour. He did it once and I went, "you are gone". Which is interesting because I work on a really high trust model.

## On why the breach of trust felt so significant...

It cut across my values. I think what it was, was that his actions told me he cared more about himself than he did the team. More about himself than he did about the enterprise and the outcome. He would have known he was not going to get the best out of me or the team by stealing work or credit. So he put his own self-interest ahead of what I think is really important, which is the business outcome, the team environment and your individual team members and helping them to be great. He would have no idea that I still even remember that conversation because the people agenda in our business is to have a very cordial, very warm relationship. I think if you asked him whether he and I are friends, he'd say "yes".

## On the insights from that experience...

I don't think you earn trust. It's fragile. It can be destroyed pretty straightforwardly. I don't think you earn trust; my sense is that you give trust. You trust people and then people will trust you back; people will repay the trust. I don't believe you've got to earn my trust. I think you are gifted trust and then you have to husband and harbour that trust because it can be fragile. Particularly when you are going against the tribe. If your self-interest kicks out against the tribe, then you really are in trouble. Particularly as a leader. Because leadership is all about having the tribes' interest at heart. That's why you get the corner office, that's why we bring you a cupcake. That's why we buy you a coffee. That's why we help you have a happier life because you're in charge and you need to have the teams/organisations interests at heart, and if you show that you don't, and that it's all about you, then it really is all over for you as a leader of a team.

## On being trusted to take a leap of faith…

I joined this organisation a number of years ago but I joined as a specialist. I was always really a consultant before I joined. My specialisms were change management, and then the organisational development side of HR. Specialist HR, not generalist HR.

I realized after having some conversations with the person that was my HR Director at the time, if you want to be an HR Director then you have to obviously have generalist HR. I was Acting of Head of Organisational Development, so acting as the most senior member of the specialist functions. Then I went away on maternity leave and I had my second child. Coming back from maternity leave, you lose your confidence, and a common experience I've found with other women who work here, is that you get a sense of "can I really do this? Can I pick back up into it? Am I a different person?", and you have all the different tensions around, "this better be really good cause I'm not with my kid".

I was about to go back to work and my HR Director rang me and said, "I've got a new job for you, I want you to be the HR business partner". Which is one of the most senior roles on the generalist side. I was like, "that's interesting. I have no skills in that area", unless I'm in there and we are doing a piece of organisational development or transformation work, in which case I'm fine. But no, at least 50% of the gig I don't know. When you are a HR business partner, you are in the business, so you can't not know answers to questions. You are very exposed.

He said "you need it for your career Katie, you need HR business partner if you want to be HR Director. I'm prepared to take a punt on you". I said, "you know I don't know how to do that", he said, "I know but I think you can do it, you'll be fine". So I came back to work now with two children, one that was two, and one that was seven months old. He got me when he said, "this is fantastic for you, this is the best career move that you can do, I'm doing this deliberately, off you go". What was interesting is that he didn't put any supports around me. He didn't put mechanisms around me, but it was enough that he was like, "I absolutely know this is the right thing for you and I know you can do it". And of course I did it.

It's a little bit like what I do with my guys. I really respect him, he is a really good judge of character, so if he thinks I can do it, I probably can. It's that idea of gifting confidence to somebody. He lent me his confidence. What was interesting, in a weird way was that the lack of supports meant he really does think I've got this. Part of it was because I knew that I could go back and ask his advice if I needed to, but interestingly, I never did. What I did do was I leaned heavily on the team. I'd go and talk to a director and I'd fudge my answer. Or I'd say, "let me have more of a think about it" and I'd sprint back to HR and go "ok, quick what's the answer?". I tell people that story now a lot when they say, "I want to do this, but I'm not sure I'm ready for it".

For six months I was dangerous, literally dangerous, but nothing broke and at the end of six months, it was cool. Which is one of the reasons having had that experience, I push my team a lot harder. I push them out of their comfort zone because that was one of the best six months of my life. I was on an exponential learning path and I use those skills today. Those skills are critical to my portfolio of skills. While I like to think I would have accepted the opportunity, I didn't seek it, I didn't ask for it, I was gifted it. It was a real vote of confidence. That's happened to me a number of times in my career.

By the end of the six months, there was a palpable sense of increased self-efficacy in general, a sense of, actually, you are better than you think you are. A greater sense of confidence, and clearly by sheer force of necessity, a much higher sense of competence, because I had to learn really, really fast and I did learn really, really fast.

I knew that it was my big opportunity to further my career, and I did jump in with both feet because I had to. I was only able to do it, because I trusted his confidence and his judgement. It wouldn't have worked otherwise.

## On the conversation's leaders need to start having to build cultures of trust…

In our organisation, there are three behaviours that we

believe mediate success; speed, simplicity and trust. So trust is at the core of what we believe is required for success, and yet, of those three, trust is the one that's hardest to go after. Because it's in the relationship, it's in the interaction between you and me as team member, between me and somebody in a different function, between me and people up and below me.

What breaks trust, is a lack of congruence between what I say and what I do. A lack of reliability. A focus on "actually, I need to be successful, therefore my self-interest takes over from everybody else". Ultimately a lack of attention spent on building the relationship, and building the foundation of trust, which is generally trying to understand each other. "Hey who are you and what do you need?"

The other component from an organisational perspective, is that organisations become functionally siloed, because we set each other up in competition by having mutually exclusive key performance indicators. So everybody unsurprisingly is coming at it from a different angle. We are driven as an organisation by metrics. We are motivated to be successful, therefore I will push as hard as I can to deliver on my metric, it doesn't matter if that guy there is doing something completely different. That creates a lot of problems from a business outcomes perspective. There are times when that tension is creative, and there are times when that tension is destructive. Those key performance indicators generate very different perspectives, and those different perspectives create tension, gridlock and lack of pace, speed and creativity.

We know as an organisation globally that trust is one of the foundation stones of great business performance and yet we don't pay enough attention to it. We don't talk about how to generate it; we don't talk about things that potentially stop trust. We don't, to be really frank, know how to generate more trust in this organisation at an organisational level. We don't know how to do it. We know how to pick things up, we know how to make things faster, we know how to simplify. Its basic stuff right, simplifying is about process management; speeding up is about removing complexity. It's mechanistic, it's relatively easy, it's structural. Trust is ephemeral, it's emotional, it's fragile, it's delicate. It's very hard to get it into an organisations culture when it's not there. Part of it is that sense of, 'who's your tribe?' In this organisation our tribe is your function.

## On how trust or its absence influences an organisation…

A number of things happen when trust exists. Decisions get made faster and they are not second guessed, they get made faster and they stick. You don't rework or re-litigate.

Things are simpler because you are not legislating for the exception, you are not going, "actually we are going to do this, but I don't trust our customers to do it right, or I don't trust my people to get it right". So I'm going to add all these complexities, whether it's legal terms and conditions, or whether is something else, or whether it's controlled across products or services etc., because we don't trust people to do the right things or the thing that we want them to do. We over complicate, and we over legislate, and we over control, in which case we reduce flexibility and I think customer experience.

I think it reduces the cohesion and collaboration and therefore the effectiveness of the team. So ultimately, I think it does drive business outcomes. I think it drives speed and I think it drives simplicity. I think without it you really are in real difficulty.

#

## Ralph - Leadership & Coaching Consultant / Programme Director Tertiary Education

### On the first time you were trusted...

I was at the School of Management as a Lecturer running a five-day leadership course which I'd designed, and it was going really badly. The participants on the end of the first day complained to my boss that it was too simple and instead of coming down on me, he simply said "OK, don't worry - I'll work with you and you'll be able to turn it around". And it was a question of him working with me, so I didn't do it just by myself.

At the end of the week, the participants all said, "best course we've ever been on, amazing!" and that was because he knew exactly what buttons to press. But he knew that if I could work with him and have that experience then I could run programmes like that in the future very well.

It boosted my confidence and self-esteem.

He didn't quite say, and I think this is quite important, he implied that you almost needed to cause a crisis; then if people trusted you and you dealt with that crisis really well, like on the programme, their appreciation was much greater than if it had run smoothly all the way through.

### On the insights gained from that experience...

First of all, the fact that there was no question about him blaming me. I think the most important thing was that I felt he trusted my intention, my willingness. He also trusted that underneath that, was a set of skills. All that was needed was simply more experience. It was his attitude towards me; which was really positive and trusting, and having the patience. In trust, patience is very important. Not passivity, but a receptiveness, an openness to other people's views. That enables them to start trusting you.

### On the ways in which that influenced your career…

The willingness to be receptive and open to where the group are; and not to panic if things are going wrong, but to allow it. Trusting the process. It's a clichéd phrase, but it's a very true phrase - if you're doing that then you can trust the process.

He was such a good role model in terms of that - he was very calm and I've learned from that.

### On building - or rebuilding - trust…

A client I was working with; I thought we had a friendly relationship and I was making jokes that weren't particularly funny jokes, but they weren't exactly negative, about what was happening with the participants. I was coming from the basis that they trusted me and that they knew it was only banter. But they didn't, and they got very upset about it and said, "you're not being very professional' and 'do you actually know what you're doing?"; things like that which really surprised me.

So I stopped all the joking, I just focused on being professional and stopped having a friendly relationship with them. I just said "OK, I know exactly what I'm going to do" and it worked. From a professional point of view, the trust was rebuilt because they saw that I was competent. I was demonstrating competency the whole time, but they didn't like - and I have some sympathy with them - the friendliness of the interaction.

## On the insights gained from that experience...

I have to be very careful about boundaries and understanding; being very clear that there is a basis of trust, and that trust has got to be about the competency first of all. Because I had assumed that they had trusted my intention as well, and that the competency was taken for granted. I think since, what I've learned to do is be very cautious about the leeway's that I have to interact with clients. Some clients when you do build up that relationship and you can joke about what's happening that's great, but sometimes it goes badly wrong. And surprisingly sometimes.

Another example - we had someone pull out of a course I was running, so I said to my client "I'll fill this space", and he went "what do you mean 'fill the space'? You're not taking it seriously. Don't you realize it's an integrated part of the programme?" And this is a guy who had made lots of jokes about the programme before. I explained that my phrase 'fill the space' did not indicate anything at all, except that, for me, running a programme is about how everything fits together, and that I was taking it extremely seriously.

He calmed down and was fine once I'd explained everything. I thought - it's the same thing, I'm coming from a basis of demonstrating competence and my intentions are 100% to do the best job I can. I also understand their side. And I think it's a misjudgment from my side and I think it's important for trust - if people are nervous, and that nervousness detracts from their trust in you then you have to be very careful.

## On breaches of trust...

I was trusting this person to do the best possible job that they could for a client and they were extremely lazy which I hadn't realized. They decided because they weren't feeling particularly energetic, they would show the clients a film. So all my respect and trust (and the two go together I think) just went out the window, and since then I haven't worked with that person again and I just don't trust them.

## On the insights gained from that experience...

Reminding myself that there are people out there who don't necessarily want to do a great job; who are there for themselves. That's almost disheartening, because most of the people I work with, and meet, almost by definition are ones that want to do a good job. So it's quite disorienting when you meet people in my line of work who aren't really up to it.

I remember one client who asked me to do a proposal for them and I spent two days in good faith and they said "oh sorry, that hasn't worked", and three months later they asked me for another proposal and I said "OK, but only if there's …", to which they said "oh yes, there will be, you're not doing it for free, I'll make certain". And again, all the work I did for free was totally disregarded. So it becomes a question of your own self-image and thinking "how could I be fooled by that?"

## On what leaders will look back on in five years and realize was unintentionally limiting trust...

I think it's about behaviours. For me, I think the key issue is that leaders come out with wonderful clichéd phrases and then they do nothing about it - they don't follow through. And that to me is the most important thing.

## On the conversation's leaders need to have now to build cultures of trust...

They need to be realistic and to only talk about things they can deliver. I heard a guy years ago talking about the round the world yacht race he was doing and going around Cape Horn with an amateur crew. One of the captains said, "it will be absolute hell, we will survive it, but we will need to pull together" and because that captain was telling the truth, and he spelt it out as it was, they got through and no one was lost. You just need trust, not clichés.

Another example was a captain trying to be positive and engaging, who said to his crew "don't worry, it'll be fine, it's rough, but we'll manage" and of course, it's incredibly difficult. And when they got through, not having expected all the hassle, one of the crew members went berserk and tried to kill the captain, which was extreme.

But what that sums up is that leaders are not telling the truth. Not because - like the captain - they're deliberately lying or trying to feather their own nest, but because they don't trust their people. They think if they tell them the truth they'll be removed, or bad things will happen, or people won't go with them. For me, the really great leaders are the ones who tell the truth, even when it's painful, but then have enough integrity so that they trust the people and then the people will follow them because they trust them.

So it's all about honesty and integrity and I don't see much of that around.

## On how trust - and mistrust - shapes an organisation...

It shapes the organisation in a really bad way when there's

a lack of trust because people watch their own backs. When there is trust, no blame cultures, trust everyone is wanting to do their best. It's fine from a theoretical point of view, but from a practical point of view, it hardly ever happens. I think there is so much pressure on performance and media interest and social media, there is so much 'criticalness' in the public as a whole that it's really difficult to be open and honest.

When you have trust, it's like a beautiful garden. When you don't have trust it's like a withered vegetable patch. For me, the trust is the warmth and the gentle rain - not thunderstorms - encouraging growth.

#

## Silao - CEO Healthcare

**On the first time you remember being trusted...**

I still remember being young around 5 or 7 in Samoa and Dad saying, "I'm so glad we can leave anything lying around and you don't take it son". It was all about money. In Samoa, the value of money is quite high. They used to leave change lying around and I never took a cent. I didn't think about it, it was just a natural thing, so I remember when he said it, thinking 'wow, I wonder why he said that'.

My background is rugby too. So, at that time, it was being given the responsibility to be the captain of a team. It wasn't a thing where I thought 'if I do this and this and this, they'll make me captain". It was just natural. I used to turn up to training early and get the drink bottles, the rugby balls and then after training, I used to help bring things in. My culture – being Samoan – you help out. It was natural for me to help; I liked it.

## On how those natural predispositions have shaped your role as leader...

I'm on this journey not just because of my professional life but because of my personal life. It's about principles.

## On building - or building - trust...

When things go wrong, people tend to run and hide and no matter what you do. When there is information missing, people fill that in with their own information and assumptions. I knew there was going to be trust issues with the changes we made because the organisation had been around for 18 years and the last five or maybe 10 years, there was already mistrust brewing. So I came on board and one of the biggest things I did was to be very up front with people.

I sat down with the Board and our Senior Management Team and I said "this is the harsh reality of what's happening at the moment" and I would say "you guys know this stuff, because you've been here a lot longer than me" And because they're so used to it, some of them picked it up and some of them didn't. I used examples and started asking questions. I was honest that the reality was we needed to change. That we couldn't keep looking at the reports and not responding to them.

The issue I was having was that if this was how they were behaving in the business, I would hate to see how they're behaving in homes when they go and visit people. They're supposed to be helping people, and that was my issue – if they're doing this in front of their managers and their peers, imagine what they're doing when no one's around.

We started with some hard facts and being honest. I wasn't vulnerable during that time because I needed to wear my

Manager's hat – the black and white stuff needed to happen. I was in my first week in the role but I'd been with the organisation for two years so I knew what the problems were. In my first week I said, this is the harsh reality of what's happening currently and I can't sit here and see this happening on my watch. What do you think we should do?' They'd been in the roles for so long – it took two meetings. But they were involved right from the start.

Last year I did a presentation to all the staff, and rather than talking about goals and the strategic plan I started talking about patients.

I talked about how my parents come here and that what they value most is the relationship of trust with the doctors. What they value has nothing to do with medication or compliance – it has to do with conversation. We have to ensure that our relationships with our families, and our clients, is meaningful. Don't see them as diabetic patients, don't see them as mental health patients, see them for them, and get to hear their stories. I came from that side and I started telling my own personal story. I wanted them to see that I'm here for the same reasons they are.

Every quarter we close the clinic and have a team huddle. We share a meal and have 'fun awards'. Every week I have a team talk email that goes out. And of that all stems from 'the South Seas way'. Our way is these kinds of principals, and you have to live by them. We've come a long way.

## On how that has changed the workplace...

People are coming to work on time. The communication amongst staff is better, you hear laughter, you hear people talking. We now have a social club committee. We have a music committee. People feel free to speak. The way they communicate – there's more thought going into it. People are keeping each other accountable. I'm getting letters and emails from patients at least once a week, thanking people. I take a photo of it and send it out to the rest of the staff.

The biggest thing I've seen is the staff that have been here a while have stepped up. They've never had the opportunity to say or do what they want. There are so many people stepping up and suggesting new things.

One of the biggest things I've seen is that whatever is happening in here is obviously filtering out to when they go out to work. Now we're getting funders wanting to come and see what we do.

### On the proudest moments as a CEO...

Probably the staff taking ownership of stuff; seeing emails from staff suggesting things, seeing team leaders stepping up and doing things. People noticing that there are people who have been here for years who've never come out of their shell until now.

We are a pacific organisation – you look at my age, I'm a 37-year-old Chief Executive. We still see people quite reserved and waiting for someone to ask their advice. One of the things we've done to get people involved, is to bring in the personal and the professional side. We celebrate the cultures and languages.

It's not about me saying everything and sending it down. That goes against what I believe as a Chief Executive, but getting other people who believe in the message to share it because they know how to articulate it to their peers.

It starts with small things. People will make a suggestion and I'll say, "that's a great idea, what's stopping us?" You've got to reinforce that. I always put it to them "have we done it before? And if not, why not?" I always ask them questions so they can think about how things have changed now and to see them take ownership and come out of their shell.

## On what leaders will look back on in five years and realize was unintentionally limiting trust...

Not having time to sit down with people face to face and have good discussions about what they're feeling. Sitting down and asking people "what are you feeling at the moment? What do you see happening? Tell me what you know about what you're doing. Tell me what you think the organisation is for. What did you sign up for? How important do you think your role is?"

Rather than focusing on us as an organisation and our aspirations and our goals, I've reframed it to be about families and patients and then using the personal stories to frame that. Because after all, these people come to work because they're passionate about making changes but somehow that passion and that empathy has been put aside for all the other stuff. But it's easier said than done because us managers don't like doing face to face when it comes to having hard conversations.

## On how trust - or distrust - shapes an organisation...

There's two things. It's a short game and I mean that we could have gone through and done nothing and just lived year by year. That would have been the short game. We were still getting our targets but the quality wasn't there. To me the outcome of this is a lot more than just our staff and ourselves and that short-term thing. People are starting to realize the bigger picture - that it's not about being a team leader or a social worker or a doctor. There is a bigger part to this. Our role in society is that we have people here who need the appropriate help, so how do we galvanize ourselves to help?

The impact of this is that it's a whole movement. I think what we're doing here is going to impact the whole health system. I think what we're doing here is long term and I can see the future for the organisation and the community that we serve.

We value relationships. And the relationships we have internally with our staff should mirror how they work in communities.

#

## Anon - (Disruptive) Recruitment Start Up Co-Founder

### On a significant break in trust...

I think most people have 'red flag' moments when something switches. For me one of these moments was when I realized my manager and I had misaligned values - I absolutely appreciate that people are individuals - but values are really important. For me this was when I realized that it was OK not to bring my whole self- heart and head- to work. Part of me disconnected and though I still worked just as hard, I think it's fair to say that my loyalty was never the same.

### On being trusted to take a leap of faith...

When we were talking about starting the business, it was a massive leap of faith - a big investment of not only money but also our time and it was a big risk. It was a new idea to market and very hard to implement. When my business partner put her trust in me to do this with me, it gave me the confidence to take that leap of faith. With this partnership of trust I've given everything I can to building our business and to driving towards change.

## On what leaders will look back on in five years and realize was unintentionally limiting trust...

Leadership today will look very different in the future. The transition from 'command and control' to leading through influence will help organisations to empower their people and thereby to realize more innovation, creativity and business potential.

One of the things limiting trust today is measuring the value someone brings to an organisation by the time they are there - or what they can see being done. Bringing an employee in to an organisation should be a mark of faith that that person can make strong contributions and that you trust them to do the job. If managers then start measuring inputs rather than outputs, the trust is obviously not there.

## On the conversation's leaders need to begin having today to create a culture of trust...

When it comes to their human capital - the humans they need to build their business, they need to begin thinking about what strategic capabilities they'll need into the future - then to entrust the role objectives with that individual. As work structures, practices and employee preferences shift to more flexibility, if a culture of trust and focus on outputs is not there, leaders will lose in the war for talent.

## On how trust - and distrust - shapes or impacts an organisation...

If trust is assumed from the beginning, and reflected in the work practices, structures and conversations which take place - employees rise to the occasion. These organisations will see the best work being done, higher discretionary effort, retention and talent attraction. Ultimately this will determine an organisation's long term success. Alternatively, if organisations take a top-down command and control model of distrust, they will fall behind and I'd say, fall into obsolescence.

#

## Wendy - Snr Managing Consultant, Consulting

### On the first time you remember being trusted...

I was the student representative on a committee of parents and teachers. The committee encouraged me to hold the Secretary role, effectively empowering me to 'have a go' in a safe environment. They trusted me to organize meetings and write many letters to arrange funding, transport, accommodation and a schedule of performances for over 50 student musicians to tour New Zealand for two weeks each year.

Looking back on this opportunity, I recognize that the committee invested their trust in me, notably giving me a long leash and forming an invisible safety net (should I have needed it). This inspires me to find ways to create safe environments for unlocking growth in others in the workplace today.

## On building trust...

Working in a client advisory role, establishing clients' trust in me and organization I represent are critical success factors. Getting started with a new (or potential) client requires a specific mindset from the outset to earn their trust. I deliberately say 'earn' – on basis it's a form of recognition for compounding behaviours and outcomes.

My best tool for building trust with new clients is my prior experience – both in terms of proven ways I've unlocked trust and knowledge I've accumulated. I especially work hard to create plenty of transparency - explaining what will happen, informing them what is happening, updating what has happened etc. – because transparency and trust go hand in hand. A key signal I look for when gauging whether trust is building usually occurs when balance tips from mostly demands (i.e., 'we must (or must not) have abc') to mostly questions (i.e., about how I've seen something work well, or inviting my advice to navigate a challenge or avoid a risk, etc.). I take this as evidence that they trust in my experience and capabilities.

## On breaches of trust...

These situations weigh my mind (and probably my actions) down and make it harder to do my best for a period of time afterwards. My nature is non-confrontational so my default position is self-sufficiency, ultimately working around the difficult individual where I can. For a period of time after, I find myself being suspicious of their motives and honesty in every single interaction, by weighing-up and second-guessing whether I can trust the exchange; whether I can reasonably expect an agreement to be honoured; whether I am risk of being compromised, and so on. Simply put, it's toxic.

## On being trusted to take a leap of faith...

Being a recognized subject matter expert in my organization means I am often approached colleagues needing help and advice for client situations. These can be tricky or troubled situations they are struggling to address, hence there can be an undertone of vulnerability or desperation to our interaction. Commonly they have been referred to me by a senior person in our organization with the sentiment that I will have a magic bullet for them. Detecting this belief in my capabilities really motivates me to try hard to find a way to move the situation forward and leave it in a better place, even if it would seem an imperfect outcome in context of a textbook situation. Being a trusted advisor in tricky or troubled circumstances is unquestionably empowering, brings me a sense of Self-importance and fresh sense of confidence.

## On what leaders will look back on in five years and realize was unintentionally limiting trust...

Leaders are likely to look back on limiting attitudes and actions related to transparency, be that towards customers, partnerships or employees. Organizations need to move away from thinking that having information is power and realizing that power comes from what you do with knowledge. Emerging technologies are fundamentally changing how we live, work and interact - this has reset customer and employee expectations and is disrupting industries and business models – and calls for greater levels of transparency.

Customers are craving transparency from the companies

they interact with – including provenance, product/service assurance, data security, and more. Employees are seeking more visibility of what matters, and what happens, through down to earth communications and evidence of consistency.

## On the conversation's leaders need to begin having today to create a culture of trust…

Cultures are ecosystems built on values and standards that can be characterized by traits and evidenced by behaviors i.e., a culture is much more than a label or instruction. Trust flourishes in an organization where 'doing the right thing when nobody is looking' becomes second nature to every employee from the top down to the bottom. To create this, leaders must lead by example - demonstrating the behaviours, providing environments that enable (not contradict) the behaviours, and telling stories that reinforce expectations.

## On how trust - and distrust - shapes or impacts an organisation…

Relationships are fundamental to doing business and trust is fundamental to building relationships, within and beyond an organization. Trust is a precious and volatile intangible asset that typically takes a long time to build but can be destroyed in a second. Within an organization, trust in leadership and staff is essential for getting the job done effectively. Beyond an organization, customers' and investors' trust is essential for business performance. New drivers of external trust in organisations are emerging, such as ability to securely handle data, posing significant implications for reputation and financial performance.

#

## Sam - CEO, Consumer Goods Retail

**On the first memorable instance of being trusted in your career...**

It wasn't my first job, but my first job where I lead people was to act as an Accountant looking after the gross profit of a large organisation but I knew I was trusted when I was given a team of people to lead who were older and more experienced than me. And I knew it wasn't about technical competence, it was about my ability to lead and manage people even though I was younger than them and less experienced.

**The strongest memories from that time...**

I remember being really concerned about being accepted. I remember being overwhelmed by the fact that I was going to have to lead people who knew more about what they were doing than what I knew. And I was concerned about how I'd develop a relationship with them that would be meaningful at one level but also one that was based on mutual respect and some recognition of my authority over them. I remember as well, one of the women was a friend's wife and she was about my age and I remember thinking, how am I going to develop a relationship with her that honours my relationship with her husband but also recognizes the nature of our relationship at work and that was really tricky.

**On embracing the opportunity despite your concerns...**

I always knew that I was an accidental accountant and I was going to be ok at the job, but I knew, even before anyone told me what leadership entailed or what management entailed, that that was where my strengths would be. I always felt like I would be a leader of teams and a leader of people. And part of the reason I felt that was because a lot of the people that impressed me and a lot of the reading that I did that prepared me for work and the challenges I faced, had nothing to do with my job, they had to do with people like Martin Luther King and Malcolm X and Marcus Garvey and all of those guys who had to mobilize people around an idea without having any specific authority over them. So I really loved the idea that you could do that and enhance people's lives through that. So I knew that I was OK technically but I wasn't a math's whizz. I had it as a safety net because I didn't know any poor accountants. But I didn't want to become a super accountant; I wanted to become a leader and a manager. So I embraced it because I knew that I had to get my head around how I did this if I was going to have the sort of career I thought I was going to be good at.

### On building or rebuilding trust on a team…

When I think about the last role I did, I came into the role without it having existed before, so everyone was nervous about what it meant for them, but they were also quite questioning as to what I was going to add to the organisation. And because the role hadn't existed before, there wasn't a huge amount of clarity around what was expected of the CEO and then beyond that, I wasn't actually sure I could do the job anyway. So part of what I did was I just told people how I felt, and that was; I think there's a real opportunity here. I've loved the idea of being able to grow my career; I haven't done this role before and I'm going to learn on the job, but here are some of the things I'm concerned about and

I want you guys to help me be successful, because if I am, you will be.

If there were dimensions to the role that were new, I let the team know that I had no concerns about asking silly questions, because if they answered them for me, I wouldn't ask them again and I was pretty confident that I would be able to add to whatever they were doing, not by having the answer, but by asking good questions. I wanted to establish an environment where more than anything, I could create an environment where they could thrive and beyond that to drive their performance by asking better questions of them. So I went in and had that conversation with everyone.

The other thing I did quite quickly was I had one to one conversations with everyone I needed to and I say that because I didn't need to have one to one conversations with everyone in the organisation. But I made sure they knew I heard them and I acted on something they told me. People realized quite quickly that I'd ask you a question, listen to what you'd say and if it needed action, then action would follow. That was my approach.

### The point where you realized you'd built high trust with the team...

I'd see them starting to challenge me, I see them starting to share things with me that I couldn't possibly have known unless they'd chosen to share them with me. I see people starting to be vulnerable and I'd see people starting to engage with me out of choice and going out of their way to do it, rather than out of obligation. People would be informal in a way that said, "I know you're the boss, but you're also part of the team". And it was those things where they were sharing with me and choosing to be informal and going out of their way to engage with me. Those were some of the behavioural traits that helped me understand that things were coming together.

The other bit is when they started doing things that were discretionary effort. They would go beyond what the job is and what it takes to do a great job, into "I heard this advert at the weekend and it made me think about this – maybe we should add that to our programme of activity". That's when I thought, "now I can see it coming together".

## On the insights from that experience and how they shaped you as a leader...

I think you have to start off by people knowing that you care about them as people rather than as just an employee or a producer of work.

It was really clear to me that I had to be humble. I was a qualified accountant and I knew a lot of technical stuff that these guys didn't know but I didn't know how to do their job. I realized I had to be humble in making the transition and I had to do more listening and asking of questions than I did making statements and observations. I had to operate to a standard that was at least as high as the best in that group. So I had to set a benchmark. And whether that was about the way I communicated, or when I turned up, or the meeting of deadlines, I realized that I had to set a standard and that gave me some credibility with the team too.

The one thing that I try and do with people when I work with them is to help them understand my philosophy. I don't have a philosophy because it's a good idea; I genuinely believe that the people who do the work will tend to have the best ideas about how to improve that work. And my job as a leader is to ask the right quality of questions to get the best out of people in the team. What people start to realize quite quickly is that that can become uncomfortable quite quickly, because I try not to do a lot of telling. I'm going to be asking you what you think and that forces you to think. But I do start by genuinely believing that if there are improvements to be made, that the guys that do the work will have the best ideas. And I try to make sure that people understand my philosophy and then I try and live into that.

## On what leaders will look back on in five years and realize was unintentionally limiting trust...

I think it's not making time for people, not being accessible. I think if you're accessible and you don't listen is another one. I think not investing in people is a big one. You can't on the one hand say you're really important to me and never spend any money on training and development. Or never actively engage in coaching.

I think the other thing is asking too much of people. There's so much that can be done now with you having constant access to your team. And pushing too hard is one of the things that could really damage trust, because it's at odds with saying that you really care about a person.

The other thing though is asking too little and not allowing that person to realize their potential. I had a conversation with my CIO this morning – her number two is 68 years old and should have retired, but we can't let him because there's so much about our systems that only he can understand. But the point I made to her was that I've seen his attitude, I've seen his level of enjoyment in the job rise directly in proportion to the level of challenge we've given him. His starting point is always to go "my gosh, you guys are going too fast" but when he gets through it and delivers, I've seen his attitude change to one of someone who's going "I think I can take these challenges on". The risk is that you push too hard, but I think a lot of people want to be stretched and they want to see what's possible but they also want to do that at the same time as being given permission to fail. And that's a biggie.

### On what makes it hard to find that balance between stretching people, while giving them permission to fail…

It's just so hard to get right and it varies by person. And it can be the same person in different circumstances who's got the ability to live with what you consider to be appropriate stretch, or pace, or breadth in their role. It's a constant double checking and second-guessing of yourself that says "am I pushing hard enough for the organisation? And am I pushing too hard for the individual, or am I pushing too hard as far as the team are concerned?". And it's very, very difficult to know what that is and what that looks like, because it could be personal circumstances that mean that that person can't cope with anymore but two weeks ago, those personal circumstances weren't there and they would cruise through that stuff.

You have to be mindful of the individual and their needs as well as mindful of the organisation and its needs. As well as being aware of what your needs are. I have a need to demonstrate progress and I have a real need to be successful and I can be blind to the implications of other people because I'm so committed to the result. And that's difficult to get right. I value that in myself and at the same time as valuing it, I have to recognize that that could be the thing that tips other people over. So I have to be introspective, I have to be challenging of myself, or critical. That's uncomfortable a lot of the time along with everything else. I have to think about the team, I have to think about the members, I have to think about our context, I have to think about our environment, the competition and then amongst all that, I have to say "who am I being" at the same time.

### On regulating who you're being in the midst of competing demands…

I have to make time not to be busy doing something. Not to be busy reading, prepping, or in a meeting or on phone calls. And I have to force myself to replay interactions and to think about body language and facial expressions and tone of voice and say "actually, is that telling me something other than what I thought it was telling me?". If someone doesn't maintain eye contact when they're talking progress against a project, is it because they're struggling with a project? Or is it because there's so much going on that it's just something else they can't cope with?

What I try to do, is to play back conversations that I might have had and think "How did he stand? How did he respond? Was he flushed? Was she stuttering when she doesn't normally? Was she disorganized when normally, she's planned? Is that because I'm pushing too hard?" I then say, "OK, what part have I played in that?" And this is where trust plays a part – other people can tell me. They can say – you're pushing too hard, there's too much on.

I've got people here who I know, if they think I'm pushing too hard, being too single minded or too one dimensional, they'll say "hang on a second, I just want you to know this looks like that" and that's how I'll pick it up a lot of the time.

**On the conversation's leaders need to begin having today to create a culture of trust…**

I think organisations need to be having conversations about the complete lack of certainty and the fact that no one really knows. If you think about how much the iPhone has changed your world in 10 years – why do we kid ourselves that we know what the future looks like? We're actually better off thinking about who we want to be in the future and making sure that that is what we're preparing to be.

One of the things for me is admitting that we don't know and just being open about that. A lot of the time a lot of the stress that people feel is that, the uncertainty that they see, they think the bosses have got a plan and they're not part of it. Or they might be part of it if they do x, y and z. And I think one of the things we need to be is just a lot more open about the fact that we actually don't know, and we're doing our best to anticipate, but it's OK not to know. What we've got to be clear about, is who we want to be in that world.

The other thing I'd say is I'm really open about there not being any job security. There's no job security in the organisation. There's job security in what you bring, in your skills, your behaviours, your attitudes. Invest in yourself and make that your job security rather than attaching it to an organisation.

For me, those are two important conversations to have. The third one is – and it's good saying this, but it's not easy to do - I always say to people, "bring yourself to work". What does that mean? Just be who you are at work, at home. But I know from my point of view it's not always appropriate to bring all aspects of myself to work. I don't necessarily talk to my boss about how I feel, I talk to him about the work that needs to be done. But really, I would like to talk to him about how I feel and I would like to bring that part of me to the table as part of our conversation. So I try to talk to people about bringing themselves to work and that that's their good stuff, and their vulnerabilities. And let's talk about the whole person and how we can help that whole person move forward, rather than it just being an interaction between employer and employee.

The other thing I'd say is – it sounds silly – but it's OK not being perfect. I know your job requires you to do all of these things, you have to deliver on all of these spheres, but you might only be good at three out of four of them. And if that's the case, that's ok, because maybe we can fill that gap with someone in your team, or we might be able to work on it with you. Increasingly you want to have those conversations that say "it's OK not to be good at everything and don't try and hide that. Let's have a conversation about what that looks like and how we might address it".

### On how trust and distrust shapes an organisation...

The way I would capture it is this – that instead of it becoming the biggest enabler of performance and growth and delivery, it does exactly the opposite, it becomes the biggest single obstacle.

And it becomes really difficult to address, because the lack of trust is unarticulated, so it manifests itself in any number of issues. And each time you address an issue, all that's happening is that you're dealing with the symptoms, so you end up spending all of your energy on symptoms of underlying issues rather than addressing the underlying issue and using that as a catalyst for everything else.

But it's not just a catalyst – I think it's an accelerator. If I've got a good team and we've kind of got half trust then we'll move half as quickly as we could have done. But if I've got a good team and we've got full trust, we might move 4x as quickly as we would have done. It's that important.

So for me, when I think about it, I always think about how much energy you've got to expend in an organisation. A lack of trust means you expend a huge proportion of your energy on the wrong things - whatever they are. I ring you up and I ask you to do something, and in a high trust environment, you take me at my word. I'm asking you to do that because it's the most appropriate thing in the circumstances and you're the best person to do it. In a low trust environment, you go "what is there behind this, and is he asking me to do it because it's a test and he's comparing me to that person over there? And how is he going to appraise me? Or is it a distraction because he doesn't want me to work on something else?".

There are all of those things that people spend their energy on instead of going "great, I've been given an opportunity, how do I put my best thinking into really doing that brilliantly?" That's what a lack of trust does. It takes away all that focused effort. And it dissipates it amongst second-guessing and anxiety and stress and questioning that needn't be there.

\#

## Martin - Executive Director, Government

### On what trust in the workplace looks like…

Trust starts at recruitment. You have to trust everyone from day one and realize that they will make mistakes, but when they do it's ultimately my fault because I hired them. I take accountability for that mistake. The next question is, when they do make a mistake, I take the hit on it, but also – how can they learn from it and how can the rest of the group learn from it so they're not fearful of making a mistake the next time? You see people make one mistake and then they start to lose their confidence and drive and certainty and they fall to bits over a period of time. You can't blame people for how they execute your strategies if you haven't explained it well enough or if you haven't built the right team with the skill sets to deliver what you need them to deliver. As long as they're confident and they've got the right capabilities, they'll be successful.

That's where trust starts for me. And it's not something you earn, it's something you lose. People lose trust and lose confidence as they make mistakes. They lose trust in themselves and lose trust in their colleagues, my job is to make sure we hire the right people, trust them from day one and when they do make mistakes, I take the accountability for it as long as the other people are willing to learn. What we don't do is when people start blaming others, that's when we change our behaviour. If someone is blaming others, I won't take the accountability. Blame is about accountability. We have a team set of rules that we play to even if you honestly don't believe you're directly accountable for the mistake that's been made you need to hold some of the accountability because you would have had a role to play. I don't tolerate people blaming others, it's one behaviour I shut out very quickly in the team. I ask – "did you communicate properly? Did you articulate what you were looking for? Did you do all you can do?" We can all do things better, and as leaders we need to take accountability for every action that goes on in the team. We take the successes, so why shouldn't we take the failures as well?

## On recognizing the absence of trust...

Hierarchy is usually a control measure to manage distrust of people. Whereas, everyone should be able to have input to a decision, to challenge people on their thinking. When people aren't prepared to be challenged on what they're proposing, or what they're working on, again that's a sign of distrust in the organisation. We like to be challenged. We've got to trust each other that we can have a robust, spirited debate that's based around the problem we're trying to solve, it's not on a personal level.

If an individual has challenged you and your thinking has stood up, you know you've validated your thinking – congratulations. And if is hasn't, someone has just given you an area to grow or improve on. They've done you a favour. They've validated your solution, or they've helped you improve it. They're the observations I look for with trust – the layout, how people work together and how people conduct themselves with one another.

## On fostering trust...

You have to lead by example. I have the ability to probably influence three or four people well. Then I need to ensure the leadership expectations I'm putting on them cascades through the business. To make sure they trust people; observing their behaviours and how they manage their leadership teams. Then also you can verify it by doing skip meetings. I walk the floor and say "hey, what are you working on at the moment? you getting what you need? What are your bosses' challenges at the moment? What's your 90-day roadmap? When was the last time you had an opportunity to input on a product that you're not working on?" I think you have to trust, but verify.

My manager said to me "when you want to look at the culture of a group, look at the culture of the leader. When you have groups that don't collaborate, they don't share things – look at the leader and you'll see those things in them". I've found that to be true. You just have to build close knit relationships, give trust, over share information. That's the other part of a non-trust culture, when people hoard information as power. I don't tolerate people who hoard information as a way to stay relevant. People are often in an organisation, not because of the information, but how they view the information. You're here for what you are going to do, not what you have done. Create a single source of truth for the information, so it can be shared and handed on, then focus on the future.

The first few months people make that shift, they're nervous. But then as time goes on and they realize they're being put onto interesting projects, good opportunities and that we're investing in their development, making sure they've got relevant skills, it transforms them. We have people who were on performance improvement plans when we inherited them, who are now high performers, they're trusted 'go-to' people in the group who – if you need to know something, or when you need something done – will go away and get it done for you. It comes back to confidence. They've never had an opportunity to be confident or to project confidence.

**On building trust in an ambiguous, complex and challenging environment...**

Don't play politics, don't have any secrets. Talk about

everything you're doing, and if you're saying it – say it to everyone. Don't say it to one person and then no one else. The only way politics catches you out is when you're not being completely honest. If you're being completely honest with everyone, and open about what you're going to do, some people won't believe you're actually going to do it.

Then, with the complexity and bureaucracy and the politics, that's where speed comes in. I did a few years in the military, in a reconnaissance unit that worked heavily with the intelligence services. You have three things around reconnaissance: power, intelligence and speed. These are the power plays that go across everything.

Big groups want you to get dragged into a power play. If I try to compete with them on power (as a smaller group) I'm going to lose. So what I have to play across is intelligence – having an understanding of the situation around you, who the decision makers are, how to influence people and drive change. What you find is that people in power don't want to drive change anyway - in a way you can compete with those. Where you're going to win every time though, is with speed. What people are trying to do with power is slow you down. Because they know they can't compete with you on speed. So what you do is maintain momentum, by saying where you are going to be, saying how you're going to get there and through the incremental deliverables, that gives you your ticket to play, it validates that you're delivering what you'd planned to.

How you remove bureaucracy is through speed. Doing stuff is the best form of change.

**On sustaining the motivation to keep focused on leading with trust in the face of pressure and pace...**

Having very high standards. Leading by example. You've got to be able to demonstrate with people that you work with, that you're credible, that you can step in and deliver that work if you really need to. There is no expectation that I set that I wouldn't do myself. You've got to know that the date is the date, and if it can't be delivered on that date, others will, or I will come in and work with them on it.

You've got to create a sense of urgency. Urgency creates focus. It also reduces inter office politics; it reduces people playing games with one another – they don't have time for it. As soon as they lose that focus, things start to drop off.

For me, it's about making sure that there's a laser beam focus on everything that we're doing. Making sure we're not focusing on too much. That we're not focusing on more than four things as a group. And we focus all of our energy and efforts into those four things. And anyone who's trying to focus their energies outside of that are brought back in to 'these are the things we're focusing on'.

So, direction, role clarity and then accountability for delivering on those dates . It's got to be that way. It's the only way it works. It's about action. It's hard work.

#

## David - ex CEO, Government

**On the first time you remembered being trusted in your career and how it influenced your leadership style...**

Trust comes in different contexts. In my university days (1970's), I was trusted because the University environment just leaves you to teach and research and do your own thing. No one actually monitors your time, your behaviour. I was doing design work for real projects; I was doing all sorts of things that other people perhaps didn't do. I was just left to do it. No one challenged or queried me on it, so I was being trusted in terms of my academic and technical ability to deliver, but also in my ability to ask if I was at the edge of what I knew. I was asked to do a whole bunch of other things in that environment, secretary for the University Research Foundation, I was the faculty representative on the Faculty Board. So those sorts of things demonstrate an element of trust. When I left the university and got into private practice, then you are trusted all the time in terms of running a business and looking after clients' money, doing design work and so on.

I grew up in an environment where your word was your bond. So that's the element of trust that always came through. My mother always used to say, "You can watch a thief, but you can't watch a liar". In other words, you've got some control on people that steal things, you've got no control over people who are intrinsically untrustworthy. You don't know whether what they are telling you is true or not. I grew up in that environment - the first critical thing in life was to be trustworthy after that nothing mattered.

## On what trusts in the workplace means for you…

Trust is equated to security. You trust people because you know you are secure in that environment. If you're in an environment where you trust everyone around you, you are going to be secure. You're not going to get a knife in the back. The antithesis of that is if you don't trust people, then you're always on edge. You are always looking for verification of what they are saying, you are always doubting the reality of what they are doing. Probably more importantly, you're querying the intent of what they are doing. "This looks like you're helping me, but are you actually setting me up?"

## On being explicit about trust and what is required in a work environment…

We need to be more explicit about trust in the work environment than ever before because we can't assume or expect that someone will come in with their own moral framework or their own ideas or expectations around what's required of them in a work environment.

I think you probably need to differentiate between integrity and trust and expediency for delivery so you can have an absolute rule. I've had debates with our kids, "I want to trust you, so that means you have to tell the truth. If you don't, if I find you've lied to me, then how will I trust you next time?" We established that as a working rule. In reality though, there are shades of grey, so wisdom becomes about the difference between better and best, as opposed to necessarily right and wrong, because some things aren't that black and white. I think there is probably a need for some conversations around that in a normal environment. The key issues are around immediate gratification when nothing is durable. On that basis, everything is going to change, so it really doesn't matter what I say or what I do, because it will be different tomorrow or rather the next week. Or determining what has lasting value and doesn't change. In this case one needs to be very considered in the position taken.

## On breaches of trust...

The first thing you've got to decide is whether the trust is broken up or the trust is broken down. If somebody is seriously ill, I would never question that. They still get paid, they still come and do work, and you manage it. That's carrying the wounded. You can get wounded at work, you can get wounded at home, you still carry the wounded. But I'm equally firm on when you betray your troops and people around you, then you don't deserve to be there, and they can't rely on you, so why would we want you around? That's my view on trust down, because I'm responsible for retaining the integrity of the business, and if it's being undermined by somebody then that person needs to go. The trust up, you don't have the same control over it. You can't. So if your board double crosses you, drops you in it, at whatever level, and remember I'm dealing in a political realm, you get public statements made that are demonstrably wrong, but you can't actually do anything about it because you can't go to the paper and actually say, well the chairman said this but he's wrong. You just don't do that. In these circumstances, you absorb it, it builds character, it makes you more aware for next time.

## On making your peace with those experiences...

You dig deep. You've got two choices in that. You either walk and say this is an untenable environment for me to work in and in my world, you may sometimes have to do that, it is sometimes better to retreat than die because you can fight another day somewhere else. But nine times out of 10, I regroup and think about how I move forward with integrity and demonstrate that integrity instead.

## On fostering thinking throughout the organisation...

I think you've got to live it yourself. You've got to demonstrate that you are prepared to be in the trench and they have got to know that you're prepared to take the bullets, so I had a policy for example that if it was bad news, I'd front it, if it was good news, you'd front it. So the staff, the senior manager, knew that. If there was a major problem, I'd talk to the media about it. But they also knew that I expected them to do that with their staff.

## On trusting others to take a leap of faith...

From a very early age I have always held the personal view - and my articulation of it was - I could build a nuclear power station if I was asked to do it. But it would take me longer than a nuclear physicist, because I'd have a bit of background work to do to get there. But I could do it, it would just take me longer. So I've had that view on anything. The flip side is also true. There's a senior manager at my pervious organisation who I promoted onto the Exec. I said "this is an internal appointment; I'm going to bring you onto the Exec and I'm going to put you in charge of this". I actually think this is going to be a big stretch for you - I will help you on the whole transition, you prove to me that it's not a bridge too far". He's still there, he's still on the Senior Exec and he just got a promotion. He texted me and he said I've only got this because you had faith in me. So it does work, but if you do it, you've got to stretch people, but not set them up to fail. There's a fine line between those two, and you don't always get it right, but nine times out of 10 you do.

**On supporting someone during stretch assignments…**

Don't make decisions for them, because they will very quickly revert to "what would you like me to do?". Then they'll feel as if they are in the position, but have actually learnt nothing. In one example, one of my team wanted a restructure, but he came up with a structure that I thought was awful, so we kept asking questions. We went through it all, and I'd ask him, "why are you doing that, how does that fit in? Go away and think about it and come back".

About six weeks later, he came up with a structure that was pretty good. And I said, "yeah, that's great, you've done really well, go and implement it". And he looked at me and said, "that's what you wanted at the beginning wasn't it?" I said yes and he said "why didn't you just tell me that?". I said, "what do you think you would have learned out of that? You would have walked out of the office on the first day and said "I'll have to do his restructure…" Now you're going to walk out of the office, having learned a lot about how you restructure and you are going to implement something that you actually believe in. Why wouldn't I have that conversation with you?" That's what it's about but you have to learn to be patient. It's a fine line because if you're too patient, you get nothing done – and I'm a little delivery orientated!

**On what leaders will look back on in five years and realize was unintentionally limiting trust…**

Somehow, we have to differentiate between trust as in personal integrity and trust as in technical competence. So there's two different types of trust and the things leading up to both are different.

The things that are happening in business that removes trust, a lot of that is actually around the professional delivery competence area, which then translates into "I don't trust you" which then you receive personally.

A personal example – I'm renovating a house, the builder who's done most of the work I trust implicitly. We've done all of the work without a single piece of paper. There's no contract and no budget. That's trust at an integrity and competence level. In a work environment, you're not allowed to do that. It was a standing joke that I was trusting him for orders of magnitude with my own personal money and I was sitting down talking to people (at work) saying, "where are the quotes? Where are the tenders? Where are the comparative evaluations?" And that to me, is where – in terms of public money in particular – it's particularly difficult.

I think in the public sector we have a zero-trust environment, because the public sector will not believe you. They want to have it verified three different ways, even if the three different ways are nonsensical. It's more important to be able to demonstrate the process and the integrity of the process than to say, "I'll trust you to do it". Because – probably - history has shown that the world is full of people that then take that and rip the system off, which I understand. So you have to have some system in place that says, "I fundamentally don't trust you, therefore I will check everything". I think that becomes debilitating in the end. I find that to be probably one of the most frustrating things in the public sector. You can't go to someone and say "leave it to me and I'll do it" because it violates all the rules.

You get beyond that when you have the right people. It's an irony (as a leader) that you're expected to be trustworthy to get there, then once you actually do get there, they do everything to fundamentally say they don't trust you.

## On what leaders could be doing differently to create high trust environments...

I don't think you ever trust anybody you don't know. And I think probably one of the biggest dangers is that we don't know who we're dealing with. Even our staff. So I would have a one on one with all of my direct reports every second week and I would meet the whole group every week in an exec meeting – which was operational.

The one on one meeting was basically a continuous improvement update. I don't believe in annual performance reviews. But those conversation invariably started with "How are you? How are the kids? How was your holiday? What did you do on the weekend?" You're never going to trust anybody, or put your trust in anybody if you don't know who they are and how they're going to perform. It's kind of working out what someone's 'algorithm' is so you can predict what their behaviour is going to be. Which is why you're doing all the psychometric tests at the end of the day. Its why I'm quite keen on those. Psychometric tests probably formalize what your gut tells you.

You have different conversations with your team because they're different people who need different things. You need to be able to read who they are and where they're at in the journey. I think that's probably one of the most important things and I think that's going. I think as we become more contractual and more digital, this whole notion about disruptive behaviour is getting lost in terms of disruptive personality behaviour rather than technologically challenging paradigms. There are a number of people out there who get a kick out of creating chaos – I'm not one of them because I think the collateral damage is often not justified.

I think Eisenhower after WW2 set up sister cities out of the shadow of the war, to say our probability of going to war with people we know is much lower than with those we've never met and know nothing about. I think the same issue is true in business. That's why you end up having companies in litigation – people don't sit down and talk to each other. In most cases, you can resolve things; if you know who you're dealing with then you never get to the point of having a problem. I think that's fundamental in terms of understanding the relationship.

The second thing is separating the right outcome from personal ego. I think there's too much time spent trying to take the credit for something and not enough time trying to optimize the outcome. That's one of the challenges that needs to be managed – pulling people back who are trying to be the hero.

To get more trust you need a higher level of competence. You have to know that people know what they're doing. You need everybody moving at the same rate. If people aren't moving at the same rate, you start losing trust between them. That's up to the General. To make sure everyone is in sync.

## On the different challenges of building trust in public vs private sector organisations...

The first thing is to work out that a politicians view of the truth is around re-election, so they have a completely different driver to everybody else. So if you report to a council, they are notionally the board. But they were put there on a popularity vote, not picked by the shareholders to be the best mix of competence for the company's direction. So you sit as the Chief Executive in that environment, and you have a group of people who may never have run a business or managed staff - then you're asking them to understand the nuances of contracts or management systems. Some of them have a degree of experience, but there's a big difference between driving a 5 metre speedboat and a 500 metre super tanker. Both of them are on the water, both of them have a skipper, but they are completely different animals. You have to be careful that you're not trying to ask the super tanker to do what you can do in a speedboat.

Part of the problem is that people don't know what they don't know. But what's even more dangerous is the people who think that they know, and they're wrong. Then you're in big trouble and that's part of the danger in the public sector. Because they're totally risk adverse, and because they don't know, you end up with the kind of hiatus you get in the public sector where no one makes a decision. It gets bandied around, it goes to multiple committees and there's enough people with their fingerprints on it, then whatever comes out at the end, no one is responsible for it, which is safe.

That's the frustration, but the system creates it, because there's no accountability. People need to be empowered to make decisions. It's all wrapped up in trust, and delivery and respect in terms of information. I don't think a lot of people have that, and I think Councillors can be particularly bad at disrespecting their staff then expecting total loyalty and obedience. That's hard to pull off all the time, yet they don't realize they're doing it. That's the challenge in the public sector.

**On how trust - and distrust - shapes or impacts an organisation…**

Trust allows innovation. No trust is no innovation, because you become risk averse. If you trust the boss, you're prepared to innovate and be proactive. If there's no trust then you become risk averse and reactionary and you shut down. 'I won't do anything until somebody tells me what to do'. As opposed to 'I'll do what I think is the right thing to do and if it's wrong I'll still be backed'.

Organisations that have interactive trust are the ones that are progressive because then people feed off each other. You get synergy, it's like a catalyst reaction – it goes faster and faster.

# ACKNOWLEDGEMENTS

This book is the work of many conversations, client work and research, so the list of thank you's is likely to be incomplete. However...

To my family, friends and colleagues... thank you for the long conversations, for challenging my thoughts and ideas, for your insights and feedback and especially your never-ending support and encouragement to complete this project. Special thank you's to Alex Lazarus, Nicole Sorrell and Sarah Laurie for the many and very special ways you encouraged me to continue when life got in the way.

To my clients... thank you for the opportunities to do this work with you over the years. For bringing this work to life day to day, and for being advocates of high-performance human workplaces. You are a powerful, game changing group of humans.

To the leaders who generously gave their time and insights... thank you for making the time, for speaking so openly, and for allowing me to share your stories here. I hope readers gain as much pleasure from reading your stories as I did in hearing them.

To the writers and researchers who have published great work in the advocacy of trust... thank you. For your perspectives, your care, your interest, your passion in sharing your work, your ideas and your knowledge. The work you do is inspiring and crucial.

And finally, to the leaders and colleagues who have shaped my worldview over my career... thank you for instilling in me the disciplines of trust, a healthy respect for treating others with dignity, and a lifelong passion for learning.

This book is for each of you, with my deepest thanks and gratitude.

*Teresa*

Printed in Great Britain
by Amazon